AN IRISH BEAST BOOK

By the same author:

Irish Wild Mammals: a Guide to the Literature.

An Irish Beast Book

A natural history of Ireland's furred wildlife

J. S. Fairley

With drawings of the mammals by Rory Harrington, of the mammalogists by Pauline Farrell and of the owls by Evelyn Drinan. Additional illustrations by the author.

Blackstaff Press   Belfast

Published by Blackstaff Press Limited, 16 Donegall Square South, Belfast, BT1 5JF.

SBN 85640 091 2 (Hardback)
SBN 85640 090 4 (Paperback)

Printed in Northern Ireland by Belfast Litho Printers Limited.

Contents

List of illustrations

Portraits of the Mammalogists

Preface

This is the first book to be devoted solely to Ireland's wild mammals and it has been written with the layman in mind. There are, in fact, several works on the mammals of the British Isles as a whole, but those published over the past half century have concentrated largely on Great Britain. Indeed, apart from descriptions of the celebrated Irish hare and stoat, they dispose of the Irish mammals with a consistent brevity. One must go back to Barrett-Hamilton and Hinton's *History of British Mammals* (1910-21) for a thorough treatment but, unfortunately, this work was never completed. Since 1921 much additional information has become available and the status of some species has altered markedly. Such broad works on the Irish fauna as there are (whose authors have had no special interest in the mammals) have, in covering their topic, perforce been limited in the amount of detail they could reasonably be expected to include. It is hoped, with the publication of the present volume, not only in some small measure to fill a literary lacuna, but to stimulate active interest in this fascinating group of animals.

This book is long overdue, for it has become increasingly the custom of those seeking knowledge on its subject to quote data from Great Britain, simply because the facts for Ireland are uncollated and dispersed through the literature. While such data may be entirely applicable in some cases, their use in others is profoundly misleading.

At the risk of insularity I have therefore relied almost exclusively on information from Ireland, except where it appeared desirable to contrast data with those from Great Britain or further afield. On occasions where it *has* been necessary to refer to outside sources, this has been clearly stated.

Such a policy has, of course, resulted in an uneven coverage of the various species. For example, very little is known of Irish hedgehogs and shrews, whereas we have learned a great deal about field mice and foxes. Furthermore a full account of our knowledge of some forms would undoubtedly make tedious reading. For instance, an inventory of sizes and locations of deer herds, past and present, or a list of the sightings of pine martens over the past hundred years, would bore all but a a minority, as would fine detail on dimensions and colouration. This book is, after all, intended to interest the non-specialist. Moreover, a consideration of price alone precludes the inclusion of much material unpalatable to the vast majority. However, I would be less than honest if I did not confess to strong bias in the extent of the treatment given to each species. I, too, would find a detailed catalogue of deer herds uninspiring, and of use mainly for reference purposes, whereas the subject of mammal fleas is, to my mind, an absorbing one.

While I would be appalled to think that I was the perpetrator of an improving book, I trust that, for sixth-formers at least, it would be considered suitable, if not altogether proper reading. In addition, as it is the only book of its kind and includes an extensive list of references (indicated by superscript in the text), it may even prove useful, in a minor capacity, in universities.

I am indebted to the illustrators for enlivening and providing relief from my prose, and to Mrs Phyllis Mercer for typing the manuscript. I am also grateful, for a critical reading, to Dr. David Bamford, Mrs Betty Gosling, Dr Vivian Gotto and Professor Michael Mitchell. They are responsible for a number of improvements. Any mistakes are my own. I would also like to thank Professor Paddy Keady for the facilities to indulge my scribbling propensities between teaching commitments. Finally, my thanks are due to a multitude who provided me with references, snippets of information and assorted odds and ends indispensable to completing the work.

In conclusion, I have aimed at accuracy and would very much appreciate hearing of any errors or omissions which may have occurred.

J.S.F.

Department of Zoology, University College, Galway.

1

The Mammals of Ireland

Indeed it is the poverty of the Irish list that makes the study of the Irish mammals doubly interesting and instructive.

A Guide to Belfast (1902)   Belfast Naturalists' Field Club

Mammals differ markedly from other animals in a number of ways but the best known of these, and most quoted, are the possession of hair and glands in the skin of the females which produce milk for the young—the mammary glands. Mammalian hair grows from small projections or papillae beneath the surface of the skin and in this, and its microscopical structure, it differs from the so-called 'hair' of some of the more lowly animals, such as bumble bees and the more alarming spiders. All mammals have hair though some, like whales, have very little of it. Again, all female mammals have mammary glands but these are often small and only apparent while the young are being suckled, when the glands are greatly enlarged. On the other hand one cannot deny that in some species they are hard to miss: those of ladies and cows come to mind as good examples. The word mammal is, in fact, derived from the Latin *mamma*, meaning a breast.

An important additional feature of mammals, and one which they share with birds, is an ability to maintain their body temperature at a constant level, commonly described as 'being warm-blooded', and mammalian hair plays an important part in insulating against the loss of heat. Along with this ability mammals can regulate the composition of their blood within narrow limits and this inner ability enables them to develop a complexity in some of their organization impossible in lower animals. This is especially true of the degree of development in the nervous system, which explains why mammals are more intelligent than other animals. (Birds, too, enjoy such a complexity but rather more of their activities are instinctive rather than intelligent. This is possibly because innate behaviour patterns require fewer nerve cells, and any reduction in weight is an advantage to animals which fly.) Being warm-blooded also allows mammals and birds to search for food in temperatures which would render amphibians and reptiles sluggish—or even freeze them: a considerable advantage. Birds and mammals thus occupy many colder regions of the globe in which amphibians and reptiles are scarce or absent.

Man, of course, is a mammal and so are a majority of the creatures with which he is most closely associated—his pets, producers of meat and wool, beasts of burden and, alas, his rodent pests. It is therefore perhaps surprising that, among naturalists, mammals are by no means the most popular group of animals. In Great Britain and Ireland there are a host of ornithologists and societies for them. There is only one Mammal Society with less than 900 members, many of whom are professional zoologists. Specialists in mammalogy in Ireland today are as scarce as the proverbial hen's teeth. Nevertheless, much is known of the Irish mammal fauna, even if the sum of our knowledge is immeasurably less than that from the neighbouring island. In a later chapter are outlined the main sources of this information for Ireland. In the remainder of this one I will attempt a sketch of the present *dramatis personae*.

There are twenty-eight species of wild mammal in Ireland today compared with fifty-two in Great Britain. The relative composition of the two faunas are shown in Table I. It is arguable that whales can also be considered as British or Irish mammals but, as they are entirely aquatic, they are more logically considered by oceans than by land masses. Whales in Ireland, in the literal sense, are stranded and soon dead!

1

There is ample evidence that seals cross the Irish Sea frequently; it would be surprising if they did not. I have therefore also considered them as, in general, outside the scope of this book. As readers will see, I have not maintained an absolutely rigid rule in respect of the latter groups of animals. Finally, in this chapter I have refrained from discussing in detail those species which are dealt with at length later in the book.

Table I

A comparison of the present day British and Irish wild mammals. Species found only on offshore islands have been omitted. 'D' indicates a definite, deliberate introduction (after Savage, 1966).

British species	Scientific name	Irish species
INSECTIVORA (Hedgehogs, shrews, moles etc.)		
Hedgehog	*Erinaceus europaeus*	+
Mole	*Talpa europaea*	
Pigmy Shrew	*Sorex minutus*	+
Common Shrew	*Sorex araneus*	
Water Shrew	*Neomys fodiens*	
CHIROPTERA (Bats)		
Greater Horse-shoe Bat	*Rhinolophus ferrumequinum*	
Lesser Horse-shoe Bat	*Rhinolophus hipposideros*	+
Noctule	*Nyctalus noctula*	
Leisler's Bat	*Nyctalus leisleri*	+
Long-eared Bat	*Plecotus auritus*	+
Barbastelle	*Barbastella barbastellus*	
Pipistrelle	*Pipistrellus pipistrellus*	+
Serotine	*Eptesicus serotinus*	
Mouse-eared Bat	*Myotis myotis*	
Natterer's Bat	*Myotis nattereri*	+
Bechstein's Bat	*Myotis bechsteini*	
Whiskered Bat	*Myotis mystacinus*	+
Daubenton's Bat	*Myotis daubentoni*	+
CARNIVORA (Carnivores: dogs, cats, bears, weasels, mongooses etc.)		
Fox	*Vulpes vulpes*	+
Pine Marten	*Martes martes*	+
Stoat	*Mustela erminea*	+
Weasel	*Mustela nivalis*	
Polecat	*Mustela putorius*	
D American Mink	*Mustela vison*	D
Badger	*Meles meles*	+
Otter	*Lutra lutra*	+
Wild Cat	*Felis silvestris*	
ARTIODACTYLA (Deer, antelope, camels, oxen, pigs etc.)		
Red Deer	*Cervus elaphus*	+
Fallow Deer	*Dama dama*	D
Roe Deer	*Capreolus capreolus*	
D Indian Muntjac	*Muntiacus muntjak*	
D Chinese Muntjac	*Muntiacus reevesi*	
D Water Deer	*Hydropotes inermis*	
D Sika Deer	*Cervus nippon*	D
D Reindeer	*Rangifer tarandus*	
LAGOMORPHA (Rabbits and hares)		
Brown Hare	*Lepus capensis*	D
Blue Hare	*Lepus timidus*	+
D Rabbit	*Oryctolagus cuniculus*	D

RODENTIA (Rodents)

	Red Squirrel	*Sciurus vulgaris*	+
D	Grey Squirrel	*Sciurus carolinensis*	D
D	Edible Dormouse	*Glis glis*	
	Dormouse	*Muscardinus avellanarius*	
	Harvest Mouse	*Micromys minutus*	
	Field Mouse	*Apodemus sylvaticus*	+
	Yellow-necked Field Mouse	*Apodemus flavicollis*	
	Black Rat	*Rattus rattus*	+
	Brown Rat	*Rattus norvegicus*	+
	House Mouse	*Mus musculus*	+
	Bank Vole	*Clethrionomys glareolus*	+
	Water Vole	*Arvicola amphibius*	
	Field Vole	*Microtus agrestis*	
D	Coypu	*Myocastor coypus*	

Table II

Typical measurements (in mm) and weights (in kg or g) of adult Irish mammals. In extreme instances dimensions may be larger than those below. Measurements marked with an asterisk are exclusively Irish. Otherwise they include, or are entirely from, specimens from Great Britain.

	Head and body	Tail	Weight
Hedgehog	179-263	17-35	800-1,200g
Pigmy Shrew	50-64	31-42	3-6g
Fox	*614-777	*222-429	*5.0-9.5kg
Pine Marten (all from Germany)	400-530	230-280	900-1,500g
Irish Stoat	*184-283	*57-117	*95-284g
Mink	302-430	127-229	565-1,020g
Badger	about 800	about 100	about 10-27kg
Otter	940-1360	350-470	5.5-16.8kg
Brown Hare	520-595	85-120	3.2-3.9kg
Irish Hare	*521-559	*74-168	*2.7-3.6kg
Rabbit	*406-457	*81-104	1.4-2.0kg
Red Squirrel	210-225	170-179	260-435g
Grey Squirrel	230-280	200-240	510-750g
Field Mouse	*78-102	*75-96	*15-30g
House Mouse	70-92	70-84	13-30g
Black Rat	*165-188	*188-208	*185-215g
Brown Rat	*203-273	*165-229	*453-516g
Bank Vole	about 90-110	about 40-60	*16-33g

	Height at withers or shoulder	Weight
Red Deer	1050-1400	95-225
Fallow Deer	about 900-950	about 60-110kg
Sika Deer	820-900	around 60kg

	Wingspan	Weight
Lesser Horse-shoe Bat	228-250	4.9-6.0g
Leisler's Bat	290-320	*14.3-20.1g
Long-eared Bat	255-265	*6.5-8.4g
Pipistrelle	*210-235	*5.0-7.4g
Natterer's Bat	265-285	(Sweden) 5.0-9.5g
Whiskered Bat	225-245	(Sweden) 4.5-6.0g
Daubenton's Bat	220-245	8.5-11.0g

In Table II I have listed typical measurements of the various animals. This is to avoid reducing the text to the level of a catalogue of dimensions. It should be borne in mind that in most species the male is slightly bigger than the female. It will be appa-

Fig. 1 Pigmy shrew.

rent that, for many forms, there is not even a respectable series of measurements available for Irish representatives.

The pigmy shrew is widespread on the Irish mainland and on several offshore islands, in virtually any habitat which is not water-logged and where there is sufficient ground cover. I have trapped one at the top of Carrantouhill, Co. Kerry, Ireland's highest mountain. They are especially abundant in grassland. In spite of the common usage of the terms 'shrew-mouse' or 'screw-mouse', the resemblance to a mouse is entirely superficial, for shrews have long mobile snouts, velvety fur, minute eyes and small ears. The teeth, which are provided with tiny needle-like cusps, are covered with bright red enamel and are well adapted to shearing up the insects on which the animals live. Studies in England and on the continent show that spiders and woodlice are also commonly consumed. The cheek teeth of most rodents are, in contrast, flattened and adapted to grinding, and they have fewer teeth anyway. Shrews are smoky brown in colour though rather lighter on the underside. Cream coloured examples have been taken on three occasions in Ireland.

The shrews are the smallest of all mammals—Savi's pygmy shrew (*Suncus etruscus*), which is found in countries bordering the Mediterranean, measures a mere 4cm from the tip of its snout to the end of its tail. The smaller an object is, the higher is the ratio of the surface area to the volume. For example, a cube of 1cm per side has a surface area to volume ratio of 6. But for a cube of 10cm the ratio is down to 0.6. As mammals maintain their body temperature at a constant level, smaller ones will lose relatively more heat than larger ones, because they have a relatively larger surface area in proportion to their size over which to dissipate the heat. Animals like shrews and mice must therefore eat proportionately more to maintain their body temperature than would a bigger mammal. But the foods, such as grain, eaten by mice have a much higher calorific value than the insects eaten by shrews, which in addition contain a greater proportion of water. It is hardly surprising, therefore, that shrews spend a large part of their life in hunting and devouring what they can catch. In a laboratory experiment[113] at room temperature two pigmy shrews ate upwards of one and a half times their own weights daily. Out of doors in cold weather this figure must be even higher.

Shrews are therefore active during most of the day and night and spend only brief periods at rest. When on the move they give the impression of intense and aggressive activity, which is augmented by the voice, a shrill twittering and chirping. Except during mating they are solitary and meetings are marked by a ritualised battle, a posturing and squeaking contest which, though decisive, brings no physical harm to either party. Like most of the small rodents, they rarely live for more than a year in the wild.

Pigmy shrews use the runways of other small mammals and burrow little themselves. They are good climbers and one Irish mammalogist found one in the upper story of his home[14] where, having scaled the curtains, it proceeded to draw attention to itself by twittering. Unseen, and suspected of being something uncanny, it was shot down as a precautionary measure.

The hedgehog or urchin needs no description as the vast majority of readers will have seen at least one. They are to be found in thinly-planted deciduous woodland, or in open country where sufficient cover is available and they have also colonised cultivated ground, gardens and parks. They are most commonly found in Great Britain in city suburbs. Hedgehogs are largely nocturnal and normally slow movers, advertising their presence by a characteristic snuffling in their search for food: including (according to work in Britain) a wide variety of invertebrate animals such as slugs, snails, millipedes, insects, young mice and birds when available, and a modicum of vegetable matter such as berries.

Hedgehogs, of course, roll into a ball for protection and will erect their spines in readiness at the slightest sign of danger. This means of defence is, naturally, futile where motor cars are concerned and thousands of the animals are killed on roads annually. However, they can move with a surprising turn of speed when so willed and I have seen one dash across the road in the headlights of a car and found it curled up on the pavement immediately afterwards. Badgers and foxes both seem to be able to kill and eat hedgehogs but foxes, at least, do this only rarely, judging from many analyses of their stomach contents (Chapter 8).

Hedgehogs hibernate during the coldest months only, as can be verified from the freshly killed specimens still commonly seen on the roads in November. Occasionally the animals are observed abroad during the winter. Hibernation in mammals is principally a mechanism for saving energy when food is scarce, in other words of avoiding adverse conditions. During winter sleep, although still controlled, the body temperature drops and the hedgehog, as a result, burns up less food. The food is, in fact, in the form of fat deposits laid down in autumn.

Extremely little is known of the hedgehog in Ireland. It is believed to have undergone a decrease in numbers in the earlier part of the century and was reported scarce in many localities in 1935.[57] It now appears to be common, though there has been no attempt to assess actual numbers.

The seven species of bat are undoubtedly the most difficult to tell apart of all the Irish mammals. So much so that reliable identifications of these animals are astonishingly scarce, the bulk of such work being completed over forty years ago. People with sufficient interest, knowledge and energy to identify them are few and

5

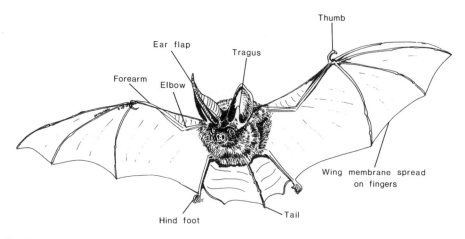

Thumb

Ear flap

Tragus

Forearm

Elbow

Wing membrane spread
on fingers

Hind foot

Tail

Fig. 2   Long-eared bat in flight showing some significant features of bat anatomy.

far between. Our knowledge of their distribution is therefore imperfect. Fig. 2 may help to clarify the following brief comments on the peculiarities of bat anatomy. These refer to the insect-eating bats to which all seven species we are concerned with here belong.

The most striking feature of bats is their wings. These are flexible membranes composed of two thicknesses of skin with a thin layer of connective tissue sandwiched between them which contains, among other things, blood vessels and nerves. The wing is stretched over the greatly elongated fingers, which serve a somewhat analogous function to the spokes of an umbrella, and it is also carried on the arm. The thumb is free and bears a claw as do all the hind toes. The wing is also continuous between the hind legs and the tail. The ear flaps are fairly large and in many species a smaller 'earlet' is obvious within. This is called the *tragus.* Some bats (only one species in Ireland) have a 'nose-leaf', a leaf-like structure around the nostrils (Fig. 3), hideously elaborated in some exotic types into flaps, frills and convolutions which are often useful diagnostic features.

One nugget of knowledge, produced with a flourish by those otherwise uninformed, is that, 'Bats have radar'. This is only approximately true. Bats find their way, and their insect prey, by emitting high-pitched sounds which bounce back off solid objects, the returning echoes being heard by the bat: more a sort of echo-sounding than radar. Plugging their ears therefore disorientates them and even stopping one decreases their powers of navigation considerably. Nose-leaf bats, or at least those investigated, can still operate efficiently with a single ear plugged. Apparently they are capable of 'beaming' the sound from the nostrils by swivelling the nose-leaf, and can thus compensate for the loss of reception of the returning sounds on one side. 'Echolocation' in bats is an extremely complex subject, for the different species of bat each have their individual peculiarities in sound production and reception, tailored to their particular habitats, hunting and general way of life.

The day is spent roosting in hollow trees, caves, old buildings and roof spaces and at dusk the bats emerge to forage. On rare occasions individuals may be seen flying during the day. I have seen this twice, once at University College, Galway, in December and again at Oughterard, Co. Galway, on a bright, sunny afternoon in

6

June. Insects are regularly taken on the wing.

Anyone who has examined a bat at close quarters has a lasting impression of the satanic grin furnished with apparently innumerable fine sharp teeth similar to those of shrews, which is only to be expected considering that both feed on insects.

As bats sleep their temperature drops and wakening them often takes time. When awake the body temperature is high, for flying requires the expenditure of energy at a greater rate. The maintenance of such a temperature for long without feeding is therefore not only impractical but impossible, and hence the drop—a kind of 'short-term' hibernation. It is worth remembering that the large surface area presented by the wings in particular results in a rapid dissipation of heat. Most bats have distinct summer and winter roosting quarters and true hibernation occurs during the winter.

One other remarkable feature in the life of most of the bats considered here is that, although mating takes place in autumn and winter, fertilization is in spring. Sperm is stored unused in the reproductive tract of the female until hibernation ends.

Without going into fine detail, which would be out of place in this chapter, it is still possible to identify four of the seven species readily.

The lesser horse-shoe bat is the only type in Ireland bearing a nose-leaf and it has no tragus. Unlike the other six, which roost against vertical surfaces, the horse-shoe hangs down quite freely from the horizontal, suspended by the claws on its feet and while hibernating it is totally enfolded in its wings. It has been found in Cos. Clare, Cork, Galway, Kerry, Limerick and south Mayo and is locally very common.

Natterer's bat has a fringe of hairs along the edge of the membrane between the legs and tail, which is an absolutely diagnostic feature. It is widespread over Ireland, but has been taken infrequently.

Leisler's bat differs from the others in the shape of the tragus which is broad at the top and narrow at the bottom. The tragus in the others is longer than broad. Leisler's is fairly common in Ireland, very probably more so than in Great Britain. In fact it may well have taken over the place occupied in Britain by its larger close relative, the noctule bat, which is absent from Ireland.

The easiest of all bats to recognise is the long-eared, which certainly lives up to its name. The ears are from 34 to 37mm long, not much less than the entire length of the head and body. When the animal is sleeping the ears are folded back along the sides of the body and are gradually erected as the bat awakens. Next to the pipistrelle and outside the districts where horse-shoe bats are found, this is the commonest Irish bat and is the one with the pleasantest disposition. It does not bite unless roughly handled and is easily tamed. It is the species most often seen under the roofs of churches and there is even a colony in the tower of the Church of Ireland on Rathlin Island, off the north coast of Co. Antrim.

Of the remaining three species, the pipistrelle is not only by far the most numerous but is that most likely to be found around houses. Large colonies, up to a few hundred, may take up residence in the roof-space of a suitable house. Their squeaking and promiscuous scattering of droppings both inside, and on the ground outside as they sally forth from the eaves at dusk, can become a definite nuisance. I have even met people who do not take to the idea of bats living in their houses anyway. In such cases I am vaguely suspicious of some lurking superstition or latent neurosis on the part of the complainant. By the way, fears that bats spread disease (in Ireland, anyway) or will entangle themselves in the ladies' hair, deliberately or otherwise, are both equally groundless. Pipistrelles also roost singly and, at times, may pack themselves into remarkably confined spaces.

Both Daubenton's and the whiskered bat appear to be widely distributed, are little known but, quite possibly, not particularly rare. Incidentally, the first documented

Head of lesser horse-shoe bat

Horse-shoe bat roosting

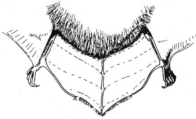

Tail-membrane of Natterer's ba

Tragus of
Daubenton's bat

Leisler's bat

Tragus of Leisler's bat

Fig. 3   *Important features in some Irish bats. Note the nose-leaf on the horse-shoe bat
and the absence of a tragus in its ear. The lesser horse-shoe bat is the only Irish
bat to hang freely from a horizontal surface while at roost. The fringe of hairs on
the tail-membrane of Natterer's bat is diagnostic, as is the broad tragus of Leisler's.
Drawings are not to the same scale.*

record of the whiskered bat in Ireland was due to a cat which, rather surprisingly, contrived to kill one at Feakle, Co. Clare, in 1852.

A description of the rabbit is entirely superfluous but the frequent variation in coat colour in the wild needs to be mentioned, since silver-grey, fawn and especially partially black varieties are not uncommon. Its general habits also are, perhaps, better known to the non-naturalist than those of any other wild mammal in Ireland. In 1954 its numbers were catastrophically reduced by the introduction of myxomatosis, spread by the rabbit flea, with marked effects on the diet of some of the erstwhile rabbit predators. Rabbits are again common in some areas, though still periodically affected by the myxoma virus; they have also been long established on some of the small islands off the coast. That less rabbits are killed by the disease than formerly is certainly true but not, as is popularly supposed, because the rabbit has acquired partial immunity. Experiments in Britain[95] show that the more virulent strains of the virus are less abundant than before and that the less severe ones (i.e. those which kill fewer rabbits) are consequently more common. A strong strain will kill over 99% of the animals infected, reducing its chances of spread, whereas a weak strain has a rather better chance of being passed on because more of the rabbits recover. Hence, as time passed, the attenuated forms of myxomatosis survived rather

Fig. 4   Irish hare. Note the white tail and that the ears are shorter than the total length of the head.

9

better than those which proved almost invariably fatal. As a result, more rabbits tend to survive the disease today.

Myxomatosis has produced at least two beautiful examples of human irrationality. First, in spite of the fact that it is manifestly an infection specific to rabbits—a few hares have contracted it but without lasting effects—it has led to a common prejudice against rabbit meat. When questioned closely, those who will not eat it confess to a fear of coming down with the disease themselves. Stewed rabbit is still a superb dish and as harmless as ever it was. Secondly, the majority of people are appalled at what they regard as the dreadful pain which infected rabbits have to bear. Anyone suspected of spreading myxomatosis is severely castigated. But, although unsightly, the suffering is not sufficient to prevent the animals from feeding and moving about. Moreover the compassion for bunnies with all their cuddly childhood associations is rarely extended to the less loveable mammals. Who, for instance, would be shocked if myxomatosis were a malady confined to, say, rats?

There are two hares in Ireland. The Irish hare is a subspecies, in other words a distinct race, of the arctic hare, an animal whose geographical range extends over northern Europe into the extreme north of Scandinavia and even to Iceland. The second, the brown hare, is found in Ireland in the extreme north-west where it has been introduced, though it may possibly occur elsewhere. The brown hare is an inhabitant largely of southern Europe including Britain and its range only slightly overlaps that of the arctic hare. It is interesting that the latter species is found on the Alps and on high ground in the north of England and Scotland, where it replaces the brown. Clearly the arctic hare is adapted to more severe conditions than its relative. There is only one distinct temperate region where arctic hares are to be seen from sea level to the tops of the highest mountains—Ireland. In this context it is interesting that the limited amount of research on the diet of the Irish hare hints at it being rather less specialized in its food habits, eating a broader range of plants than its Scottish cousin. The stomach contents of twenty Irish hares shot in the highlands of Co. Antrim in winter[201] showed that the food was 28% heather, 15% bog cotton, 10% other sedges, 44% upland grasses and 2% other plants. Scottish hares eat much more heather and it forms 90% of their diet in winter.

The brown and Irish hares differ in several ways. The Irish form is smaller, has a larger head, is rather slimmer and is clad in a more reddish-brown coat. However, the most clear-cut features are the colouring of the tail and the length of the ears. The tail of the brown hare is brown on the upper side, and when running, it is tucked down so that the white under-surface cannot be seen. The Irish hare's tail is entirely white. The ears of the brown hare are long and, if turned forward, could be made to extend beyond the end of the nose. Those of the Irish hare are short and barely reach the nose-tip when stretched towards it. Curious to relate, going on this criterion, the hare on the old Irish three-penny piece was not an Irish hare!

The arctic hare in northern Britain is generally known as the blue or mountain hare. It differs from the Irish subspecies in being smaller and having a dusky 'bluish' brown coat. Furthermore it turns white during the autumn moult. Some Irish hares undergo winter whitening too, but this is nearly always only partial. Entirely white specimens are rare, but not unknown. There are also a few recorded instances of black or buff Irish hares. The Irish hare has also a rather longer breeding season, from about February to October.[82] In its Scottish cousin breeding declines in July.

Hares, unlike rabbits, do not burrow and live life entirely above ground. Nevertheless, there are a few odd reports of their going to ground when pursued. The normal resting place is a *form* or hollow in ground vegetation made by the

Fig. 5   Brown hare. Notice the long ears and that the upper surface of tail is dark.

animal's body. Again, unlike rabbits, their young are born at an advanced stage of development with their eyes open, and are fully haired. They shelter in forms while the mother is away feeding. Precocious development is naturally an asset in a defenceless animal which lacks the protection of a burrow.

The Irish hare is a more social species than the brown and is sometimes seen tógether in groups. Often several are to be seen on the landward side of the North Bull Island in Dublin Bay, sometimes running across the mud flats at low tide. Up to quite recently herds exceeding 100 grazed regularly beside the runways at Aldergrove Airport, outside Belfast.

Of the two squirrels, the red is thinly distributed over most of the country, but locally common, and said to have increased in numbers in recent years. Because it is shyer than the grey, and therefore not seen as often, and because no systematic work on it has been completed in Ireland, its precise status is uncertain. It is typical of coniferous and mixed woods, normally scarce in entirely deciduous woodland.

An introduction, the grey is only to be found in eleven counties namely Armagh, Fermanagh, Kildare, Leitrim, Longford, Meath, Monaghan, Offaly, Roscommon and Tyrone with a single example from Co. Wicklow. It may be found in all types of woodland but generally requires hardwoods somewhere in the vicinity.

Although both squirrels eat a variety of mainly vegetable food, a substantial proportion of the food of reds appears to be conifer seeds and, of greys, seeds of

11

hardwoods, especially acorns. The two squirrels are readily differentiated simply on colour and size. In addition reds usually have tufts of hair around their ears during most of the year. *Both* species can become pests and can cause serious damage to trees, but this happens rather less often with the reds simply because they are usually scarcer.

A widespread misconception regarding squirrels, and one enthusiastically imparted to children in Nature Study classes until fairly recently, is that they hibernate. It is hardly remarkable. An Irish Professor of Zoology stated it as an accepted fact in a text-book of 1933. No doubt some readers can confirm that squirrels are often out in winter from personal experience. I have seen them foraging after a fall of snow myself.

The brown rat is possibly the most familiar of wild mammals and is unloved by all. It is found throughout Ireland, usually in or near human habitation or on cultivated ground, but seldom wanders far from these habitats. It has colonised a number of the off-shore islands and is often well-established around streams and rivers, where it may live a semi-aquatic life. The 'water rat' of Ireland is merely a brown rat in the water. The brown rat is the most serious of all mammal pests, destroying incalculable amounts of grain and stored products, either by eating or fouling them. It will, indeed, eat almost anything and is therefore the omnivore *par excellence*. It spreads disease and its fecundity is a byword, though by no means exceptional in the rodent world. The success of rodents in general is, as a matter of fact, largely due both to this remarkable rate of reproduction and to their small size. The two factors have enabled them both to exploit numerous niches not available to larger mammals, and to build up large populations swiftly. Strangely enough, the brown rat is a poor climber and does not store food.

The black rat competes unsuccessfully with the brown and is confined to temporary settlements at sea ports. It is also to be found on Lambay Island, off Dublin. It arrives on board ships, where it is the commonest rat. It is a smaller animal and, comparatively, more handsome. It may be distinguished from its larger relative by a rather less shaggy coat and especially by the length of the tail. The tail of the black rat is always as long, or, usually, longer than the length of the head and body. The tail of the brown rat on the other hand is shorter, usually about 70% to 90% of the length of the head and body. Despite the names, colour is not a feature to be relied upon and brown varieties of the smaller species are not uncommonly met with.

The black rat has virtually as catholic a diet as the brown and is no less a pest, though fortunately present in such small numbers. It is a good climber, and when encountered in buildings, this is often in the upper stories. The oil from its fur leaves tell-tale smears at the back of the shelves it uses as runs and similar marks may be left below roof beams. Outside the British Isles it is frequently arboreal (i.e. tree-dwelling). Descriptions of phenomenal climbing powers in rats usually concern the black species. I remember, as a fascinated child, my father vividly recounting how a rat descended, head first, a vertical steel girder in a machine shop in the Belfast shipyard. I also recall a description of an incident in a Dublin hotel at breakfast concerning an uninvited rodent and horrified guests, but this might be hearsay and would hardly serve the interests of tourism.

The house mouse is rather less abhorrent to most than rats. This is in part, at least, due to insidious conditioning in youth from children's literature and to cartoon films. The animal is, none the less, a serious pest, consuming a vast range of foods, and is a vector of disease. Its motto, concerning eating, is, 'Little and often and anywhere' (H.N. Southern), for mice, even with excess food on all

12

sides, will scuttle about, nibbling here and there. The house mouse is a diffuse, light, wary and erratic feeder. The ancestors of today's mice, which lived on the steppes of Asia, fed on the seeds of grasses which were scattered on the earth and had to be searched for individually. Adapted to such a way of life originally, their descendants continue to dine in much the same manner. This not only results in their contaminating much more food than they devour, but also makes for problems in controlling them, notably in poisoning, for they must consume a fatal amount of a prepared bait.

As well as feeding behaviour which gives an impression of an inability to concentrate and having to be constantly on the alert for predators, the stresses of existence as a house mouse include a deplorable social life. Fierce conflict rages between unrelated male mice when they first meet. Eventually an order is established with a dominant male, the other males tending to keep out of his way but forming a hierarchy among themselves. Mice high up on the list are chased by fewer and chase more of their associates and *vice versa*. Not surprisingly, stress on 'bottom' mice affects their health and recent work in the U.S.A. shows that stressed mice are much more susceptible to parasites and disease.[166] There is, happy to relate, rather less aggression between members of the same family. Altogether house mice seem to lead a highly-strung life.

In appearance house mice are usually grey-brown or grey above and grey, sometimes tending to white, beneath, but odd colour varieties occur from time to time, even in wild mice. This is reflected in the extraordinary range of colouring produced by mouse fanciers through selective breeding. In the National Museum there are orange and black skins of wild mice caught in Dublin.

House mice, despite the name, are not uncommon in the countryside around farms and in hedgerows in cultivated ground, especially in summer, and can sometimes be trapped in sand dunes. Individuals moving into human habitation on the onset of colder weather in the autumn are sometimes referred to as 'field mice' but should not be confused with the long-tailed field mouse (*Apodemus sylvaticus*) which is probably the commonest of all the Irish mammals.

A famous population of house mice lives on the North Bull Island in Dublin Bay, an expanse of mainly sand dunes and salt marsh. At the turn of the century it was discovered that many of these mice were of a sandy hue on the upper surface which harmonized so closely with their surroundings that this was taken to be a case of special protective colouration, a camouflage which might have rendered them less visible to the predatory birds of the island.[124] There is no shortage of the latter;

Fig. 6 House mouse

13

I have seen the kestrels (*Falco tinnunculus*) and short-eared owls (*Asio otus*) there myself. Trapping on the island undertaken a few years ago confirmed that mice fitting the original description were still resident. I would stress that not all of the house mice on the island have sandy fur, some showing it only slightly and some not at all, and would remind readers of the great variation in colour already mentioned. However, the 'Bull mice' are still an interesting facet of the Irish fauna, worthy of further study.

The bank vole, which was only discovered in the south-west ten years ago, has not been much studied in Ireland, though there is an impressive accumulation of data on it from elsewhere. Bank voles look rather like mice but are rotund and have shorter ears and muzzles; their tails are about half the length of their bodies. Their fur is a rich chestnut on the head, back and flanks, fading to a creamy grey beneath. The voice is used often, at least it is when they are handled or in captivity, and it is a rather flat, querulous squeaking. The animal is a good climber. Work in Britain indicates a diet of seed, insects and a high proportion of green plant material, such as shoots, leaves and buds. Bank voles are found, almost exclusively, in vegetation affording dense cover and are numerous in overgrown banks, hedgerows and patches of bracken and bramble in woodland. Measurements of the skulls of the Irish voles suggest that they have minute peculiarities of their own.[78] For example, the distance across the *occipital condyles*, that part of the skull which fits into the uppermost of the back-bones, is rather larger than those of English and Scottish voles so far measured. I would hasten to add that such differences are in the order of fractions of a mm.

Badgers are sadly maligned animals. Inexplicably, many country people slander them without ever having seen one. The animal's supposed crimes can usually be laid at the fox's door and are often the result of an overactive imagination. That such animosity is almost traditional is shown by a statement in 1714 by Arthur Stringer, huntsman to Lord Conway on the shores of Lough Neagh: 'The badger is a very melancholy, fat creature, sleeps incessantly and naturally when in season very lecherous.' Though outstandingly perspicacious in most of his zoology, Stringer was blatantly contemptuous of badgers. He also writes

> When he is [dug] out the greatest use he is for is to kill him with hounds or mastiffs or if you have young terriers that you would enter, the best way is to cope or muzzle him so that he cannot bite and put him into an earth.

Badger digging is still practised. I have no wish to become embroiled in a controversy on field sports but will say this. In most of these, when properly carried out, the quarry is eventually dispatched fairly rapidly. The badger is a powerful beast, tenacious of life and, when forced to it, a formidable opponent. Killing one with dogs, especially a few dogs, is bound to be a protracted, bloody business for both sides. I have known experienced fox-shooters take their terriers away from holes where they believed badgers were in residence, preferring to give up the opportunity of raising a fox rather than risk a confrontation between their dogs and a badger. At the same time, I would be surprised if badger-digging, at the moment, constituted any real threat to the Irish badger population as a whole.

How much of a nuisance is a badger? Studies in Great Britain and my own efforts with foxes both suggest that the killing of poultry by badgers is, at most, an uncommon occurrence and that a fox is the culprit in most suspected cases. The evidence for lamb-killing is practically non-existent, although badgers may well consume ovine carrion on occasion, including dead lambs. Judging by the vast exaggeration of the depredations by foxes on lambs, it would be surprising if at least some blame

Fig. 7 Badger

did not finally reach the badger, whose name is already blackened.

The damage done by badgers to game birds is also probably small. The most reliable figures are those from the Eley Game Advisory Service (now the Game Bird Conservancy) at Fordingbridge in Hampshire. This is a research centre formerly run by the major manufacturer of shot-gun cartridges in the British Isles, which is basically interested in the best methods of raising the maximum number of birds for shooting. One would therefore expect plain speaking regarding predators. In their 4,000 acre (1,600 ha) shoot from 1948 to 1959, a total of 3,133 partridge (*Perdix perdix*) nests were located. Of these only thirty-nine, slightly over 1%, were shown to have been lost to badgers. To put this in perspective the relevant passage in the Eley booklet No. 16 *Enemies of Game* (1967) needs quoting.

> Badgers are not usually harmful to game interests, though on one occasion we lost eighteen known partridge nests to one rogue animal. The normal badger is an asset to the countryside, and should be left in peace.

One useful fact in determining whether damage is attributable to badgers is that they eat their food where they find it and do not carry it home.

Badgers are bulky animals, appearing grey at a distance, the head being marked with broad black and white stripes. In fact the body hairs are banded with black and white and consequently look grey when seen some way off. Often the 'white' is yellowish or reddish. Such 'red' badgers are sometimes remarked by country folk.

The badger digs a sett, a series of deep interconnecting burrows perhaps at several levels which may ramify far into the ground. These may be occupied by many generations and, in time, may take on the appearance of something of a fortress. Mr. C.D. Deane wrote of seeing one with thirty-five entrances.[39] The presence of dry grass or other vegetation scattered around the mouths of the holes is a fairly reliable indication of badgers as, unlike the fox, they are fastidious, change their bedding and keep their houses comparatively tidy. Setts are typically in copses or small patches of, usually, well drained scrub or agricultural ground but also in banks, sand dunes and on hillsides. Deane mentioned one in an abandoned farm-house in Co. Wicklow

15

and another under a road in Co. Down, which eventually caused part of the surface to collapse under a lorry.

Badgers usually emerge at dusk to feed and their menu is decidedly *a la carte*. The single most important item in Irish investigations appears to be earthworms[60] but young rabbits, mice and birds (possibly as carrion), slugs, snails, insects, fruits, seeds and even fungi are known to be eaten too.

A supposition, first mentioned by William Thompson in the middle of the last century, attributed to Thomas Pennant in the previous one, and still widespread is that there are two varieties of badger: the dog-badger, which is largely carnivorous, broad-jawed and truculent, and the pig-badger, mainly a herbivore and relatively inoffensive. The precise details I was informed of as far apart as Glencar, in Co. Kerry and Rathlin Island, Co. Antrim. It remains a supposition still.

Fig. 8 Pine marten

There is some reason for believing that the badger was scarcer in Ireland at the turn of the century than it is today, in the north especially. There are specific notes in the literature of around that time of badgers being sighted, suggesting that they were sufficiently scarce for their appearance to be noteworthy. Today badgers are exceedingly common, practically all over the country.

The pine marten, the rarest of all the Irish mammals, is not unlike a stoat or ferret in general body form, but is larger and has a bushy tail. The fur is a rich chocolate brown with a cream patch at the throat extending over part of the chest. The marten is often arboreal but is also found in rocky country, an extreme example being provided by the Burren, in Cos. Clare and Galway. Nothing particularly precise is known of its distribution although it appears to be common in a few districts, notably in the west and and particularly in Clare.

A study in Scotland[140] revealed that the bulk of the marten's food consisted of small birds and rodents but rabbits, hares, insects, fruit and other items were consumed as well. An analysis I made of a collection of droppings from a lair in the Burren[92] showed that the martens had eaten small birds, a field mouse, almost certainly a lizard (*Lacerta vivipara*), a snail, a beetle and several ivy fruits. 90% of the rodents eaten in Scotland were field voles (absent from Ireland), which are relatively easy to catch. Field mice are extremely agile and have surprising leaping powers. It is hardly odd, therefore, that only one was found in the Irish analysis. Current work on martens in Co. Clare, in which I have assisted in a minor capacity, includes extensive examinations of droppings. From this it is obvious that young hares, field mice, small birds, beetles, bees, earthworms and fruit are the main items of diet but that the odd lizard, frog (*Rana temporaria*), snail or woodlouse are not ignored. The consumption of fruit is, of course, seasonal and included were hazel nuts, cherries, blackberries, rowan berries, ivy fruits, raspberries and wild strawberries.

Arthur Stringer considered the food of the marten to be, for the most part, birds, rats, mice, snails and berries, and that they took poultry when they could. In his time, when martens were apparently more numerous, the latter was not unlikely. Though rats seem to be at variance with other results, the common rat in Stringer's time was the black species which, being arboreal, would present itself to the marten much more frequently than the brown does today. As it is also smaller, it would have been easier to tackle.

Martens are often known as 'marten-cats' and are, quite probably, the 'cats' referred to in Irish placenames and in ancient Irish poetry.

Mink are a recent addition to the mammal fauna, an unwelcome one, and can be confused with otters as both are dark brown, somewhat similar in appearance and live in and around water. Mink are smaller, have a white patch on the lower lip and sometimes a few other white spots on the underside. The head is more pointed than the broad face of the otter, and the otter's tail is thicker at the base and markedly tapered. Several colour varieties of mink are farmed in Ireland and may be seen in the countryside when they escape. After a few generations in the wild, however, the colouration reverts to the normal one.

The food of mink consists chiefly of mammals, birds and fish but with smaller quantities of frogs, insects and crayfish (*Astacus fluviatilis*). Available information on the food from Britain is conflicting. A study in England and Wales[36] indicated that mammals and birds were the main prey, with fish secondary and of only local importance. There was no evidence that salmon (*Salmo salar*) or trout (*Salmo trutta*) were taken. In Scotland,[2] research revealed that fish predominated in the diet though mammals and birds were of importance, and that salmon and trout were the most common species taken! Obviously work in this field is needed in Ireland as mink are clearly a potential

Fig. 9   Fallow deer stag. Notice the palmate (flattened) antlers.

pest. Nothing has been done yet. The only information is a list of sightings in the wild.[41]

There are three species of deer in Ireland. Red deer are the largest, have a red-brown summer coat and a more brownish winter pelage. The antlers, which only stags carry, are well developed in older animals and may bear over twelve 'points' in all, that is, six on each antler. The Japanese sika is similar in appearance but smaller with less complex antlers. The hair is not as red and there is faint but quite obvious white spotting on the summer coat. Unlike the rump of the red deer, which is yellowish, that of the sika is white and the upper part is bordered with black. Fallow deer range in colour from fawn with white spots to dark grey-brown, almost black in some cases, without them. Specimens of the latter extreme can be seen, among other places, at Randalstown Forest, Co. Antrim. The male is instantly recognisable from the antlers, which are flattened or palmate. The rump is similar to that of the sika but the tail is long, dark and edged with white. At Grangecon, Co. Wicklow, there is a herd of white-coloured fallow.

Red deer are to be found in a wild state in Ireland in three places but this is not to suggest that park deer are normally tame in the usually accepted sense of the word. There are probably nearly 1,000 head of wild red deer at Glenveagh, Co. Donegal, though estimates vary. Glenveagh is the only enclosed deer forest. 'Forest', in this context by the way, does not necessarily imply trees at all, but a fenced area. Maintaining a strict enclosure round a vast area is very difficult and escapees may be seen in surrounding districts. There are possibly about 200 red deer around Killarney and an equal number (perhaps) in the Wicklow mountains, but more of the latter in the next chapter. There are five red deer parks and at two of these the animals are kept for hunting purposes, namely the Montalto Estate at Ballynahinch, Co. Down, and at Ashbourne, Co. Meath. Mr Rory Harrington informs me that outliers from the latter have established themselves in the Boyne Valley. There are other parks at Moycullen, Co. Galway, Doneraile, Co. Cork, and Caledon, Co. Tyrone. In the last of these the deer have been interbred in the past with wapiti (Canadian red deer—*Cervus canadensis*) and, consequently, carry particularly fine heads of antlers.

Fallow deer are widespread though localized over much of Ireland, except in the extreme north-west, south-west and south-east. All are park deer or those descended from herds originally kept in parks which have gradually been allowed to escape as the parks were abandoned or allowed to fall into disrepair.

Japanese sika deer are present in very large numbers in the woods around Killarney and as far away as Kilgarvin and Killorglin. They are something of a pest, their browsing causing damage to young trees. They undoubtedly impede proper regeneration of the woodland. More recently they have extended their range to the Glengariff district of Co. Cork. Sika are also abundant in the afforested areas of the Wicklow mountains. There are herds at Colebrooke, Co. Fermanagh, and Baronscourt, Co. Tyrone, as well and a few from the latter have been established at the Gortin Gap Forest Park in the same county.

2

. . . and how they arrived

There is no need to begin with any general description of Ireland . . . But it may be desirable to recall a few topographical features . . . There is, first of all, its unique position—an island out in the North Atlantic, doubly cut off from direct continental influences by intervening seas. At the same time, it lies, along with the adjoining and larger island of Great Britain, on a shallow platform . . . so that a slightly higher level of the land, by spilling the water off the shelf, would allow, and has allowed at certain periods in the past, free immigration from the continent. These times were too long ago to have affected human affairs . . . but they had a considerable influence as regards the peopling of the land with the animals and plants which still occupy it.

The Way that I Went

R.L. Praeger

Every Irish child knows that, outside of the Phoenix Park and Bellevue Zoological Gardens, there are no snakes in Ireland whether directly due to saintly intervention or not. Indeed an attempted introduction of the said reptiles to Co. Down in 1831 resulted in at least one sermon on the imminence of the apocalypse. But that Ireland is serpentless is a single example of the poverty of her fauna, for this is reflected also in the relatively smaller numbers of the species of birds, fishes, insects and virtually all other animal groups compared to those in Great Britain. From the previous chapter the reader will have learned that there are several English mammals which are unknown in Ireland. But on the continent there are about 150 species of mammal, many more than in Great Britain. These facts are worth pondering—they provide scope for almost unlimited speculation, but one possible theory appeals to most: that Ireland received her fauna from the rest of Europe via Britain and that whereas some species made both stages of the journey others only managed the first.

Any account of the origins of the present Irish mammal fauna must start some 600,000 years ago at the beginning of an epoch in the world's history known as the Pleistocene Period, more commonly spoken of as the 'Ice Age'. During this time the ice caps at the poles expanded over much of the world which is not now covered by ice, though we are concerned exclusively with the northern hemisphere. The coverage was by no means permanent. There were four main phases (or glaciations) separated by warmer periods when the ice retreated to the region of the pole. In fact the combined length of time of these warmer periods was greater than that of the glaciations. Each of the latter was again interspersed with shorter, relatively temperate periods. Furthermore on some occasions the ice moved back further than its limits today and the climate was then warmer than the present one.

The vast fields of ice effectively lowered the level of the sea. This was for two reasons. Firstly the water which formed the ice cap came from the sea and secondly, to a lesser extent, the pressure the glaciers exerted on the earth beneath them resulted in other ice-free areas being pushed upwards. For part of the time, therefore, not only was Britain linked to Ireland but to the continent as well.

The advance of the ice sheets was accompanied by a deterioration in the climate and their retreat by a corresponding improvement. As the weather became colder in Europe, the animals characteristic of the temperate regions were forced south and they were replaced by those of colder climates which had been driven down from the north. The process was naturally reversed as the ice receded. This cycle of events was repeated a number of times.

The penultimate glaciation completely covered Ireland and the chances of any mammals having survived it are remote. During the last glaciation, which ended some 8,000 years ago, the coverage is not thought to have been so complete, but the exposed areas would have been little more than tundra when the ice extended to its southern limit. As it finally melted the sea level rose and Ireland was cut off from Britain. The land-link between Britain and the continent was, in contrast, severed at a much later date. We know this largely because whereas a lowering of the present sea level by 30m would render a channel tunnel obsolete, a drop of 60m would be needed to connect Britain and Ireland—by a land bridge between Co. 'Derry and Scotland. It is believed that when such a link existed the climate was still a cold one. This conclusion, like many others concerning the Pleistocene, is drawn from the geological evidence regarding the position of the ice and the shoreline at the time and extensive work on pollen analysis. The structure of the pollen of most plants is extremely characteristic and it often remains preserved in the earth in large amounts. So an analysis of pollen in soil levels of known age may yield an accurate picture of the prevailing vegetation of the time and therefore, indirectly, of the climate as well.

It follows from this that the present mammal fauna in Ireland is made up either of animals which were already there before the glaciation, arrived before the Ulster-Scottish land bridge was lost, have managed to cross the sea themselves, or have been introduced by man, whether accidentally or deliberately. The importance of sea crossings and especially introductions by man has frequently been overlooked or, sorry to state, played down in the past. So there have been numerous attempts to interpret the composition of the Irish fauna (including the anomalies between the list of mammals found in Britain and those in Ireland) largely in terms of survival from earlier interglacials and orderly post-glacial colonization. However, these alone cannot be made to account for everything. Ireland has no moles, for instance, for they would have been unable to burrow in frozen soil (a satisfactory explanation) but there *are* hedgehogs. As noted in the last chapter, the hedgehog, though found in open country, requires cover. It is practically unknown above the latitude of 60°N. Moreover it hibernates and is active largely at night. It therefore seems a most unlikely candidate for arrival in Ireland in severe post-glacial conditions. Again, long-tailed field mice are common in both Britain and Ireland but field voles are absent from the latter island. Field voles extend into the tundra of northern Europe whereas field mice are never found north of the tree-line. It is highly unlikely, therefore, that the mice would have colonized ahead of the voles after the last glaciation and so have reached Ireland ahead of them. Such examples must be explained by introduction, and man is known to have settled in Co. Antrim nearly as far back as 8,000 B.C.

There have, in fact, been several efforts to explain the Irish fauna in terms which often stretched the geological and zoological evidence beyond its limits, including such wonderful theories as land bridges to Spain and hypothetical ice-free lands off the south-west coast with comparatively temperate climates. Such lands have now, needless to say, conveniently sunk beneath the waves and their former existence is difficult to disprove! The simpler explanation was seemingly regarded as insufficiently ingenious. That it was largely rejected up to quite recently is, regrettably, partly due to its offence to the ingenuity of some scientists and, in the case of Irishmen possibly (dare I say it?) because it has been regarded as, in an oblique way, a slight on the respectability of their country's fauna. A quotation from Dr. G.B. Corbet,[29] of the British Museum, the present authority on such matters, seems pertinent.

The Irish fauna as a whole is of such an erratic composition as to suggest a series of chance introductions rather than an orderly sequence of arctic, followed by more temperate, faunas, until at some stage the supply has suddenly stopped due to severance of the land connexion. The absence of voles suggests that the last connexion (to Scotland) was severed at a very early climatic stage. However, a narrow channel or wide river would effectively bar small mammals while allowing unrestricted passage to many insects, birds and plants. Thus a south-flowing river could have allowed such selective colonization in the southern Irish Sea region while a truly terrestrial bridge in the North was inaccessible to most species because of the climatic severity.

Although bank voles are now known from part of Ireland, they are almost certainly a fairly recent introduction and, as such, in no way invalidate the above argument.

During the Pleistocene and in early post-glacial times there were a number of mammals in Ireland which are now extinct. Most of the evidence for their presence is in the form of bones excavated from clay deposits beneath bogs and from caves. The list included[177] lemmings (*Dicrostonyx gulielmi* and *henseli*), reindeer (*Rangifer tarandus*), arctic fox (*Alopex lagopus*) and lynx (*Felix lynx*), all of which are characteristic of the colder parts of northern Europe today. There were also brown bear (*Ursus arctos*), spotted hyaena (*Crocuta crocuta*), wolf (*Canis lupus*), mammoth (*Mammuthus primigenius*) and the celebrated giant Irish deer (*Megaceros giganteus*). The latter beast was as big as a horse and had antlers spanning sometimes nearly 3m. (Larger measurements, often quoted, refer to the distance *round* the antlers.) Deer shed and regrow their antlers annually! Reconstructed skeletons of this awesome animal can be seen on prominent display in Irish museums. The giant deer was, in point of fact, widespread in the rest of Europe at the time but remains have been found in largest numbers in Ireland. Besides those mammals already mentioned there may have been others such as wild boar (*Sus scrofa*), but their presence is doubtful. Precise reasons for the extinction of the animals listed above are not known. Doubtless the change in climate and consequent change in vegetation and food supply were the cause in many cases, either directly or indirectly.

Of the mammals present in Ireland today, the pigmy shrew, fox, marten, stoat, badger, otter, red deer, Irish hare and all the bats are usually regarded as indigenous. Of these the hare, the stoat and the shrew could all have been early post-glacial colonizers. The Irish hare, as explained in Chapter 1, is a subspecies of the Arctic hare and the present range of the stoat also extends into the arctic. The pigmy shrew shares an almost identical geographical range with the common shrew on the continent but extends up to higher altitudes, suggesting a greater tolerance of extreme conditions. It may have been able to cross to Ireland before the common shrew arrived on the scene. On the other hand it may, as may the hare and stoat, have survived the ultimate glaciation. Again, it could quite well be an introduction by man.

Red deer, remains of which have been found in Pleistocene cave deposits, are quite likely to have been present during the last advance of the ice. In any event, a short sea crossing would have posed few problems for them. Formerly widespread, the the only native stock remaining are those in the Killarney district and even these may possibly have a small measure of foreign blood from imported animals. There are records of red deer being brought to Ireland from as far back as 1244. Elsewhere Irish red deer died out, probably before 1850, and the other herds are all derived from introductions.

A long swim would present no problem for many otters and they probably still cross the Irish Sea. An alleged account of such an incident was published in 1950.[146]

Bats, needless to say, can fly and some specimens have been taken at lighthouses and lightships at considerable distances from the coast. In 1891 a long-eared bat was caught at the Teeraght lighthouse and, in the same year, a Daubenton's bat was seen on the Lucifer shoals lightship, both of which are 16km (9 miles) offshore.

Fig. 10 Red squirrel

In 1898 a pipistrelle was picked up dead on the South Arklow lightship, 11 km (7 miles) from land.[17] So the Irish Sea might have been crossed by all seven species, especially when the gap between the two islands was narrower. That the lesser horseshoe bat has been met with only in the south-west is, however, in need of some further explanation. It is by no means impossible that other species of bat will reach Ireland in the future. In this context it is interesting that a continental vagrant, Nathusius's pipistrelle (*Pipistrellus nathusii*), was found in an English roost in 1969.[191] Little can be said of the origins of the fox, badger, marten and red squirrel save that they have been here since before historic time. Maybe some of them could have suc-

Fig. 11 Grey squirrel

ceeded in swimming a narrow channel and human introduction is a possibility, the skins of squirrels, foxes and especially martens being prized from early times—but this is mere speculation.

Augustin, in 655 A.D., mentioned foxes and badgers in Ireland and he made a quaint and enigmatic reference ('sesquivolos') which may have been to squirrels. Strange to state, his squirrels were not, in all probability, the progenitors of the squirrel population today. Of the red squirrel's abundance in time past there is conclusive proof in the records of the levies on its skins for export, but the latest of these was in 1662. Whether through overhunting by man or not the red squirrel apparently died out after this although the precise date of its disappearance is unknown. From about 1815 there were extensive importations, accurately documented, throughout much of the nineteenth century,[15] so that, by 1910 all thirty-two counties had resident populations.

As argued earlier, the field mouse is certainly an introduction. Much the same, indeed, can be said of its presence on other islands off the coast of Britain where voles are absent. Certainly it is found on more of these than any other small mammal, which would tend to suggest that it is more readily introduced. Trade between the

24

British Isles was considerable in pre-historic times, and included *inter alia* the carriage of sheep and cattle (presumably with fodder for them), peat and roofing turf, all of which could have concealed small mammals. Trade of this kind with larger islands would have been much less because they would have had resources of their own. This probably accounts for the landing of field mice in Ireland but not of voles and common shrews, or, at least, not voles and common shrews which survived.

As already reasoned the hedgehog too has probably been brought to Ireland by man. It appears unlikely that this was accidental as the animal in question is much larger, usually slower and much more conspicuous than a mouse. This is not to say that it would have been impossible. In 1974, for example, one turned up in a Bournemouth ironmonger's shop among a consignment of kettles from Poland.[9] Yet the hedgehog may have been introduced to Ireland intentionally, possibly as a source of food or for use in processing wool for cloth. That hedgehogs have been domesticated in Europe since the fourth century B.C. is implicit in Aristotle's writings. The Romans used their spiny coats for hackling cloth or in wool-carding. So much so that at one time an anxious Senate passed a law to regulate their destruction. The ancients could have eaten them as well. It would be surprising if such gastronomical experimenters as the Romans did not. The earliest actual record of their use as food in Britain is of 'hyrchouns' (urchins) being served at a feast in 1425 but there are many others, especially from the last century. For example the naturalist and fisherman-extraordinary Frank Buckland told of a farm where they were consumed regularly and of a market in the City of London at which dealers sold them in large numbers. That gypsies ate hedgehogs, at least until fairly recently, is fairly widely known. No doubt they were esteemed a delicacy for a very long time. An acquaintance of my own who lives close to the land has recommended the dish with enthusiasm.

The domestic rats and mice were all imported by man. Perhaps this is being unfair as it is really a case of seafaring rodents coming ashore of their own accord. It is not difficult to see how this happened (and is still happening) but, rather, hard to see how it could have been avoided.

Fig. 12 Hedgehog

25

The original home of the house mouse was in the East and it is still to be found there, living on the seeds of wild grasses, on the steppes of central Asia, Turkestan, and Persia, where remains of man's earliest agricultural settlements have been found. House mice had the appropriate feeding adaptations and were around at the right time and place to take advantage of agriculture. As they were small, unobtrusive, nocturnal and extremely prolific, Neolithic man was unable to shake off his unwelcome messmates. On the other hand the mice were sufficiently pugnacious to chase off possible competitors of similar size. Eventually the house mouse spread by trade routes to Europe and may have reached Ireland in prehistoric times.

The celebrated eastern house mouse might equally be entitled 'the mouse that never was', in Ireland at any rate, though reference is generally made to it in accounts of the Irish fauna.[75] The history of this intriguing quadruped began in 1935 when the the late Eugene O'Mahony, of the Natural History section of the National Museum, claimed to have found a new race or subspecies of the house mouse in Ireland, on the basis of a number of skins from individuals caught on the east coast. It was sandy-brown above, white beneath and had white feet. He compared his finds with as many examples of the various subspecies he could find (and there are many, both real and imaginary), even travelling to the British Museum in London to do so. Finally he was sent two skins from Cairo which he considered indistinguishable from his specimens. He concluded that the 'subspecies' had come from Egypt and was *Mus musculus orientalis*, as distinct from the common Irish *Mus musculus domesticus*.

In the late 'sixties it occurred to me that the whole business was rather suspicious. That O'Mahony's mice looked like the Egyptian ones was not conclusive proof that they, too, originated in Egypt. Furthermore, how could a race of mice retain its characteristic coat colours if it interbred with native mice? O'Mahony . . . 'found nothing to suggest interbreeding', but one does not often see house mice mating. They are fearful of man at the best of times and, up to a few hundred years ago, it was widely accepted that they did not reproduce sexually anyway but came into being through spontaneous generation. If the two races did not interbreed, how did the foreign one compete successfully in small numbers with so near a relative? Lastly, if sandy coloured individuals appeared on the North Bull Island, what was so surprising about the odd sandy mouse on the nearby mainland? Moreover a search of the literature revealed that at least two authors had considered these *orientalis* mice to be nothing of the kind.

In 1970 I examined the skins in the National Museum and found them much as O'Mahony described. However, there were others, some with *domesticus* colouring on the upper surface and *orientalis* under surfaces, and *vice versa*. A few *domesticus* specimens had white hair on the feet and one, which had not, was like *orientalis* in every other respect. It was obvious that material typical of the two 'subspecies' had been considered and possible intermediates had been ignored. In other words, there were not two races. O'Mahony's description was of one extreme kind of variation of the 'ordinary' house mouse. I sent coloured photographs of the mice to Drs. R.J. Berry and M.E. Jakobson in London who, in the course of their researches, had examined thousands of wild house mice. Both were quite sure that the supposed *orientalis* were well within the normal range of colours shown by the mouse in Britain. The Ulster Museum has several skins of specimens caught in one garden in the suburbs of Belfast. Even these show the same variety of colouration as between the two 'types'. The Eastern house mouse was manifestly an artefact.

In 1937 O'Mahony described two further subspecies, both just as invalid. To be fair to him, he worked at a time when 'splitting' (the excessive sub-division of animal groupings) was still in fashion among mammalogists, and there were many emi-

Fig. 13 Black rat

nent splitters. He carried out fine research on birds and insects, especially parasitic insects, and some on mammals.

The black rat was formerly distributed in south-east Asia but has been carried all over the world from the Middle Ages onward, bringing with it the sinister flea, *Xenopsylla cheopis*, the vector of bubonic plague. Giraldus Cambrensis mentioned the presence of rats in Ireland in 1185.

The brown rat population, too, expanded from eastern Asia, probably China and Siberia, but it was a latecomer, reaching the British Isles only in the early eighteenth century. Vast hordes were reported crossing the Volga in 1727. Rutty (more of whom in the next chapter) wrote that they began to infest the Dublin district about 1722. A statement in *Walsh's Impartial Newsletter* dated 1729 also seems pertinent.

Fig. 14 Brown rat

This morning we have an account from Merrion that a parcel of those outlandish Marramounts which are called Mountain Rats, who are now here, grow very common; that they walk in droves and do a great deal of mischief—the writer describes how they ate a woman and nurse child in Merrion. People killed several who are as big as Katts and Rabbits. This part of the country is infested with them. Likewise we hear from Rathfarnham that the like vermin destroyed a little girl in the Field; they are to be seen like Rabbits, and are so impudent that they suck the cows—nay abundance of them are to be seen in Fleet Street.

It is a moot point whether mendacity and sensationalism in the press have waned to any extent since then. The brown rat rapidly replaced the black and the latter is now, as stated in Chapter 1, only found in temporary settlements at ports. By 1744 the brown was indisputably the common species since a statute passed in that year offering bounties for the killing of several animals including 'water rats, commonly called "Norway rats" ' made no mention of the black rat, which can therefore have been of little importance.

The ancient Irish took hunting very seriously and wrote at length of beasts of the chase, including hares, but never of rabbits. Presumably there were none. Although the Romans are sometimes credited with first taking them to Britain there is no solid evidence for this and it can be assumed that the Normans were responsible for their introduction to both England and Ireland. It is significant that there is no mention of warrens in the Domesday Book (1086). Warrens in Ireland were first written of at at the time of Edward I, between 1274 and 1307. A record of 1282 informs us that twenty skins from Ballysax, Co. Kildare, were priced at 1s 4d (6.7p). By the fourteenth century skins were being exported regularly.

During the nineteenth century there were several attempts to populate Ireland with brown hares but, in most cases, the stocks died out.[12] However, those put down at Strabane in Co. Tyrone in 1876 thrived and similar introductions in the same county, and in Cos. 'Derry and Donegal, also met with success. It is generally accepted that brown hares are still at least locally common in these three counties (although I have no direct personal knowledge of this) and that they may occur in other parts of Ireland. Attempts to establish mountain hares from Scotland have failed. In any event, even it they had survived, they would presumably have interbred with the native

Fig. 15 Rabbit

Fig. 16 Red deer

form and the foreign blood have been rapidly diluted within a few generations.

Of the species of introduced deer, the fallow has by far the longest history, although the exact date of its arrival is uncertain. The earliest record appears to be of a gift of twelve animals in 1296 to Eustace le Poer (an ancestor of the Power family of Curraghmore, Co. Waterford) from the Royal Forest of Glencree in Co. Wicklow. The original introduction must therefore have been before this. Fallow deer were also stated to be living in Ireland by Ranulphus Higden in his *Polychronicon*, written during the fourteenth century. Fynes Moryson in his *Itinerary* (1617) remarked

> The Earle of Ormond in Mounster, and the Earle of Kildare in Leinster, had each of them a small Parke enclosed for Fallow Deare, and I have not seene any other at the time, yet in many Woods they have red Deare, loosely scattered . . . They have also about Ophalia and Wexford, and in some parts of Mounster, some Fallow Deare scattered in the wood . . .

suggesting that, even then, fallow had escaped and established themselves in the wild.

The arrival of Japanese sika is recent and much better documented. At the end of the eighteen-fifties Viscount Powerscourt tried to acclimatize various deer in his estate in Co. Wicklow, including axis (*Axis axis*), sambar (*Cervus unicolor*), and wapiti, but with scant success. It is reported that the wapiti had to be destroyed when the stags 'became savage'. In 1860 he released four sika into his demesne, which by 1834 had increased to a herd of 100 head even though a few were regularly shot or exported each year. Animals transported from Powerscourt formed the basis of the other herds in Ireland today.

The final consequences of bringing those four sika to Ireland may be most unfortunate if the species is not properly controlled by a reasoned, selective shooting policy, which will likely have to be an intensive one in some areas. Speaking generally, deer in Ireland may be regarded either as a nuisance, as game, as a natural resource or as an embellishment to the scenery. The latter attitude is readily understandable but their graceful movements, appealing liquid eyes, apparent harmlessness and the regal associations of the antlers sometimes provoke a response more emotional than rational. Complete protection is quite illogical and some form of management programme is essential if sika, at any rate, are not to become a pest.

Viscount Powerscourt succeeded in mating red deer with sika in his park and the offspring proved fertile. As a direct result in Wicklow today, a hundred years later, there are probably very few, if any, pure red deer, the 'red deer' of the mountain tops being largely hybrids.[106] (Hybridization between the two species has also been observed at Colebrooke in the last century, and in Great Britain and quite recently in Cos. Fermanagh and Tyrone.)[107] While the initial unions were admittedly in captivity, it is clear that once such a link is forged between the two populations—a hybrid no doubt mating easily with either species—interbreeding can continue in the wild. Both species co-exist in Killarney at the moment in a pure state, but there is at least a possibility of the vital initial crosses taking place or of a hybrid animal being introduced from outside. So the integrity of the only native deer in Ireland may well be in danger. In my opinion they *are* worth preserving as such. That interbreeding has not occurred to date in Killarney is no guarantee that it will not happen in the future. Quite possibly it may not, but we know so little of the necessary conditions that the opportunity for a cross cannot be ruled out. This latent threat, along with the damage to woodlands of considerable beauty and of great intrinsic and scientific value, invites drastic measures. While precipitate moves are never desirable, it must be remembered that the sika is an alien of not

Fig. 17 Sika deer

much more than 100 years standing, so that it could probably be exterminated in Co. Kerry with no very serious ecological repercussions. A compromise would be to remove some of the red deer to a sanctuary area and keep out the sika. Perhaps current research will point to the best course of action.

Attempts, too, were made to introduce the roe deer to Ireland during the nineteenth century, for example at Colebrooke. These were unsuccessful except at Lissadell, Co. Sligo, where a herd was built up in the eighteen-seventies. Some of the later generations had particularly heavy antlers, sometimes said to have been

Fig. 18 Mink

the finest in Europe.[151] Nevertheless, all of them died out within some fifty years—hearsay has it through mismanagement and poaching. Rumours persist that there are still roe deer in the wild in Ireland. This is only a remote possibility.

A further three species of mammal were added to the Irish list during the present century. American grey squirrels were, sad to state, set free in the neighbourhood of Castle Forbes in Co. Longford in 1911 and have since spread to ten other counties.

A recent addition is the American mink. Mink were first ranched in Ireland in 1950[41] and by 1960 there was a thriving industry with a total of forty farms throughout the country. Legislation to control such farming was introduced by the respective governments in 1965 and 1968, prohibiting the keeping of the animals without a licence. By 1969 there were only twenty-four farms but in a total of fifteen counties; two of the former contained over 10,000 animals and one was

Fig. 19 Bank vole

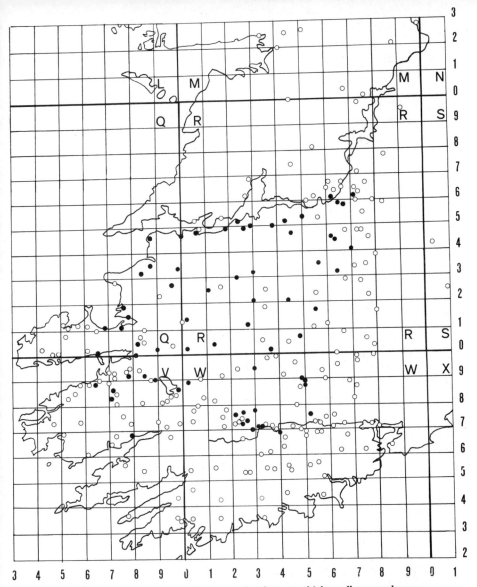

Fig. 20   Map of south-west Ireland showing localities at which small mammals were trapped from 1964 to 1970. Blocked circles indicate localities where bank voles were caught, open circles where they were not (with acknowledgement to the Royal Irish Academy).

reported to house over 50,000. With such large numbers of these intelligent animals in captivity some escapes were inevitable, whether due to damage to the cages, vandalism or the difficulties inherent in handling them. By this time (1969) mink had been sighted in the wild in eleven counties and were known to be breeding in at least one, Co. Tyrone, where thirty-five individuals had escaped earlier. Mink are well established in Great Britain. The same will soon, no doubt, be true of Ireland.

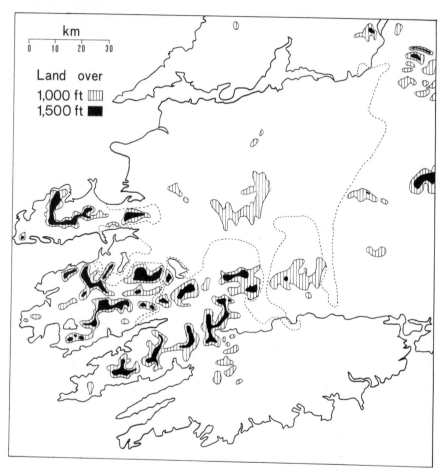

Fig. 21   *Map of south-west Ireland showing the main areas of high ground and the probable range of the bank vole in 1970. The suggested limit of its range is indicated by a broken line (with acknowledgement to the Royal Irish Academy).*

In August 1964 a research student at University College, Cork was trapping rodents at Listowel, Co. Kerry, when he caught an unusual 'mouse'. It was dumpier than a field mouse and had red-brown fur, quite unlike the usual wood brown of that rodent. It turned out to be a bank vole, contradicting the oft-repeated statement that Ireland has no voles. A few people have trapped in the south-west since, providing further information on where it does and does not occur. In 1969 I decided to start an intensive trapping programme to determine its distribution. Thus by late 1970 there were results from a combined total of over 250 localities[77] where small mammals had been trapped in the south-west from 1964 to 1970. These sites are shown in Fig. 20 and from this a tentative map of the distribution was produced, depicted in Fig.21. As the traps were always set in heavy cover, voles were by far the most common species caught—when they were caught. On balance, therefore, it seems reasonable to infer that they were not present at most of the points where only mice and shrews were taken. Fig. 21 is necessarily

34

a reasoned interpretation of the results and there are minor alternatives.

Since the vole is restricted to one part of Ireland and there is nothing to prevent its advance—mountains and rivers are the only real barriers and these perhaps temporarily—so it is logical to suppose that it is a relatively recent introduction. One can also legitimately postulate that, as it was almost certainly only introduced once, it must have arrived somewhere in the middle of its present range: in northeast Kerry or north-west Limerick. Since no one has measured the rate of its spread, estimates of its time of arrival are merely speculative. Even so, some people seem to thrive on futile conjecture of this kind. It seems reasonable to conclude that the bank vole reached Ireland within the past 150 years. However it *could* have come in the last twenty.

Mention has now been made of the appearance of all the extant mammals, but there were other unsuccessful introductions, besides those already noted. Indeed the list can be continued to an inordinate length if we consider single representatives of each species. The one which came nearest to success was the musk rat (*Ondatra zibethica*), a rodent of lakes, streams and marshes in North America. A single pair of these animals, which are rather larger than brown rats and something similar in appearance, were brought from Canada to Nenagh, Co. Tipperary, in 1927. They proceeded to gnaw through the wire of their cages and escape, presumably to the Nenagh River. Nothing more was reported for nearly six years but, in the meantime, the rats had been busy and reproduced themselves at a rate little short of splendid. Inquiries, after two had been shot at Dromineer, Co. Tipperary, in 1933 revealed, alarmingly, that they were quite common over an area of some 415 sq km (150 sq miles).

Escapes from fur farms in England and Scotland had already taken place in 1929 and the escapees had not only bred but had seriously undermined river banks with their excavations. Control measures had been introduced and the rats were finally exterminated in 1937. With the situation across the Irish sea in mind, the

Fig. 22 Musk rat

government moved with commendable swiftness and almost immediately introduced legislation for the extermination of the musk rats, on 24th July 1933. By May 1934 the job had been completed with an official tally of 487 killed.[101] Apart from a few fine skins, salvaged from the massacre, and now mostly in the National Museum, the musk rat is merely (an admittedly lesser-known) part of Irish history.

Numbers of another rodent, the coypu or nutria from South America, which is bred for its fur, escaped in Co. Tyrone in 1944 but all of these were quickly killed. Great Britain has been less fortunate and coypu have been living in the wild in East Anglia since before the second world war.

Various attempts have been made to acclimatize other mammals in Ireland including rocky mountain sheep (*Ovis canadensis*), mouflon (*Ovis musimon*), musk oxen (*Ovis moschatus*) and bison (*Bison bonasus*). Even dormice and greater horseshoe bats have been released in an ill-conceived effort to augment the impoverished Irish fauna. These were all regrettable and, happily, unsuccessful. One of the most curious instances was of the mongooses (an unsettling if accurate plural) on the port areas of 'Derry and Belfast 'to keep rats away from the sides of bacon'. The last of these were killed in 1954. Strangely enough, three mongooses were captured in Belfast within a short space of time in the first few years of the present century. The last of these was trapped after the loss of a number of domestic fowl from a house on the Cavehill Road.

In the middle of the last century an armadillo was found wandering about the fields in Co. Meath, having been thrown out for dead from a travelling menagerie.

Three zoological curiosities would hardly be amiss in rounding off the chapter. They will, perhaps, serve as a warning to those who might jump to the wrong conclusions concerning the presence of mammals in Ireland on too little evidence. The first is the only instance of a mole in Ireland. As will be discussed at length in the chapter on owls, birds of prey often regurgitate the hair and bones of their mammalian prey in the form of pellets. Such a pellet was picked up by the late R.J. Welch in 1905 at Benevenagh, Co. 'Derry, and proved to contain the skull of a mole.[1] Presumably the unfortunate animal had been eaten by a migrant predatory bird which had just arrived from Scotland.

Welch, it may be said, besides being a photographer of almost legendary repute, was an inveterate collector and supplied many useful finds to naturalists, especially around the turn of the century, besides assembling the finest of all individual collections of Irish shells. These, together with his photographic negatives, are in the Ulster Museum. In 1933 he published some correspondence he had had with the finder of a dead common porpoise (*Phocaena phocaena*) in the river Cusher, near Tanderagee, Co. Armagh, Welch's attention being first drawn to the incident through an account in the press. The discovery was an extraordinary one as the Cusher flows into Lough Neagh, a freshwater lake drained to the north coast by the River Bann. The animal would seem therefore to have swum over 80km upstream before expiring. Abroad, some species are found well up river and indeed there were instances in the nineteenth century of porpoises as far up the River Suir as Waterford, but so long a swim for a common porpoise was unprecedented. Some time later Welch came upon the explanation, which he again published. The animal had been brought from Ardglass on the Co. Down coast on a lorry, but being rather 'high' for exhibition, had been tipped off the vehicle into the river.

The third oddity is an instance of blue hares in Ireland. In the nineteen-fifties, golden eagles (*Aquila chrysaetos*) nested for eight consecutive seasons on sea cliffs in northern Co. Antrim. An examination of the site by Mr. C.D. Deane of the Ulster

Museum revealed that rabbits and hares were the principal prey.[38] The latter were not Irish hares, or even brown hares, but blue hares. Presumably the eagles, which had no doubt originally come from Scotland, were returning to hunt on the Mull of Kintyre, a journey of at least 43km (27 miles) for the return trip. Stranger still is a reference to similar events a century and a half earlier. For in 1811 a Rev. Dr. William Hamilton Drummond published the poem *The Giants' Causeway* which, musing on the eagles of North Antrim, runs

> Far o'er the seas with level wings he skims,
> Sports in the clouds, or through deep azure swims,
> 'Till near Cantire he wheels his rapid course,
> Or mid th' Ebudae, with the lightning's force
> Darts sudden down to pounce the trembling hare,
> Or from the shepherd rend his fleecy care.

3

The Irish Mammalogists, what they wrote and where they wrote it

Although the lives of studious men may, generally speaking, present fewer striking incidents than those of warriors, navigators and politicians, yet the memoirs of naturalists are always extremely interesting, on account of the connexion in which they are necessarily placed with whatever is curious, beautiful or sublime in creation.

Lives of Eminent Zoologists   William Magillivray

A mammalogist is someone who studies mammals, but few of the Irish mammalogists have been this alone and even fewer have had the reputation of specializing in the field. This is hardly surprising, for it is only within the past forty years that so many naturalists have come to concentrate their energies on a single aspect of flora and fauna. For breadth of knowledge in natural history our Victorian and Edwardian great-grandparents would put most of us to shame.

The scientific attitude is, historically speaking, a recent one and the true spirit of scepticism, an unwillingness to accept any assertion whatsoever unless grounded on proven fact, is not much more than 200 years old. True, it was evolving much earlier, but scientists were then very much the exception. Even the members of the Royal Society in the seventeenth century, although striving after the truth of natural phenomena, were, when baffled, quite likely to fall back on irrationality or mysticism. Some were merely engaged in a hunt for the bizarre.

Well into the beginning of the seventeenth century the study of animals was a most inexact science. Based on the writings of Aristotle and Pliny, filled out with allegory and superstition, zoology was the handmaiden of ethics. Animals were studied almost entirely as moral examples either in their appearance or behaviour. Verification by direct observation never seemed to occur to anyone. No doubt the majority preferred entertaining falsehood to the more prosaic unvarnished truth, and a tendency in this direction still lingers with us. The attitude was epitomized by Sir Thomas Browne who pointed out that many '. . . impossible falsities do notwithstanding include wholesome moralities and such as expiate the trespass of their absurdities'. Even as late as 1675 the learned Jesuit Kircherus catalogued griffins and mermaids among the passengers in Noah's Ark. This approach is not yet dead, even today. During the past year I have in Belfast twice heard from the pulpit, in children's addresses, liberties taken with widely recorded zoological facts which made me squirm in my pew.

In earlier times the existence of the chimera, basilisk, unicorn and cockatrice were unquestioned. It was universally accepted that, for example, beavers bit off their testicles when pursued, tigers' whiskers were deadly poison and that pelicans fed their young with their own blood. So it was not until the beginning of the eighteenth century that the first data on Irish mammals appeared which had the marks of an objective study, and more than a hundred years later before any sustained flow of information. In contrast, botany made headway much faster than zoology, for wild plants were studied more seriously, often with a view to their therapeutic value.

The early writers Augustin and Giraldus Cambrensis were referred to in the last chapter. Augustin is sometimes given the honorary title of the first Irish naturalist, on a thin enough offering to be sure. In 655 he wrote his *Liber de mirabilibus Sanctae Scripturae* and included in it the earliest known list of Irish animals.

Quis enim, verbi gratia, lupos, cervos et sylvaticos porcos, et vulpes, taxones et lepusculos et sesquivolos in Hiberniam deveheret?

or

Who indeed could have brought wolves, deer, wild swine, foxes, badgers, little hares (?) and squirrels (?) to Ireland?

For many years his work was confused with that of St. Augustine of Hippo and it is probably due to this fortunate error that it was preserved.

Giraldus Cambrensis was a Welsh ecclesiastic of the twelfth century who first visited Ireland in 1183. In 1184 he joined the entourage of Henry II where he spent part of his time as tutor to Prince John (the future 'bad King John' of school history books), with whom he returned to Ireland in 1185. A few years afterwards he completed his *Topographica Hibernica*, the only major contemporary account of Ireland, which has proved of great value to historians, if rather less to zoologists. Giraldus himself was obviously very pleased with his efforts and so, no doubt, were many Irishmen, who are ever ready to inform a credulous foreigner. Giraldus's main ambition in life was to hold the see of St. David's, possibly because of a sentimental desire for his uncle's bishopric but more probably to bring about some sort of independence from Canterbury for the Welsh church. At any rate he never achieved it, being rejected twice, perhaps because the authorities saw that the appointment of a Welshman to a Welsh see was a way of making a rod for their own backs. His main achievement seems to have been his literary work, though he was coadjutor with the bishop of Ely, who was entrusted with administering the state when Richard *Coeur de Lion* was off crusading.

The *Topographica Hibernica* is an amalgam of fact, fibs and fantasy and much of it is patently absurd. It is undoubtedly of much use but, from the scientific point of view, so apocryphal a document is not to be relied upon without supporting evidence. One has only to read the more palpable nonsense to realise this. For instance, Ireland is said to be low lying around the coasts and mountainous in the centre. It is also suggested that the view of Ireland from England is clearer than that of England from Ireland, because of the distance. There is an extensive list of miracles including, *inter alia*, a fish with three gold teeth, a floating island and an animal half-ox, half-man.

Of the mammals Giraldus writes (and the Wright translation is quoted here):

This island contains nearly all the species of wild animals which are bred in the western countries. It produces stags so fat that they lose their speed, and the more slender they are in shape the more nobly they carry their heads and branching antlers. In no part of the world are such vast herds of boars and wild pigs to be found: but they are a small, ill-shaped, and cowardly breed, no less degenerate in boldness and ferocity than in their growth and shape. There are a great number of hares, but they are a small breed, much resembling rabbits both in size and the softness of their fur. In short, it will be found that the bodies of all animals, wild beasts, and birds, each in its kind, are smaller here than in other countries; while the men alone retain their full dimensions. It is remarkable in these hares that contrary to the usual instincts of that animal, when found by the dogs, they keep to cover like foxes, running in the woods instead of in open country, and never taking to the plains and beaten paths, unless they are driven to it. This difference in their habits, is, I think, caused by the rankness of the herbage in the plains, checking their speed. Martens are very plentiful in the woods; in hunting which the day is prolonged through the night by means of fires. For night coming on, a fire is lighted under the tree in which the hunted animal has taken refuge from the dogs, and being kept burning all night, the marten eyeing its brightness from the boughs above, without quitting its post, either is so fascinated by it, or, rather, so much afraid of it, that when morning comes the hunters find him on the same spot.

Of the badger he said

39

There is also here the badger or melot, an unclean animal, which bites sharply, frequenting the mountains and rocks. It makes holes under ground for its refuge and protection, scratching and digging them out with its feet. Some of them, whose natural instinct it is to serve the rest, have been seen, to the great admiration of the observers, lying on their backs with the earth dug out heaped on their bellies, and held together by their four claws, while others dragged them backward by a stick held in their mouth, fastening their teeth in which, they drew them out of the hole, with their burthens.

. . . some of these servants are to be found remarkable both for their degeneracy and uncouth shape, and for the manner in which the shaggy fur on their backs has been rubbed and worn off.

This is, needless to say, the veriest twaddle but it was probably sincere and one must at least admire the confidence of the writer, perhaps because the possibility of an authoritative contradiction was remote. He continues

There are some other wild animals which are not found in Ireland, such as roebucks, goats, hedgehogs, hermins and polecats.

There are few or no moles in Ireland, either because they have never existed, or on account of the extreme humidity of the soil.

The larger species of mouse is found here in great numbers, and the smaller kind swarm to such an amazing degree that they consume more enormous quantities of grain than anywhere else, and are very destructive to clothes, which they gnaw and tear, however carefully they may be locked up in chests. Bede describes the island as possessing only two sorts of ravenous animals. To these I have added this third, which is most destructive.

From the twelfth to the beginning of the eighteenth century is largely a void as far as mammalogy is concerned, though some other areas of natural history received attention. True, there are occasional references to mammals in some books, for instance regarding the export of furs, to wolves and to deer and deer-parks, but no attempt at concentrated study. One volume whose title has often excited the interest of of tyros (myself included) is *Irelands Naturall History* (1652) by Gerard Boate (1604-1649), clearly published posthumously. But they will search it in vain for any enlightenment on the contemporary status of wild animals or plants, for though sections on botany and zoology were projected, they were never written. Although Boate (a Dutchman also known as De Boot, Bootius or Botus) had apparently never been to Ireland, he produced a worthwhile geographical text, but not one of natural history as we would understand it. Later editions contained additional papers, among them one by Sir Thomas Molyneux (1661-1733) on the giant Irish deer. Molyneux, who was Professor of Medicine at Dublin University, was the first to treat in detail of the remains of this magnificent species and, incidental to his findings, are some of the earliest records of whale strandings on the Irish coast. He also described, in another discourse, the remains of a mammoth unearthed in Co. Cavan.

Sir Thomas Molyneux's elder brother William (1656-1698) was the founder of the Dublin Philosophical Society, a scientific body which flourished in Dublin between 1683 and 1708. In 1684 he read to the society the only paper in their proceedings of any mammal interest: an account of the anatomy of a bat which he had dissected. However he is noteworthy in another context.

In 1682 Moses Pitt, a London bookseller who was processing material for an English Atlas (which included Ireland!), was directed by Robert Hooke, his principal scientific adviser, to include regional descriptions as well as maps. The latter eminent scientist may have suggested Molyneux as a likely contact in Ireland. At any rate Molyneux agreed to provide such descriptions and forthwith proceeded to dispatch questionnaires (or *'Quaeries'*) to those whom he considered reliably informed. Among the sixteen questions, the second reads 'What Plants, Animals, Fruits, Mettals or other

Natural Productions there are peculiar to the Place and how Order'd?'

Work went ahead smoothly until at least the summer of 1684 but, in the following year, Pitt was arrested for debt and the whole scheme fell through. By the end of the year Molyneux knew that there was little chance of publishing, and '. . . burnt all that I had written myself on the subject, but I have still by me the rough papers of many other persons.' It is regrettable that what might have been a very interesting work foundered. Several descriptions have survived in manuscript form and are in the Library at Trinity College, Dublin. Notes on 'Rare Animals in Ireland' shows 'Quadrupeds as before undertaken by Dr Gwithers' and

Quadrupeds in Ireland and not in England
    Wolf Dog Wolf
Quadrupeds common in England and not found in Ireland
    Otter Stag
Quadrupeds in England and not found in Ireland
    Frog, Toad, Mole, Water Rat, Roe in Scotland
Quadrupeds common in England and rare in Ireland
    Pole-Cat Fulmart or Fitchen

Some descriptions were eventually published, but the above shows the extremely primitive state of contemporary knowledge on the subject.

One of the foremost contributors was Roderic O'Flaherty of Galway who produced from his notes *A Chorographical Description of West or H-lar Connaught.* But this was not actually printed, by the Irish Archeological Society, until 1846. The pertinent passage therein is brief and is therefore quoted in full.

The land produces wild beasts as wolves, deere, foxes, badgers, hedgehogs, hares, rabbits, squirrells, martins, weasels and the amphibious otter, of which kind the white-faced otter is very rare. It is never killed, they say, but with loss of man or dog, and its skin is mighty precious. It [i.e. West Connaught] admits no rats to live any where within it, except the Isles of Aran, and the district of the west liberties of Galway.

O'Flaherty was not a scientist.

In 1714 Arthur Stringer, huntsman to Lord Conway at Portmore, Co. Antrim, published *The Experienc'd Huntsman* at Belfast, which was republished in 1780 in Dublin. This little-known and extremely rare little book went unmentioned by the Victorians and Edwardians and I can find no reference to it in natural history books or scientific journals. Nevertheless it is a remarkable piece of work and contains copious notes on the habits and means of hunting deer, hares, badgers, foxes and martens in the north of Ireland. Stringer did not care much for badgers, which are only briefly covered. His methods, here and there, are undoubtedly cruel but were typical of his age. They are outweighed by the wealth of detail and the undoubted originality of many of the author's observations. Stringer was a man far in advance of his time and he does not deserve to have been forgotten. His work merits republication at least.

He was a great believer in the evidence of his own eyes and scorned hearsay.

I do not find that any author who has wrote on this subject, has (as I have here attempted) set down his own practice and experience, but has satisfied himself in collecting what he has found scattered up and down in books, who like himself have taken upon tick from others as to the subject of his writings.

His scepticism is perhaps best illustrated in his willingness to credit minimal powers of reasoning to animals and to accept only the simplest explanation for any train of events. A little of his general information is likely based on insufficient data and perhaps, occasionally, the truth may not be entirely ungilded. But while modern zoologists would not agree with all that he has to say, it is remarkable that so much of his mammalogy is in tune with contemporary ideas.

The following is a typical excerpt.

The hare is kindled or bred in every month, from February to November [probably October] . . . I have known a hare have young three times between February and November . . . When the hare doth gender . . . they do resort together, sometimes two or three, or four brace; where I have seen them fight with each other several times, as also heard them cry (when fighting) with a small shrill voice. The hare does not lie or sit with her young, but comes to them, and gives them suck . . . if it be in an open plain country, and no covert, they have their young in old caves . . . in the bottoms of old walls, or any such like hole or vault, that she can find in February, March, April or May; in the other months she commonly breedeth or kindleth in meadows or high rank grass or lying rank corn, fern or lying rushes.

I have had occasion to quote him at length elsewhere and readers will have ample opportunity to compare his thoughts with modern views.

In complete contrast was the Rev. John Keogh (1681?-1754) who held a living at Mitchelstown, Co. Cork. In 1739 he released his *Zoologica Medicinalis Hibernica*, a preposterous work, purely medicinal in nature, which lists the alleged therapeutic properties of Irish animals. Although it makes hilarious reading today, it may have been quite plausible in its time. We learn, for instance, that hedgehog fat is good for ruptures, that hare's blood applied warm to the skin has a cosmetic effect and that the dung of the 'weasel' cures the falling sickness. Again

The Flesh of a Bat, medicinally taken, is good against a Scirrhus of the Liver, the Gout, Rheumatism, Cancer, and Leprosy, it has greater Virtue to cure the above disorders, when taken after this Manner. Take of the Flesh pulverized half a Dram, Powder of Hogs-lice one Scruple, mix for a Dose.

It was not until 1772 that a systematic list of all the mammals was compiled with brief informed observations, as it happens, for County Dublin. In that year John Rutty (1697-1775), a physician from Wiltshire who had made his home in Ireland in 1724, published his *Essay towards a Natural History of the County of Dublin* in two volumes. Copies of this can still occasionally be picked up at well under three figures, even from book-dealers, and can be regarded as an investment. It is a true 'Natural History' in the modern sense and boasts sections on botany, geology and meteorology besides a comprehensive account of the zoology of the district. Samples of the compilation on quadrupeds, including domestic animals, are given below.

Echinus The Hedge-hog.
The flesh is good food and said to be scarce inferior to the Rabbit. It feeds on Apples, Nuts and other fruits, and on Worms.
In the beginning of Winter it conceals itself in the earth, and is seized with so profound a sleep, that it appears to be dead, the pulsation of the arteries and the respiration, as is said, not being sensible, and the same is the case of the Marmotte, Dormouse, and some other Quadrupeds.
Mus aquaticus The Water Rat, here commonly called, the *Norway* Rat, which first began to infest these parts, about the year 1722, and which, tho' it has devoured our pease, grain, &c. has at the same time, in great measure, rid us of other Rats [the black rat], and partly destroyed the Frogs. It also feeds on fish, nor does it wholly spare Birds, Rails having been devoured by it.
The *Norway* Rat is amphibious, and burrows in the ground, under the water, yet lives dry as the Beaver, and tho' it dives, it cannot live long under water, its claws being only a little webbed at the bottom . . . It has been eaten.
The Bite is not only severe, but dangerous, the wound being immediately attended with a great swelling, and is a long time healing.
Mustela. The weesel [stoat]
It may be very useful, as it kills rats and mice better than cats do . . .

42

Taxus suillus . . . The Badger, *Gray, Brock* or *Bawson.*
Besides the medicinal use of its Fat, the flesh, when roasted, is good food, like pig's flesh, and makes a good Ham; and the skin is tanned for Breeches, Waistcoats, &c. and is sometimes dressed with the hair by Furriers.
The Hair makes pencils for Painters.
Vespertilio. The Bat.
It attends us all summer in the evenings, and in warm weather . . .
Otherwise it retires into caves, ruined buildings, the roofs of houses or hollow trees, where it remains the whole winter in a state of inaction . . .

Similar notes are included on the hare, rabbit, field mouse, squirrel, otter, marten and fox and the house mouse is mentioned. The dormouse is erroneously stated to be native to Ireland but, as the description of the colouring tallies with that of the field mouse, and that of the field mouse clearly indicates the pigmy shrew, no doubt the field mouse is the animal in question. Rutty's book is refreshing in that he clearly made a genuine attempt at producing an informed and critical account of his subject.

As Ireland entered the Victorian era, there was a quickening of interest in natural phenomena. Men of ability and originality appeared, who relied primarily on the evidence of their own senses or those of trusted colleagues. Societies too sprang up under their influence, facilitating intercourse between them and lesser lights. The Belfast Natural History and Philosophical Society was formed in 1821, the Belfast Naturalists' Field Club in 1863, the Dublin Natural History Society in 1839, the Dublin Microscopical Club in 1849, the Dublin Naturalists' Field Club in 1885 and a sprinkling of less spectacular organizations founded, like the various other field clubs, the Cork Cuvierian Society and the Dublin University Zoological and Botanical Society.

In these organizations there thrived that admirable spirit of self-help which manifested itself in so many facets of life of the time, however excessively lampooned today. It was taken for granted, for instance, that members would undertake their own research, that it would be worthwhile, that papers would be read regularly and, in the vast majority of cases, by the members themselves.

The Belfast Natural History and Philosophical Society was not atypical. On 5th June 1821, the eight founders met for the first time. By the end of 1826 there was a membership of sixty. Rules provided for the reading of papers in rotation, the subject to be announced two meetings in advance. Omitting to make a declaration punctually resulted in a fine of 1s 3d (6.25p), and 2s 6d (12.5p) for failure to read the paper on the appointed date. There was no occasion to operate this punitive law until 1824. Eventually the society, which had been making use of members' houses, acquired rooms, accumulated specimens and opened a museum which was the basis of the present Ulster Museum. The B.N.H.P.S. is still meeting.

One member of the B.N.H.P.S. was Robert Templeton (d. 1894), who joined in 1833. His father, John Templeton (1766-1825), was possibly the earliest of the modern Irish naturalists. He worked steadily and mainly on his own on the flora and fauna of the north-east, predominantly in the Belfast area and around his home 'Cranmore' in the present Malone district of that city, where, incidentally, King William III was entertained on his way to the Battle of the Boyne in 1690. The *Belfast Magazine* (1808-1814) contained his monthly 'Naturalist's Report' but, apart from that, he committed little to print. Luckily most of his manuscripts were preserved and his writings on animals published by his son Robert, including a list of the mammals with notes on their abundance.[197]
Another participant in the B.N.H.P.S. was William Thompson (1805-1852),

43

WILLIAM THOMPSON

certainly the most distinguished Irish naturalist of his time. It is a cliché that there were giants in those days but there is, none the less, little doubt that Thompson was a giant. Though no botanist, his shadow still stands over Irish field zoology and in particular ornithology. In a relatively short life he had an outstanding output of original work.

Thompson was the son of a Belfast linen merchant and was educated to fit him for a career in the same business. He was apprenticed to the trade in 1821. Although showing no great inclination for the work, he was efficient and strictly methodical, traits which are clear in most of his later writings. Friends in the business aroused his interest in local birds and consequenly a great deal of his leisure was spent in rural walks.

In 1826, then twenty-one, he set out on a tour of the continent lasting some four months. During this he maintained a journal which, again, provides evidence of his acute powers of observation. On returning he was persuaded to join the B.N. H.P.S. and, in the year following, read his first paper, 'The Birds of the Copeland Isles' (off Co. Down). Some time after he had returned from his travels, he set up business on his own account. It did not appeal to him and in 1832, being comfortably off, he retired and, living with his widowed mother in a house in Donegall Square, devoted his entire time to natural history. He was elected vice-president of the society in 1834 and president in 1843, which he remained until his death. During this latter period as full-time naturalist he made frequent visits to Great Britain and took part in a scientific excursion on H.M.S. *Beacon* in 1841.

He worked steadily and accurately and published some hundred papers from his studies, a few of which pertain to mammals. At this point I should, perhaps, digress and explain the significance of publishing papers.

Although books are traditionally the first source for *general* scientific information, they usually contain only a moderate percentage of data available for the first time in print. For the most part they bring together, in an abridged and collated form, the knowledge from a number of *original* papers cemented with the authors' expertise in the subject. These papers are most often the results of first-hand study on a particular topic and are published in scientific journals normally after perusal by independent and appropriately qualified referees. However, review papers are by no means unusual. Frequently the journals are the organ of some learned society—for example the Royal Irish Academy or the Zoological Society of London—in which case non-members are rarely disqualified from contributing. Independent periodicals of this kind are, nevertheless, by no means uncommon. Subscriptions for such scientific publications are often high and they are not normally taken by municipal libraries. To obtain them it is easiest to consult a library in a university, research institution or of a learned society. Fortunately authors acquire, at the time of printing, a supply of copies (reprints or offprints) of their papers and these are sent out free, on request, to *bona fide* workers in the same or related fields. A few journals are inexpensive and are worth the support of the amateur, not only because they will keep him *au fait* with the latest developments, but also because they commonly hold their value. An example is the *Irish Naturalists' Journal*, with a subscription of a mere £3.00 *per annum*. I shall deal at greater length with the periodicals relevant to Irish mammalogy later.

One final word. It is axiomatic, though often unrealized, that unless research *is* published it might just as well never have been undertaken in the vast majority of cases. Information must be disseminated to be of any value. While some exaggerate the significance of their efforts, others, through too modest an assessment or through sloth or procrastination, never transform their findings to print—and the knowledge is lost for ever.

As Thompson's reputation spread, he came to be regarded as an authority and so correspondence on wildlife flowed in from interested observers all over Ireland. This he began to arrange, with his own work, in preparation for a *magnum opus, The Natural History of Ireland*. The first three volumes, all on birds, appeared in 1849, 1850 and 1851. However from 1847 he had been suffering from heart trouble and in 1852, while visiting London to make arrangements for the projected visit of the British Association to Belfast, he had a fatal heart attack.

Thompson had prudently made provision for the posthumous publication of the remainder of his work, should it be necessary, but this proved a difficult task. The manuscript was fragmented and sometimes consisted of brief notes on minute scraps of paper or on the backs of envelopes, so marshalling the facts was indeed tedious. The resultant volume, on *Mammalia &c.*—in other words everything else besides birds—is therefore understandably disjointed in places. Nevertheless it is a mine of information, crammed with original and usually personal observation, the section on mammals alone running to sixty closely-printed pages. Mammalogists will also find the accounts of the raptorial birds worth reading as they include details of mammalian prey. Thompson always maintained a strict impartiality, carefully sifting the evidence and never making a definite judgement unless this was justified. Viewed from 120 years on, it is astonishing how often his conclusions were correct.

It is uncertain how many copies of *The Natural History of Ireland* were pro-

45

duced but they are, even now, not infrequent in antiquarian book-dealers' stocks and are often modestly priced.

Thompson and Templeton were the finest of the early nineteenth-century naturalists, but while Templeton was obliged to work alone, Thompson lived at a time when there were others as keen, if not as active, as himself. His labour resulted in some thousand species being added to the list of Irish animals. His work is a model of painstaking precision and must be looked on as the basis of modern mammalogy in Ireland.

Many of the Victorian naturalists applied themselves briefly to the study of mammals, though relatively few specialized in that direction. Facts on the bats, nearly always in the nature of simple identification and distribution, were supplied from several individuals. Principal among these were three Dublin men. J.R. Kinahan (1828-1863), a lecturer in zoology and botany at Trinity College, Dublin and a man of wide interests in biology, reviewed the knowledge of Irish bats in 1859. The paper had the remarkable title of

Mammalogica Hibernica: Part 1. Sub-Class, Lissencephala; Order Cheiroptera, Insectivoridae;— or, a general review of the history and distribution of bats in Ireland; with remarks on Mr. Foot's discovery in Clare of the lesser horse-shoe bat, a species hitherto unrecorded in Ireland.[131]

Even with such a grandiose title it is doubtful whether Kinahan seriously contemplated compiling a complete work on the Irish Mammalia.

H. Lyster Jameson (1875-1922) was responsible for further study and published this in bits from 1893 to 1897, including a summary.[123] It was Jameson also who discovered the sandy-coloured house mice on the North Bull Island. Apparently he had a sense of humour which occasionally extended to practical jokes. The late A.W. Stelfox (1883-1972) who was the foremost Irish naturalist of the mid twentieth century, informed me that, at the time, there was unofficially some doubt about where the North Bull mice had really come from, and of a suspicion that Jameson might have been involved in a little surreptitious leg-pulling of the scientific community in Dublin.

Nathaniel Alcock (1871-1913), a medical man, spent most of his life abroad and carried out research on the human nervous system. While in Dublin he published, in 1898, 1899 and 1901, a total of six useful papers on the bats, some of which were extensive. He again summarized the then known facts on distribution.[3]

The Patterson family of Belfast were a force in the Irish natural history world over much of the nineteenth and well into the twentieth century, for three generations. They were all engaged in the mill-furnishing business: Robert (1802-1872), his son Robert Lloyd (1836-1906) and grandson Robert (1863-1931). Robert, the elder, was one of the eight founder members of the B.N.H.P.S. He had broad zoological interests—even reading a series of papers on 'The Insects in Shakespeare's Plays' and publishing school text-books on Zoology. His single claim to mammalogy was a note on a bottle-nosed whale (*Hyperoodon rostratus*). But he was chiefly responsible for the publication of the last volume of Thompson's work and, for that alone, he is entitled to inclusion here.

Robert Lloyd Patterson's contributions were in a narrower category. He concentrated his energies on local sea-birds, fish, whales and dolphins, presenting his findings in 1880 in the book *Birds, Fishes and Cetacea commonly frequenting Belfast Lough*, and, up to 1901, his mammalogical efforts totalled a few additional notes on the marine forms already mentioned and a brief communication on bats. His book is well worth reading and captures all the colour and enthusiasm of Victorian natural history, although the chapter on whales and dolphins is short. Included is a brief but graphic description of a meeting with a school of killer whales (*Orcinus orca*) at the mouth of the lough one day while out fishing. The anxious fisherman who was Patterson's companion, begged him to make no noise, fearing the 'Becker dogs' which sometimes made mischief with boats.

Robert Patterson, the younger, was mainly an ornithologist but found time for other living things. His *Ulster Nature Notes* (1908) included his own and those of friends. It was published by Mullans of Belfast, who are still selling books in Donegall Place. It contains passages on bats, badgers, stoats, and wolves. His remaining efforts were mainly notes on the distribution of bats and pine martens, but his best-known paper on mammals deals with the extinction of the fox in Co. Antrim.[167] He also wrote a regular nature study column in the Belfast newspaper, the *Northern Whig*.

There are several other Victorians with some claim to minor mention including Robert Ball (1802-1857), an all-rounder, R.J. Ussher (1841-1913), an oologist (a Victorian euphemism for a birds-nester) who eventually became the finest bird-man of his time, and Robert Warren (1829-1915), one of Thompson's correspondents and mainly an ornithologist. Ussher and Warren wrote *Birds of Ireland* (1905), the first standard text since Thompson's and not destined to be displaced for nearly fifty years. It also contains records of mammals as the food of eagles, hawks and owls. Our list would be incomplete without reference to James Edward Harting (1841-1928), a quite outstanding personality in natural history and field sports in the British Isles during Victorian and Edwardian times. He was what can only be described as an all-round specialist, equally at home in the fields of classical zoology, field study, hunting, hawking, shooting, fishing and the literature associated with them all. He was on the staff of *The Field* from 1869 to his death, where he wrote on natural history, falconry, shooting, country houses and legal matters—2,326 articles in all. He edited the *Zoologist* from 1877 to 1896 and was the author of several books, including the widely acknowledged standard texts on falconry. In 1882 he was appointed to organize the zoological library in the then newly built Natural History Museum at South Kensington. He afterwards became librarian for the Linnean Society. He wrote several notes and papers concerning Irish mammals and his book *Essays on Sport and Natural History* (1883) contains an excellent review of early works on Irish natural history.

At Queen's College, Galway, as it was then, R.J. Anderson (1848-1914), Professor of Natural History and still affectionately and awefully remembered as 'Dickie John', entertained an interest in marine mammals. He read papers on them as far afield as Monaco and Berne at zoological congresses and his finds still lie in the Zoology Department. He was an eccentric with an extraordinarily broad field of interest in natural science. He also published some lengthy pieces of zoological doggerel, sketched and invented, among other things, a revolving microscope arrangement.

Four important figures dominated mammalogy in Ireland from the closing years of the last century into the early decades of the present one: R.M. Barrington (1849-1915), G.E.H. Barrett-Hamilton (1871-1914), R.F. Scharff (1858-1934) and C.B. Moffat (1859-1945).

Richard Barrington was born in Wicklow of a family with scientific leanings and, as a delicate child, was rapidly drawn towards natural history. The resultant fresh-air and exercise helped in transforming him to a vigorous and energetic adult. He was interested chiefly in botany, birds and mammals, the latter from an early stage. In one of his notes he mentions that:

> When a boy nearly all my pocket money was earned by rat-catching, my father allowing me one penny per head, so I soon became expert at the trade, and well acquainted with the habits of rats.

47

G.E.H. BARRETT-HAMILTON   R.M. BARRINGTON

In 1866 he entered Trinity College and in the same year published his first paper, concerning the food of the wood-pigeon. In 1875 he was called to the Bar but soon found the occupation of land-valuer more to his taste, in that it kept him in the open air. After his father's death he became more closely concerned with running the family farm in Wicklow. He was, to a large extent, a gentleman of leisure and devoted his time to natural history. He was a popular man.with many friends and a great sense of fun. R.L. Praeger tells how Barrington and H.C. Hart went botanizing at Powerscourt, Co. Wicklow, by prior arrangement in what turned out to be dreadful weather. Though soon soaked, neither would admit discomfort and Hart made a point of walking through briars and tall vegetation to discourage his companion. The latter calmly stepped into the river, seated himself and began to eat his lunch. Hart joined him, rivalry ceased and friendship prevailed.

Barrington's major work was in recording bird migration as seen at Irish lighthouses and lightships. This was done by recruiting the lightkeepers in a scheme to list all of the unfortunate birds which had perished by dashing themselves against the lights, and a few bats as well. All went well when the lightkeepers were persuaded to corroborate their notes by sending in specimens of wings and legs. The final tome was published at Barrington's own expense but only 350 copies were issued.[17]

Barrington still found plenty of time for the mammals. His most significant labour was in compiling a comprehensive catalogue of the dates and localities where red squirrels had been reintroduced after their extinction in Ireland.[15] This necessitated considerable correspondence, checking and ferreting-out of detail and is a

48

sound piece of work. He also kept field mice in captivity and chronicled their breeding habits[16] and even inadvisedly attempted to introduce dormice to Ireland, an exercise which happily foundered. His other published notes deal with bats, rabbits and rats, including an absorbing account of the 'Difference in mode of attacking turnips by rabbits and rats'.

Major Gerald Barrett-Hamilton differed in one important way from all the naturalists alluded to so far in this chapter, for he was primarily a mammalogist. Born in India of Irish parents, his family returned home to Kilmanock in Co. Wexford in 1874. He took an interest in nature at an extremely early age. Notes had to be made for him when he was too young to write and he was keeping a diary of his activities at the age of ten. He went to Harrow in 1885 and was encouraged by his house-master, himself an enthusiastic ornithologist. Two years later he began correspondence with Alexander More (1830-1895), who was then keeper of the Dublin Natural History Museum. More, who had a perceptive mind and a wide knowledge of most branches of natural history, advised and encouraged him considerably. In 1887 Barrett-Hamilton had his first writings on mammals printed, a note that black rats were not uncommon around Kilmanock.

Before leaving school he began a natural history column in the *Irish Sportsman*, a weekly newspaper of the time. He wrote several articles for it which embodied much original material including a remarkable series on the Irish hare, packed with useful data. Appropriately enough, he appeared under the *nom de plume* of 'Lepus Hibernicus'.

In 1894 he took a science degree at Trinity College, Cambridge. The following year he pointed out the peculiar characteristics of the Irish stoat[198] and visited Morocco where he became interested in geographical variation in the house mouse. He was appointed a commissioner on the British Bering Fur Seal Enquiry in 1896 and gathered information at the seal rookeries over two years. Fur seals (*Callorhinus ursinus*) migrate annually to their breeding grounds on the Pribilof Islands in May and remain until November, spending the rest of the year at sea. Barrett-Hamilton took the opportunity of travelling during these latter periods to Japan, Kamachatka, various North Pacific Islands and, during one journey home, to Egypt. Throughout his journeys he worked incessantly, publishing nearly all his observations eventually, including those on the Maydoom fresco in the Ghizeh museum, possibly the most ancient ornithological illustrations in the world.

After three years work on European mammals and service in the Boer War, when he was able to make further collections, he lived at Kilmanock from 1903 to 1913, quietly farming the family property, breeding dachshunds and producing numerous papers on British and Irish birds and mammals. He was also gathering his material for a definitive work on the mammals of the British Isles. 1909 saw him in the Clare Island Survey, an exhaustive biological examination of Clare Island, Co. Mayo, by leading field natualists of the time. In October 1913 he sailed for the Antarctic, commissioned by the Colonial Office and the British Museum to investigate the indiscriminate killing of whales round the Falkland Islands and South Georgia. The following January he developed pneumonia, which proved fatal.

Barrett-Hamilton, more than any of his contemporaries, had the opportunity and education to succeed and, taking full advantage of this, he made a brilliant career. He published nearly 170 papers, thirty-seven of them directly concerned with the mammals of Ireland, some of considerable length and lasting significance. Furthermore, he built up a large collection of mammal skins and skulls for the British Museum. He is even now an important figure in mammalogy, sixty years after his untimely death.

His book *A History of British Mammals* began publication, in parts, in 1910. Owing to his death it was never finished. The final part, the twenty-first, was brought out in 1921 and, in fact, the last six parts were completed by M.A.C. Hinton, curator of mammals at the British Museum. About half the species in the British Isles were covered: the bats, shrews, mole, hedgehog, rabbits, hares and rodents, but even the unfinished work is of a high standard and is still the most significant single reference work. The text is worked in minute detail, though thoroughly readable, and is profusely illustrated by Edward Wilson, the naturalist and artist who died with Scott on the return journey from his ill-fated expedition to the south pole.

Barrett-Hamilton was a confirmed 'splitter' and named numerous subspecies of mammal which are not all considered valid. However, he was quite frank about it and prompted by the best motive—a keenness to record variation, rather than a preoccupation with coining trinomials.

Even if I were to find that I had made numerous bad subspecies I would vastly prefer to be on the side of those who attempt to unravel the mysteries of variation . . . rather than to cultivate the icy scepticism of the modern school of lumpers to whom the many phases of animal variation are like the ripples of the ocean to the navigator—things to be detested in proportion as their magnitude makes them troublesome.

A.W. Stelfox, who met him on the Clare Island Survey, spoke to me of his boundless enthusiasm and terrieresque tenacity when confronted with a problem. Stelfox recalled, while walking with him one evening at dusk, seeing what was apparently a large mouse disappear into a dry-stone wall and of an ensuing eager, strenuous, protracted and entirely fruitless hunt for the retiring rodent.

Barrington and Barrett-Hamilton were both, from all accounts, warm, friendly and humorous. The same could not always be said of Robert Francis Scharff who, though pleasant enough at times, was of a more ruthless and rigid disposition. Certainly he did not always accept criticism gladly.

Scharff was born at Leeds, of German parents, and studied at the universities of Edinburgh, London and Heidelberg and at the marine stations of St. Andrews and Naples, taking zoology as his main subject. He was one of the rare Ph.D.s in Ireland in Victorian times. He joined the National Museum in Dublin in 1887 as assistant keeper and succeeded to the post of keeper three years later, when A.G. Moore left, where he remained until his retirement in 1921. He thus held an important position and worked industriously, swiftly becoming a commanding figure in Irish zoology. His breadth of knowledge was seldom matched and he worked on virtually the whole spectrum of animal life including birds, fishes, turtles, molluscs, wood-lice, leeches and tapeworms. His continental background and linguistic ability kept him in touch with international events and he published in several languages. He had over thirty publications on the native Irish mammals. Most of these were, however, only short notes, some of which were sound but a few given to rash speculation. He also published informative accounts on the origins of the domestic mammals.

Scharff's consuming interest in later life was in animal distribution, and he wrote three books on the subject, *The History of the European Fauna* (1899), *European Animals* (1907) and *The Distribution and Origin of Life in America* (1911), none of which contain very much on the mammals of Ireland. In them he plunged into very deep water indeed. Enough has been said in Chapter 2 to give an idea of the pitfalls besetting those who would unravel the history of the Irish, British or continental fauna. Scharff pursued the subject with a resolution and, lamentable to relate, a degree of indifference to inconvenient facts. He, like many another, found great difficulty in accounting for the present distribution of animals because of the barriers

R. F. SCHARFF   C. B. MOFFAT

offered to their movement by the seas. In spite of all evidence on the permanence of
ocean basins and numerous geological anomalies, he invoked former land-bridges as
an explanation with procrustean abandon. As far as Ireland was concerned, he
believed that the Ice Age was not a cold, but essentially a wet period and that much
of the present fauna must therefore have survived the glaciations. *Geomalacus macu-
losus*, a spotted slug discovered in Ireland in 1840 and confined to a small area in the
south-west, caught Scharff's imagination for, though it occurs on the continent, it
is absent from Britain. The 'Kerry slug' figured in several of his theories. Miss Geraldine
Roche, who went to work at the Natural History Museum in 1930, told me that
Barrett-Hamilton is said to have remarked, whimsically, 'And *Geomalacus* said, "I
have discovered Scharff"!'

Scharff was also greatly involved with the collection and examination of fossil
bones in Irish cave deposits at the turn of the century. Stelfox talked of his occasionally somewhat high-handed behaviour on the subject of bones. One of the attendants at
the museum was James Duffy (1861-1934) who, though he left no trace in the scientific literature, from 1884, when he joined the staff, made a life-long study of the
bones in the museum. Stelfox had the highest opinion of Duffy's abilities and R.L.
Praeger, probabaly the most famous of all Irish naturalists, recorded his invaluable
assistance in sorting the various bits and pieces dug from the caves. Apparently Scharff
resented Duffy as an amateur, as one who had risen above his station in life and, according to Stelfox, probably because of Duffy's superior knowledge of the subject. Scharff

51

was, reputedly, not above consigning particularlay troublesome fragments to the dustbin.

Another interesting peculiarity was Scharff's insistence that wild cats (*Felis* spp.) were indigenous to Ireland and if they were actually extinct, had lingered well into historic time. Moreover he seriously entertained a notion that they might still have survived in the mountain fastnesses of the west. He even went as far as publishing a request for any relevant information in 1905. In this he was far too credulous and was ready to swallow statements where he should, at least, have expressed some scepticism, for every alleged specimen of the wild cat so far produced in Ireland has invariably proved to have been a domestic pussy which was living off the land. On one occasion he wrote: 'Indeed Mr. F.C. Wallace assures me that he saw a magnificent Wild Cat near Annaghdown, Co. Galway, about 1883, when rabbit shooting.' He should never have accepted such an unsubstantiated statement on such a doubtful matter.

His investigations led to his examining bones of cats in cave deposits and to measuring their skulls and teeth. Although the bones always occurred at levels where the remains of other domesticated animals had been found in abundance, he pounced on the cat material he located as supporting data for his theory. He even went as far as describing two distinct types of cat from the remains; a larger, more powerful race and a smaller, more slender one. Unfortunately, as Stelfox pointed out in a paper in 1965,[192] two such types still exist, because tom cats are bigger than queens (or female cats)!

All this must, of course, be seen in perspective. Scharff, over his lifetime, made some valuable contributions to science.

Charles Bethune Moffat was a Manxman but his parents moved to Ireland and were residing at Ballyhyland, Co. Wexford, when he was in his third year. He was educated on the Isle of Man and privately in Ireland. He went to Trinity College, Dublin in 1875 and had a distinguished undergraduate career, taking a first class standard throughout, culminating in his B.A. degree in 1879 when he was twenty-one. He entered law, was called to the Bar in 1881, but, after only one brief, forsook it for journalism and for many years was connected with Dublin newspapers, especially the Dublin *Daily Express.* Shortly after joining the staff of the latter paper, he began writing articles on natural history (he was known as the 'Bugman'), mainly on birds and mammals, which were his chief interest. This was by no means the limit of his abilities and indeed he was often entrusted with political leaders. During his journalistic career he made frequent trips to Ballyhyland and spent long holidays there. He probably continued writing for the *Daily Express* until the last issue in June 1921.

He threw himself into all the natural history activities in Dublin with enthusiasm. He was a member of the Dublin Naturalists' Field Club, in which at various times he held the posts of president, secretary and treasurer, of the Royal Irish Academy and the Zoological Society of Ireland. But he was most closely associated with the Irish Society for the Protection of Birds and with Mr. S. Brown, K.C., a senator at the time, he managed to have a bird protection bill passed in the Senate and Dail in 1930.

Moffat was possibly the finest field naturalist that Ireland has ever produced and a perfect example of the theory that naturalists are born, not made. Not only had he acute powers of observation but the patience to watch and wait for events to take place. His experiments on the factors affecting the emergence and return of bats to their roosts, many of which were undertaken at his friend Barrington's home, often involved him in all-night vigils. In 1916, when Summer Time was introduced, he complained that it 'put the bats back to such monstrously late hours'. After finishing his articles for the morning's paper at around 2.00 a.m. he would, as like as not, set off for Phoenix Park and ornithological observations as day was breaking. Moffat was critical of his work, logical in his conclusions, had a retentive memory and wrote precise yet beautiful prose. All this was combined with a comprehensive knowledge of the literature on his subject. As secretary to the I.S.P.B. he never took notes at committee meetings but wrote minutes and reports.which were literary productions.

Moffat never seems to have collected anything and he was credited by his contemporaries with publishing rather less than was expected from his vast experience and encyclopaedic knowledge. Other mammalogists often wrote of him providing them with information and much of this he never put in print himself. Yet he did publish a lot. His best mammal work was that on bats, already mentioned, on the three commonest species: the pipistrelle, long-eared and Leisler's bat[153] and on Daubenton's. His other papers dealt with virtually every other species of Irish mammal, with a strong emphasis on field study. He produced one book *The Life and Letters of Alexander Goodman More* (1898) which contains the few notes More had made on mammals. From an examination of his personal papers, stored in the vaults of the Royal Irish Academy, it appears a second book was projected: *The Wildlife at Our Doors* based on selected items of his in the *Daily Express*, all earlier than 1912. His most significant paper, of sixty-nine pages, 'The Mammals of Ireland' in the *Proceedings of the Royal Irish Academy* (1938), is a review and essential reading for aspiring Irish mammalogists.

Moffat was shy, self-effacing and excessively modest, which has resulted in his receiving rather less recognition than was his due. Stelfox remembered him as almost looking about for somewhere to hide when being thanked or complimented, such was his embarrassment, and that he was unmistakeably bird-like in his demeanour. A colleague of his *Daily Express* days recalled

> To some of us he seemed to possess bird-like characteristics. Even in the way he entered the sub's room every evening there was something bird-like—at first poking his head round the door as if to explore that the coast was clear, and then a dash forward and a pleasant 'good evening' to all. One of the staff once remarked that he would not be surprised if Moffat flew in and lighted on the gas bracket.

Miss Roche remarked that he sometimes used his shyness to advantage in avoiding bores. Perhaps because of it, he never married but had rooms in Baggot Street in Dublin where, Stelfox said, when a meeting was to be held he had to remove all the books and papers which had somehow accumulated on the chairs. However he *did* take tea regularly with a lady of about his own age and also from Co. Wexford. Stelfox believed him too shy to propose. There are several indications that lead one to suppose that, secretly, Moffat was intensely generous and a confirmed altruist, though he himself lived a life of Spartan simplicity.

Only a handful of twentieth century naturalists have written more than an occasional note or paper pertaining to our subject. G.H. Pentland (1850-1932) of Blackhall, Drogheda, produced ten in his later years all dealing with short personal observations and, from his other efforts in print, seems to have been equally interested in birds. Pentland came of a family who owned a considerable area of land in the Drogheda district and was, apparently, sufficiently well-off to indulge his interests. He was a founder member of the Baltray golf club, had a keen interest in sailing and built his own boats for the purpose. One correspondent informed me that he even constructed a home-made car which had a flat base, a wicker-work chair to take one person and a tiller for steering. He left Ireland in the early 'twenties and went to live near Guildford in Surrey.

Major R.F. Ruttledge, the doyen of Irish bird-study, has published several notes on mammals as well, mostly on bats but also on the distribution of the red squirrel and pine marten.

Eugene 'Bugs' O'Mahony (1899-1951) has already been referred to in discussing the enigmatic eastern house mouse. He was a Dubliner who became interested in the animals of the sea shore, probably having been stimulated by a period spent amongst the fishermen at Kilmore Quay, Co. Wexford, when a boy. He became a regular visitor to the natural history section of the National Museum and joined the staff as technical assistant in 1922. Contact with his colleagues broadened his horizons and he applied himself to the study of mammals, birds and insects, notably beetles. After 1924, when two of the senior staff retired, O'Mahony and A.W. Stelfox held the fort alone until 1930, when a keeper and assistant naturalist were appointed. So well did the two maintain the collections, deal with enquiries and attend to the general running of the museum over the intervening six years, that the general public never realised the lamentable state of affairs prevailing.

O'Mahony kept up a fairly steady stream of items in print during his lifetime on a variety of topics. Those of relevance here, besides the unfortunate efforts on the mice, were one on the mammals of the North Bull Island,[163] in which he confirmed the presence of Jameson's sandy mice, and a remarkable series on fleas and lice which are the basis of our knowledge of these parasites in Ireland.

O'Mahony never received any recognition in the museum in terms of promotion or salary and he was still a technical assistant when he died in 1951.

Up to quite recently mammalogists were still scarce. Mr. C.D. 'Jimmy' Deane, now Deputy Director of the Ulster Museum, has always maintained a lively interest in mammals but definitely as a second string to the feathered folk. He has written regularly for the daily newspapers, and readers may well be familiar with the name. Besides writing, he is an accomplished wildlife photographer, both in cine and still, and an informative, unorthodox and entertaining lecturer.

Dr. A.J.M. Claassens, a Dutchman, while for a few years a research student at University College, Cork in the early 'sixties, added materially to the known facts on the distribution and abundance of Irish mammal fleas. It was he, too, who discovered the presence of bank voles in Co. Kerry. He published his find jointly with Fergus O'Gorman, who has also been involved, to a greater or lesser extent, in a number of other projects on Irish mammals.

The most recent research has concentrated on deer. Mr. J. Riney and Mr. J. Larner have been working on, respectively, the red and sika deer in Killarney. Rory Harrington, whose illustrations adorn this book, studies deer in the Wicklow mountains with an enthusiasm which knows no bounds, has a particular interest in hybridization and cherishes a romantic desire to see the wolf reintroduced to Ireland. Research on the pine martens of Co. Clare is undertaken by Paddy O'Sullivan. The latter two researchers are in the Forest and Wildlife Service of the Department of Lands. The formation of the Irish Deer Society indicates an increasing interest in at least some of the mammals. Christopher Smal works on the mice and voles of the Bourne-Vincent National Park at Killarney. David Norris studies otters. As this book goes to press, a further two zoologists are commencing work on Irish mammals: Janet Grainger on pigmy shrews at Galway, and Eden Thompson on the stoat populations at Killarney.

A few books have been published pertinent to our subject by authors who themselves did little actual study in Ireland. Notable among these is the *Mammals of Great Britain and Ireland* (1904-6) by J.G. Millais, a sportsman, naturalist, author and artist. This massive production, limited to 1,050 copies and in three sumptuous folio volumes, is a mass of information but rather less technical and more artistic than Barrett-Hamilton's standard work. This is especially true of the illustrations, which are profuse and exceedingly attractive. Some are by Millais himself, some by Archibald Thorburn—to my mind the finest of all wildlife artists—and there are numerous superb photographs. Ireland is well covered and Millais is particularly useful for the groups not discussed by Barrett-Hamilton. Many libraries possess a copy but those who covet fine books will save themselves much anguish by not examining it. Millais also produced *British Deer and their Horns* (1897), another lavish publication and recommended reading for deer-men, who should also find the carefully-researched publications of Kenneth Whitehead of use: *Deer and their Management in the Deer Parks of Great Britain and Ireland* (1950), *The Deer Stalking Grounds of Great Britain and Ireland* (1960) and *The Deer of Great Britain and Ireland* (1964). Thomas Bell's *A History of British Quadrupeds including the Cetacea* (1837) was the standard Victorian mammal manual. The second edition (1874) is advised as being more comprehensive.

Finally, on the subjects of books, those wishing to search for individual publications, or simply hell-bent on wallowing in the literature, both books and papers, can do no better than consult *Irish Wild Mammals: A Guide to the Literature* (1972) by the author of *An Irish Beast Book!* The former contains 970 references, many of which are annotated, and a subject index.

Turning to the literature in periodicals: even if we exclude newspapers, this is scattered through some seventy different journals. Many of these contain only one or two items of interest over many years and it would be unrealistic to try to include them all here. I have therefore concentrated on the more important sources, commencing with the major ones.

The *Natural History Review* was published in Dublin from 1854 to 1860 and in London from 1856 to 1865. After 1860 the Irish flavour was virtually extinguished. Originally the *Natural History Review* was a *pot-pourri* of reviews, notices and proceedings of societies, mainly of Irish interest, notably the proceedings of the Dublin Natural History Society, which was an august body in its hey-day. Apparently the members were dissatisfied that their activities should come out second-hand, so to speak. In 1860 they commenced the *Proceedings of the Dublin Natural History Society*; volume I was for 1849 to 1855. The four subsequent volumes (1863-1871) continued to run a few years late, their affairs always appearing in the *Natural History Review* beforehand. From 1860, when they were dropped from the latter, they can still be followed in the society's own journal. A single part of a sixth volume was all that was produced. A notable contributor was J.R. Kinahan and his bat paper of the brobdignagian title appears there. Bats were, indeed, the principal subject of mammalian interest.

The *Zoologist*, a London publication, became a major vehicle for Irish work. It ran from 1843 to 1916, when it was amalgamated with *British Birds*. The editor for nineteen years was the inestimable J.E. Harting, who consequently wrote lengthy articles and many notes for it himself. Other distinguished contributors were Barrett-Hamilton, Barrington and, briefly, Moffat, Pentland and Scharff.

In April 1892 was launched the Dublin-based *Irish Naturalist*, which supplanted the *Zoologist* for many Irishmen. It began well, all the Natural History societies in the country passing resolutions according it a hearty welcome. The *Irish Sportsman*, however, gave it a frigid reception, implying that the *Zoologist* and its own Natural History columns already met all needs in this direction. In fact the *Sportsman* was a weekly newspaper, and although the nature notes are worth the reader's attention, notably those by 'Lepus Hibernicus', they quite often amounted only to chit-chat.

The *Irish Naturalist* was edited by R.L. Praeger and, save for the last two years, by G. H. Carpenter, who worked with Scharff in the Dublin Museum until he was given a chair of Zoology in the Royal College of Science for Ireland in 1904. There was an issue nearly every month, and, turning its pages, one is struck by a spirit of amateur enthusiasm and personal endeavour which is more muted today. It provides enthralling material for browsing.

Up to 1914 it looked in a healthy state, volumes of 200 to over 250 pages appearing each year. It then began to lose weight. In 1916 there were only 172 pages, and in 1920 the final 135th page bore a notice that the price was to be doubled from 6d (2.5p) per number, which had never changed since the first issue, to 1s, due to increased costs. This did not ease things sufficiently and, in a leaflet with the November issue for the following year (printed in red), Scharff informed the readership that a deficit of over £50 *per annum* was still being incurred. Reputedly funds were then guaranteed and the printers volunteered to reduce costs but the next volume contained only 148 pages and, in 1923, it had shrunk to 128, November 1924 saw a notice that publication was to cease in December.

Stelfox told me, quite bluntly, that the *Irish Naturalist* died of mismanagement and that it should have been perfectly viable after reorganization. Apparently Barrington subsidized its publication for several years. This is borne out by the fact that the journal first began to get thinner in the year after his death. From a different source I find that Stelfox himself did a great deal to keep it alive. His opinion on management is supported by the facts, for, at the insistence of the Belfast Naturalists' Field Club, a committee was formed of representatives of the various societies to organize a replacement organ. In September 1925 the first number of the *Irish Naturalist's Journal* came off the press. It was produced under the editorship of J.A.S. Stendall, then assistant curator at the Belfast Museum. The valiant efforts of the founders were fully vindicated for the *Irish Naturalists' Journal* is fifty, and still going strong. The giant Irish deer motif on the front cover of the *Irish Naturalist* was retained. The size was increased from 8½ x 5½ inches (21.5 x 14 cm) to 10½ x 7 inches (27 x 18 cm) but the price was equivalent to that of its forerunner at 6s (30p) for the year's subscription of six issues. These two periodicals effectively form a chain from 1892 and are the most important from our point of view.

There are several other journals where relevant papers are scarcer but, quite often, comparatively more bulky. The *Transactions* (1787-1906) and the *Proceedings of the Royal Irish Academy* (1836-) both fall into this category, the latter containing Moffat's recommended review paper. *The Scientific Proceedings of the Royal Dublin Society* (1878-, formerly the *Journal*, 1858-1878) can boast *inter alia* of Barrington's treatise on the introductions of the red squirrel. The *Proceedings of the Zoological Society of London* (1830-), renamed *Journal of Zoology* in 1965, is the best-known international zoological periodical and contains a very fine scattering of items appropriate to our subject. Mention must also be made of the *Annals and Magazine of Natural History* (1837-). In its early stages it was the *Magazine of Zoology and Botany* and then the *Annals of Natural History*. Recently the title has been changed again to the more prosaic *Journal of Natural History*. The 'Annals and Mag' was favoured by William Thompson and his personal set is now in the Science Library of Queen's University, Belfast. He also read papers at meetings of the British Association, which were published in the *Report of the British Association for the Advancement of Science* (1831-). Although of peripheral interest, there are also some sizeable reports therein of research at Irish whaling stations in Co. Mayo from 1910 to 1916. Strandings of whales on the Irish coasts are detailed in *Reports of Cetacea on the British Coasts* (1914-) and published by the British Museum (Natural History).

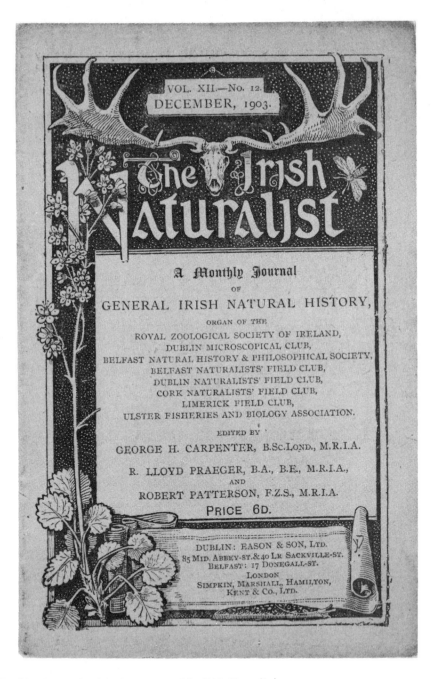

VOL. XII.—No. 12.
DECEMBER, 1903.

The Irish
Naturalist

A Monthly Journal
OF
GENERAL IRISH NATURAL HISTORY,

ORGAN OF THE
ROYAL ZOOLOGICAL SOCIETY OF IRELAND,
DUBLIN MICROSCOPICAL CLUB,
BELFAST NATURAL HISTORY & PHILOSOPHICAL SOCIETY,
BELFAST NATURALISTS' FIELD CLUB,
DUBLIN NATURALISTS' FIELD CLUB,
CORK NATURALISTS' FIELD CLUB,
LIMERICK FIELD CLUB,
ULSTER FISHERIES AND BIOLOGY ASSOCIATION.

EDITED BY
GEORGE H. CARPENTER, B.Sc.Lond., M.R.I.A.

R. LLOYD PRAEGER, B.A., B.E., M.R.I.A.,
AND
ROBERT PATTERSON, F.Z.S., M.R.I.A.

PRICE 6D.

DUBLIN: EASON & SON, LTD.
85 MID. ABBEY-ST.&40 LR SACKVILLE-ST.
BELFAST: 17 DONEGALL-ST.
LONDON
SIMPKIN, MARSHALL, HAMILTON,
KENT & CO., LTD.

Fig. 23   Facsimile of the front cover of the 'Irish Naturalist'.

The Mammal Society produced its own bulletin from 1954 to 1969, the *Bulletin of the Mammal Society of The British Isles.* Although intended for private circulation among members, it has found its way into some libraries and contains several snippets of Irish data. The British Deer Society publishes *Deer* (1966-), and the deer of Ireland are by no means ignored in it.

The vast accumulated bulk of *The Field*, in publication since 1853, contains numerous small notes of interest to us but thinly spread, and though many are valuable, a few tend to anecdote.

Finally, most of the facts on Irish fleas, lice and other parasitic insects which are, after all, intimately associated with the mammals, have been set down in the *Entomologist's Gazette* (1950-) and the *Entomologist's Monthly Magazine* (1864-). In the latter appeared most of O'Mahony's findings.

4 The Field Mouse

In the hedge-sparrow's nest he sits,
When its summer brood is fled,
And picks the berries from the bough
Of the hawthorn overhead.

Sketches of Natural History   Mary Howitt

The first reaction of most people to the setting of mouse traps in a wood is to suspect that the would-be trapper is suffering from at least a temporary mental aberration. Though the exercise may seem absurd, it is nonetheless usually crowned with success for, after dusk, the woods and hedgerows of Ireland bustle with, quite literally, millions of field mice. The long-tailed field mouse, *Apodemus sylvaticus*, is almost certainly Ireland's commonest mammal. It is widespread throughout the island but is rarely seen, as it is small and almost exclusively nocturnal.

The name 'wood mouse' is often used instead and it has become increasingly frequent recently in the scientific literature. The 'field' is, admittedly, somewhat misleading, for it is not employed in the modern topographical sense, in other words it has nothing necessarily to do with agriculture, but as in the biblical 'beasts of the field', meaning wild as distinct from domestic animals. The same sense is also intended in the term 'field work'. In short, it is intended as a direct contrast to 'house mouse'. Because the animal is so little known in Ireland, there is no generally recognized common name. As mentioned in Chapter 1, 'field mouse' often refers to feral house mice, especially those which enter houses in autumn, but the term is most usually applied to pigmy shrews. 'Wood mouse' is unheard of but 'dor mouse' is known, though there are no true dormice in Ireland. The Gaelic name is '*Luch fheir*', but this is used no less indiscriminately than the English names.

Fig. 24   Field mouse.

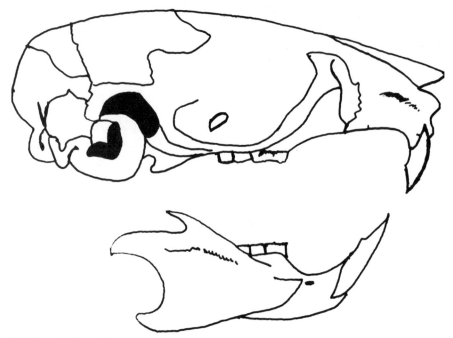

Fig. 25   Skull of field mouse.

Even those who shudder at the thought of a house mouse, are often charmed by *Apodemus* for it is an indisputably handsome animal. Slightly larger than the house mouse, it resembles it in general proportions, though the eyes, ears and hind feet are bigger. The fur is a soft, wood brown above, mixed with black and yellow and the latter hue is intensified along the flanks. The overall brown colour varies, in extreme instances, to a distinct rufous tint or to a sandy orange. Beneath, the hair is white but there is almost always a yellow-brown spot at the throat, sometimes lengthened into a stripe. Divergence from the general pattern of colouration is rare but a 'black and white' specimen was reported as exhibited at a meeting of the Dublin Natural History Society[206] in 1858 and other variations have been recorded outside Ireland.

The tail is relatively sparsely haired, the skin above dark brown and whiteish beneath, though the whole of the tip is white on some specimens. Of over 300 I examined in Co. Down, about 5% were thus affected.[71] The phenomenon of albinism of the tail tip also appears in some other mammals, notably the fox. It has been suggested that, as the end of the tail is probably the coldest part of the body, perhaps the temperature is sufficiently low in some individuals to inhibit the normal production of pigment. In this context it is interesting that a mouse I once caught had a small white patch of hair on top of the head, an area which, with the skull directly beneath, may also be comparatively isolated from body heat.

The tail is remarkable in quite another way: it comes off. Those who have no knowledge of this are taken aback, if not horrified, by an accidental, practical demonstration. When the appendage is seized, the sheath of skin separates at some point and the rodent escapes with the organ partly denuded. There is little bleeding and the exposed section eventually dries up and drops off. Mice in this undignified condition are not uncommon. Conceivably the mechanism may have some protective value. For example it might save a mouse's bacon if a pursuer happened to catch it by the tail. For this reason the animal is best held by the scruff of the neck and naturally should not be 'tailed' like laboratory mice.

The coats of immature field mice are quite unlike those of their elders, a dark smoky grey above fading to a lighter grey beneath. They can easily be confused with house mice and even Barrett-Hamilton mistook some juveniles he was sent from Cos. Kerry and Galway for representatives of a distinct race of the species[13]—his tendencies to 'split' have already been emphasized—to which he assigned the sub-species *celticus*, a trinomial which he had later to retract. His action was probably prompted by the writings of Rev. L. Jenyns, an English zoologist, who obtained field mice from Co. Kerry in 1841 which were smaller and darker than normal.[126] These were undoubtedly young mice too.

The skull, shown in Fig. 25, is of the usual rodent type, having a pair of continuously-growing incisor teeth at the front of both the upper and lower jaws separated from the cheek teeth by a gap, the *diastema*. The constant growth of the incisors is matched by a corresponding loss in wear. Should one become broken, the opposing tooth will have nothing to grind on and will continue to lengthen, later preventing the animal from feeding and so eventually killing it. The outer surface of each incisor is coated with enamel, the hard substance which covers all of those parts of our own teeth which project above the gum. The inner surface is, however, exposed and relatively soft. Consequently each tooth is worn at an angle, giving it a keen cutting edge which is automatically resharpened by working against its opposite fellow. The teeth in the cheeks are used to grind up the food and this is facilitated by the wide degree of lateral movement allowed to the lower jaw.

Apodemus, like other rodents, has a cleft upper lip, the halves of which can be pulled aside so that action of the front teeth is unimpeded. The lips can also be closed behind the incisors when the animal is gnawing, but not actually feeding, and so keep unwanted, chewed-off particles out of the mouth.

There is something exceedingly attractive about *Apodemus* at rest, poised, alert, and quivering. There is a distinct impression of sharply tuned senses imparted by the large eyes, the ears, twitching at the slightest sound, and the long whiskers. Indeed the animal will jump away at the first hint of danger, and obviously flight is of extreme importance to a defenceless small mammal. Although field mice may walk or run, the characteristic means of progression is by leaping, when the large hind feet are employed to advantage. The actual performance is difficult to describe briefly, the mouse bounding along in a peculiarly erratic manner. There is only an approximate directional correction at each leap so that, although the general movement is in a straight line, the path is a zigzag one. At a single bound the mouse can reach an altitude of over 0.5m, if so willed, but very often the jumps are much lower. The spoor in snow of a hopping field mouse is easily recognized. The prints of the four feet lie close together in groups and there is also a more or less obvious drag mark made by the tail which is probably an important organ of balance in this type of movement. The impression of the tail is also fairly clear in snow or sand where the animal has been walking.

At rest the mouse may sit upright, leaning back on the tail for support, which leaves the fore-paws free for the manipulation of food.

Field mice climb well and are tolerably good swimmers, the stroke being the usual mammalian 'dog paddle', in other words the action does not differ essentially from walking. The main problem in swimming for man is caused by his normally erect posture, necessitating his head being turned at right angles to the body in order to face forward. A man must raise his head almost clear of the water to breathe, causing loss of buoyancy, so that this is done only intermittently in most strokes. In contrast, when most mammals take to the water, they can submerge almost completely and still keep their nostrils above the surface. It is therefore hardly surprising that the vast majority of mammals can swim.

The voice most often heard from the field mouse is a high-pitched piping made when the animal is upset, for example when it is grasped roughly, and doubtless at other times, '. . . a chirping cry that almost reaches the dignity of a song,' as Moffat put it. But softer squeaking or chuckling noises are also made.

That mice are almost entirely nocturnal has been demonstrated convincingly in experiments in England and it has been my experience both when trapping outdoors and while keeping individuals in the laboratory. Nevertheless, some are abroad during the day. I encountered one in full daylight in January on a path at the Giant's Causeway, Co. Antrim, and I once saw two young mice feeding at the roadside near Pontoon Bridge, Co. Mayo, on a brilliant June afternoon. Barrington wrote of spying a pair sunning themselves outside a hole in one of his clover fields[16] and Dr. Brian West has told me of seeing them from time to time in the open during the daytime on the close-cropped sward which covers much of the island of Inishkea South, Co. Mayo.[93] While the large eyes of *Apodemus* may be correlated to its nocturnal habits, it should be remembered that efficiency of the eye is not related to its size relative to the body but to absolute size, each of the light-sensitive cells bulking much the same in any mammalian eye. To my mind and experience the mice are much more sensitive to sound than sight.

Normally the day is spent below ground in tunnels which the mice excavate for themselves. These may have more than one entrance and can extend for some distance. O'Mahony[163] dug out burrows on the North Bull Island and found them as long as 2.7m and that they went down to depths of as much as 1.5m. He also noticed freshly turned-out sand at the mouths of the holes, covered with mouse footprints. Such piles are often the mark of a hole in occupation, but they are not always present, for sometimes an entrance is made by an *Apodemus* digging itself out from below. Along the tunnels are storerooms and a chamber containing a nest of finely shredded grass. Occasionally nests are built above ground, for example in tussocks of grass. Thompson found two of them in a beehive at Fort William (now in Belfast), a somewhat surprising and, one would imagine, potentially uncomfortable site. In Britain Harting even found one in a rook's nest, high up in an elm.

The mouse is found in a wide range of terrain but this must fulfil three requirements. First, it must not be entirely built up. Just the same, field mice extend well into city suburbs. I have had a specimen from within a mile of the centre of Belfast. Moreover in 1964 they were found to figure in the diet of some short-eared owls (*Asio flammeus*) which were living on the unclaimed waste ground in the Belfast Harbour.[56] Secondly, a minimum of cover is required, but not necessarily ground cover. Mice can be trapped under dense stands of sitka spruce in forestry plantations, under rhododendrons or even beeches, where there is no ground cover at all. Thirdly, the ground must not be permanently damp or, at least, there must be dry patches, where the animals can presumably make their homes. Dry stone walls are often important refuges in bogland and mice normally occur on open bogs at extremely low densities or not at all. Experiments at the Peatland Experimental Station at Glenamoy, Co. Mayo, indicate that improvement in the form of drainage and fertilizing can result in an increase in numbers.[133]

The mice are common in woodland, scrub, gardens and hedgerows, and are also present on dunes, even those which are only lightly colonized by plants. I have caught them in the Murlough sand hills at Dundrum, Co. Down, where the sole vegetation consisted of marram grass or a low covering of sea buckthorn.

In Britain field mice are sometimes taken in grassland but usually only where field voles, the most abundant rodents in long grass, are absent or around only in small numbers. It is no surprise, therefore, that the mice live in this habitat in Ireland, where there are no field voles at all. However, extra cover, for instance in the form of a few fronds of bracken, makes long grass demonstrably more suitable, or so I have concluded from live trapping.[63]

Field voles are numerous on high ground in Great Britain and have been trapped at the top of Scottish hills. Mice do not extend above the tree line and indeed are not found north of the tree line in Europe. Exceptions in Britain can usually be traced to food left behind by hill walkers on mountains which are frequently climbed.[28] In Ireland *Apodemus*, in contrast, is to be found at high altitudes. One of the Rev. Jenyns's specimens was reputedly collected at 760m (2,500 ft). Prompted by this knowledge in 1964, I decided to try trapping mice on a mountain and selected Carrantouhill in the Magillycuddy Reeks in Co. Kerry, which at 1,041 m (3,414 ft) is Ireland's highest mountain. I was rewarded with three mice.[55]

An unusual type of country is provided for field mice by the pavements of the Burren in the mid-west. This is an area of rounded limestone hills, quite bare and seamed with joints which have been enlarged by solution. Most of these, together with many hollows in the rock, contain a thin soil which supports a dense characteristic flora, predominantly because of the prevailing high humidity. In May 1963 I did some live trapping in some of the deeper joints or *grykes* and from this it was clear that field mice were common enough in them.[62] The bottom of the fissures are too constricted to allow for the entry of most predators. Only stoats could enter them at all and even they might have difficulty in negotiating some of the narrower parts. The grykes are therefore almost ideally secluded from the mouse's point of view. However, crossing the exposed limestone from one gryke to another is probably a somewhat hazardous undertaking

Field mice do not take up residence in houses as readily as house mice but this is by no means unknown. Having lent traps to friends in Galway one autumn to remove unwanted rodent visitors which were clattering about in cupboards at night, I was eventually presented with two bodies, both of them *Apodemus*. Dr. West found that field mice on Inishkea often crept into the only inhabitable cottage on the island to pilfer foodstuffs.[93] The first thief to be apprehended was dispatched with the aid of a bedroom slipper.

Field mice are found on many other of Ireland's offshore islands. Most likely they owe their presence there to accidental introduction by man, being brought in with supplies from the mainland. They occur[79] on Rathlin (Co. Antrim), Bere, Cape Clear, Sherkin (Co. Cork), Lambay, North Bull (Co. Dublin), Tory (Co. Donegal), Inishbofin, Inishmore (Co. Galway), Great Blasket, Valencia (Co. Kerry), Achill and Clare (Co. Mayo). Other islands require further investigation. On the wind-swept islands of the west, dry-stone walls are probably very important for cover, and, on the exposed terrain of Inishkea South, they were never seen far from walls or ruins.

On the mainland, field mice of 30g can be considered as quite exceptionally heavy, and any over 25g are regarded as big. On Rathlin Island they are considerably larger.[53] Of seventeen I caught there in early summer in 1963 (when, admittedly, one would expect a large proportion of the population to be old adults), only three weighed *less* than 30g. One turned the scale at 36g, and doubtless a more intensive search would have produced even bigger ones. The dimensions of the body and skull were, naturally, correspondingly greater. Having handled over two hundred mice before going to Rathlin, the first specimen I caught there came as something of a shock. Very few specimens have been caught on most of the other Irish islands and it is conceivable that there may be populations of mice of similar proportions on some of them as well.

On some of the islands of Great Britain the mice and voles are also larger than on the mainland. As size is heritable, presumably there is some factor promoting natural selection for a larger rodent on islands. It has been postulated that this is the absence of ground predators.[29] All things being equal, this should favour an increase in size, for bigger mice are able to compete more successfully with their fellows. The presence of the predators favours small size, for escape is then possible into holes inaccessible to them. This is, of course, merely a hypothesis. It should be rememberd too that the progenitors of most insular populations of small mammals were almost certainly few in number, maybe only two or three, brought in hiding in provisions. The potential for inbreeding and consequent abnormalities is therefore greatly increased. A possible case of this is provided by the seventeen field mice caught on Tory Island in 1964.[162] Nine (over half) had white tail tips, as opposed to the usual minute fraction.

What Irish field mice feed on has been fairly well documented, both in a number of casual observations and in a small systematic investigation. In the latter I examined the stomach contents of fifty-nine specimens caught in snap-traps over one year in woodland in Co. Down.[61] Coconut was used as bait, not that it is any more appetizing than a range of other eatables, but because it stays on the prongs of the trap well and is easily distinguished from other materials in the stomach when they are being examined under the microscope. (At this point it is worthwhile turning aside to point out that there is no bait which is outstandingly attractive to mice. That cheese has any particular merit is an error perpetuated by popular tradition, nursery stories and the feebler sorts of journalism. That aniseed will render food unusually appetizing to rodents is a similar unfounded delusion.) The food from each stomach was identified and was classified under six general headings. The percentages of the mice which had fed on each class of food were as follows: seed 69, fruit 12, green plant (shoots, buds and leaves) 3, roots 3 and insects 51. Evidently seeds and insects were the chief foods, though the quantities of the former in the stomachs were nearly always greater than those of the latter. Fruit is also clearly of some significance. Other items were taken sparingly and less frequently. The results are much the same as those obtained in other countries.

In woodland a sizeable part of the diet is composed of the seeds of both deciduous and coniferous trees and it is possible that the feeding activities of the mice may be a factor in checking tree regeneration in some Irish woods. From the analysis above, it is plain that green plant material is not much bothered with and so seedlings are rarely destroyed. The term 'seed', of course, includes nuts and in eating these the mouse must first deal with the shell. To do this the nut is pressed against the ground, for most are eaten after they have fallen, and any unevenness on the shell is used as an anchorage for the upper incisors. A hole is duly gnawed by the lower ones. Should the nut become dislodged the process is recommenced, but not necessarily at the same point. In other words the animal may start again from scratch. One cannot expect too much brain-work from a field mouse. Once the case is perforated, the bottom incisors are inserted and the hole enlarged from the inside until the kernel can be extracted. This is done with the upper and lower incisors, which are used rather like tweezers to winkle the kernel out. It can then be managed by the fore-paws while the mouse nibbles at it. Softer food, such as grain, is similarly held and all of the husk and other coarse material are daintily dropped aside, uneaten.

Moffat[156] found the remains of acorns, ash keys and beech-mast at the respective entrances of three mouse holes in a field, concluding that the occupant of each hole had cleared out unwanted rubbish from the interior of its home, and that each of them had been fairly constant to its own preferred food.

Dandelion seeds are sometimes eaten and O'Mahony came across a large pile of these on the North Bull[163] in a hollow where two mouse tracks met. Placing a trap at the centre, he caught an *Apodemus.*

Ripe haws are a great attraction and Moffat[156] wrote of seeing the animals on the uppermost branches of a hawthorn hedge at dusk making a supper, or rather a 'vespertinial breakfast' of the fruits. I have twice come across piles of haw remains mixed with mouse droppings in hedges, the left-overs of such feasts. On one of these occasions the remnants were in a heap under the hedge. On the other, three old birds' nests had been used as dining rooms and all three were almost full of yellow and red fragments. This use of deserted nests is well known and scraps of other seeds from hedgerow plants are sometimes found there too. Commonest are perhaps rose-hips, the mice having carefully chiselled off the end of each seed to reach the kernel. The bird's nest habit inspired the scansionless verse at the beginning of this chapter, which was written as long ago as 1834. It is quite probable that the nests, within a hedge, may afford some measure of protection from predators. There is adequate cover from aerial ones, and ground predators would be obliged to climb.

Since uneaten food is also to be found along with the leavings, the habit may simply be an extension of the extraordinary food-storing propensities of the mice. Even when kept in captivity with surplus food they will hide quantities of it in various parts of their living quarters. Barrington[16] noticed that his pets covered up a wheat grain or other tit-bit with the nose, after the manner of a dog burying a bone. Sometimes the hind feet were used to scrape material from the floor of the cage over a food item. When live trapping, it is quite common to find that the entrances to traps have been carefully stuffed with twigs and dead leaves, presumably securing the bait as a cache of provisions. In the 1962 spring edition of the *Countryman* appeared a letter from a reader in Co. Down who described a hole in a bank under a beech tree with a large pile of beechmast beside it, the cases mostly empty and some nuts peeled white. Undoubtedly this was a field mouse food depôt too.

The field mouse can be regarded only infrequently as an agricultural pest of any importance, and it is rarely if ever found in corn stacks. But it can be a serious nuisance to the horticulturalist and, on occasion, the scourge of the kitchen-garden. Bulbs are sometimes attacked—I have seen those of bluebells in woodland unearthed and partly eaten—but the main trouble is with peas and beans, so much so that in parts of Britain field mice are known as 'bean mice' or 'beaners'. They will often go along a row of freshly-sown seeds, digging them up, devouring them on the spot or carrying them off, so that the gardener must resort to soaking the seeds in paraffin beforehand to make them distasteful or to setting traps for the felons. The mouse's custom of hoarding, needless to say, makes things worse, for far more peas and beans are excavated than are required at the time. The habit, incidentally, testifies to the field mouse's well-developed sense of smell. Thompson wrote of a text-book example

In gardens a short distance from Belfast, I have known them to commit very extensive depredations on the early crops of peas and beans. Although annoying, it was at the same time amusing, to observe how completely they had carried off every bean of the first crop. These had been planted in double rows, and above every bean there was a cylindrical hole excavated, by which the mice had gained access to it. Traps made of a single brick were successfully used for their destruction.

A more drastic measure is prescribed in the curious booklet *The Pests of the Farm*, by H.D. Richardson, published in Dublin in 1847. This contains some notions which, from the distance of over a century, are faintly amusing. To stop the mice digging up freshly sown corn, the following concoction was recommended. The recipe was taken, almost verbatim, from an earlier work, also produced in Dublin.

> . . . a peck of barley meal, a pound of powder of white root, and four ounces of powder of staves-acres, and when these are all mixed together by sifting through a coarse sieve, add half a pound of honey, and as much milk as will work the whole into a paste. Let this be broken in pieces, and scattered over the field at the time when the mice are coming. They will eat it greedily, and it is certain death to them . . . The mice will be kept from digging after the corn, and, at the same time, will be killed by the ingredients.

It should perhaps be repeated that serious trouble of the latter kind from field mice is unusual.

Barrington wrote of the range of vegetable foods his captives would take. He often put a sod of grass into the cage for them to root through and they fed readily on oats, wheat, barley, chestnuts, beech-mast, walnuts, arbutus berries, gooseberries, apples and grapes. Most of the fruits in my own analyses were almost certainly blackberries.

There are rather fewer observations on the carnivorous side of the animal's diet in Ireland, but only through a lack of observers. Moffat witnessed two determined attacks on frogs in spring, in both cases drawn to his attention by the screams of the luckless amphibians.[156] Thompson found that in winter mice broke into beehives and ate the honeycomb. Molluscs are eaten too, though my sole experience of this was a half-eaten snail which I caught in a live trap along with a mouse.

Cannibalism is not unknown, and this is sometimes the result of the rare occasions when two mice are caught in one live trap and finish off the bait. An animal killed in a snap-trap may also be dined on by his relatives and neighbours. In most cases the diner starts with the eye; then the skull is broken open and the brain at least partly devoured.

In *Apodemus* the sexes are easy to tell apart. Males have a band of fur separating the urinary opening and the anus whereas in females the area between them is quite naked. As in other rodents the male sex organs, the *testes*, enlarge greatly when the animal becomes mature and move down from inside the body into the scrotum. At the end of the season the testes regress and move back into the body. Fecund males have therefore a marked outpushing just in front of the anus, which is very easy to spot. The female reproductive opening, which is quite separate from the urinary one, is closed over in juveniles, and in adults it is only open in the breeding season. It is also scarred over for a short time during pregnancy. It is thus possible, not only to learn the sex of an individual without harming it in any way, but also to determine its reproductive condition. Sexually mature mice rarely weigh less than 15g. It is a simple matter also to recognise a suckling female, for then her six mammae are quite prominent.

Extensive data are available from Britain on field mouse reproduction. The gestation period is around 25 days and the young, though born naked and blind, can cling to their mother tenaciously with their mouths and feet when she is disturbed. Weaning takes about 21 days and the young first venture out of the nest at approximately 16 days and are then about 6g in weight.[189] The mother can become pregnant again shortly after giving birth. It was Barrington who made the first detailed observations on the reproduction of field mice, in 1880 and 1881 on two females in his captive colony. He found that intervals between litters varied from 23 to 29 days, a close reflection of the established gestation period. One female was believed to have produced six families in four months. There were from three to five young in each litter, the average being four precisely.

I had the opportunity of comparing, with these figures, the number of young carried by the females before birth.[72] Altogether I dissected thirty-nine expectant mothers, many of which were killed during an investigation to find whether field mice carried Weil's disease (a severe form of jaundice) in north-east Ireland. The mean number of embryos at the height of the breeding season was 5.4., with a range of from five to seven, which does not differ from comparable observations in England. While these figures are somewhat higher than Barrington's, I found that the numbers of those mice near term were generally less than five. The explanation is doubtless that some of the unborn young die and are reabsorbed in the uterus of the mother. This remarkable phenomenon probably takes place in many mammals, though this has only been appreciated relatively recently. It is particularly well documented for the rabbit.

The breeding season usually lasts from April to September, though a small proportion of the animals are fecund for a few weeks in March and October. There is some variation. A population under study in a wood near Athenry, Co. Galway,[87] stopped breeding in October, but were mostly in condition again by early January. In Great Britain it has been known, in one wood at least, for there to be no winter break at all and it is thought that continuous breeding may be induced by an exceptionally heavy fall of seed.[202] Much more research is needed to sort out the problem.

Several birds and mammals eat field mice. They are regularly taken by owls and stoats, and are a minor but consistent prey of the fox. Fuller details are given under the appropriate chapter headings elsewhere in this book. It will be recalled from Chapter 1 that martens hunt them and that they are consumed by badgers too, though adult field mice are far too nimble for badgers to catch often in the open.

Perhaps surprisingly to the non-naturalist, the kestrel is a major predator. Those who have watched one hanging in the air, with its wings beating rapidly as it scans the ground, are sometimes puzzled as to what it must be looking for. The answer is 'mainly mice'. Like owls, kestrels regurgitate parts of their prey in the form of pellets, which are often dropped around their nests and at roosting places. An analysis of the pellets will give a reliable indication of the bird's food. Unfortunately many bones are discarded uneaten and so the detective work must be done mostly by identifying hair under the microscope.

During the summer of 1964, with considerable help, I was able to obtain over 400 pellets from seven nesting sites,[90] and to collect with them uneaten scraps of prey—mainly birds' wings and a dead field mouse which provided additional clues. It was plain from the analyses that the kestrels were subsisting principally on field mice and small birds, particularly young starlings (*Sturnus vulgaris*). House mice, rats, shrews and rabbits (presumably young ones) were eaten as well and even ground and especially dor beetles (*Carabus* sp. and *Geotrupes* sp.). Confirming these conclusions are the observations of C.D. Deane, who watched parent birds bringing food to their young in the shape of two field mice, a house mouse, a young rat, a newt (*Triturus vulgaris*) and a frog.[37]

During the winter of 1972-73 I was able to make regular collections of pellets from a kestrel roost in a ruin on the banks of the River Corrib, outside Galway.[81] As before, field mice and birds were the most important foods but, once again, other small mammals were eaten, as well as the odd frog and, in a warm spell in March, lizards. A lot of beetles, comprising at least eight different species, were taken but the bulk of them were, once more, dor beetles.

That *Apodemus* should be eaten by kestrels so frequently seems strange in view of its nocturnal habits. Probably the birds are particularly adept at picking off the odd individuals abroad in daylight. Furthermore, it is well known that they can hunt in very low light intensities. Quite probably many mice are captured at dawn and dusk. Thompson

> ... remarked the kestrel abroad at a very early hour in the winter morning; and Mr. Poole notes his having observed one on the morning of 11th November before 7 o'clock when there seemed little enough light for an owl to plunder.

Cats out hunting probably kill many field mice, the mouse's agility meeting its match in pussy's suppleness, speed and cunning. However, to some extent this must be conjecture, for people who can be relied upon to identify a field mouse with certainty are few and far between. Most 'field mice', on enquiry, turn out to be shrews. Cats are much more inclined to carry about and bring in shrews, for these have scent glands which make them unpleasant to eat; on the other hand *Apodemus* may well be devoured on the spot. Nevertheless, I have four Irish accounts of cats playing with field mice which I have no doubt are genuine. In two of these I was able to examine the victims afterwards myself.

There are no further predators of any importance. Other raptorial birds are likely to account for only a few mice, but it is worth mentioning that I was once allowed to examine some pellets of the peregrine falcon (*Falco peregrinus*) which contained a little field mouse hair. I was also informed by Mr. J.W. Greaves, former-ly of the Ulster Museum, that he had found their remains in pellets of buzzards (*Buteo buteo*), collected on Rathlin Island. I did not see these myself. Very young mice, especially those in a nest above or near the surface of the ground, are likely to fall prey to animals which have little opportunity to devour the adults, such as hedgehogs and brown rats. Mr. F.W. Fox of Tallaght, Co. Dublin, wrote to me some years ago of seeing rooks (*Corvus frugilegus*) and herring gulls (*Larus argentatus*) taking broods of young field mice turned up by the plough.

While some mice end up as dinners for hungry predators, virtually all of them provide meals for equally ravenous parasites. Field mice carry a rich and varied super-cargo of creeping things, though not all of these are harmful. Their nests usually abound with the same livestock. Making their living off Irish field mice are four species of flea (see Chapter 9), a louse (*Polyplax serratus*) and at least eleven differ-ent kinds of mites,[79] though a few of the latter appear to be scarce or localised. In fact no attempt at all has been made to discover whether Irish mice suffer from the smallest types of parasitic mite, which live in the skin and are not normally removed by brushing the fur, so the list may be extended in the future. More sophisticated techniques are needed to collect these lesser mites or, indeed, to obtain lice in any numbers.

One of the larger mites, *Laelaps agilis*, about 1mm long, I found on half of all the mice I examined. The record was sixty-seven from a single individual. While some of the mites are parasites, others feed only on particles of dead skin or take blood from abrasions when it is available. Still others are predatory, feeding on the other mouse associates. The loose nature of the relationship between some mites and the mice was well illustrated during an expedition by some naturalists to the Great Blasket Island[47] where the commonest mite on *Apodemus* was *Poecilochirus necro-phori*, a species usually found on dung beetles. One individual yielded 200 of them.

In areas where ticks are common, they are sometimes found attached to mice, mostly around the mouth and ears. In most cases these are simply immature stages of the common sheep-tick (*Ixodes ricinus*), a species which will feed on a wide range of mammals and birds, despite its name. Usually the ticks lie in wait in vegetation and embark when the mouse brushes past them. They bury their mouthparts in the skin and proceed to suck blood. Once engorged, they drop off, so the acquaintance is a comparatively brief one.

Perhaps the queerest of all the hangers-on is the beetle, *Leptinus testaceus*, which is quite often seen scurrying over field mice. This flattened, brown, eyeless insect is only about 3mm long and has also been found in rotten wood, among dead leaves, in bumble bees' and birds' nests and, more rarely, in the nest of a species of ant. On the continent it occurs occasionally on moles and hamsters and has even been seen on sap flowing from trees.[25] What its business is with *Apodemus*, no one knows. But there is no lack of theories. It may be a casual parasite. It might prey on the mites. It may eat organic debris in the mouse's coat or selected morsels from the rubbish in its nest. Or it may only use the mouse for transport.

A single mouse can carry an astonishing load of passengers. The most varied list, in my experience, comprised four beetles, eight fleas and fifty-one mites (of four different species). The activities of the citizens in the anarchic world of field mouse fur and nest are imperfectly known and would repay the researcher looking for 'something completely different'.

None of the dependants bite man, which is fortunate, for field mice make ideal pets in all but one respect: they rarely become tame. They should be given plenty of space; a box of about 40 x 30 x 30 cm is right for a pair. It is a dismal thing to see *Apodemus* confined in one of the tiny cages used for laboratory mice. Because of their skills in jumping, climbing and gnawing, one must ensure that their home is escape-proof and wooden boxes are not recommended. The floor should be covered with sawdust. The provision of food presents no problem and, other than supplying fresh drinking water in the usual feeder-bottle used for white mice, there is little to do. *Apodemus* does not have the same offensive smell as house mice and the quarters need only be cleaned out each month. Bedding material should be provided in the form of hay or wood-wool, preferably, a nest box.

The mice are sociable and rarely squabble, even when several of each sex are kept together, but space and seclusion are necessary if it is intended that they should breed. Barrington gave a delightful account of the domestic life of his colony.[16]

> ... we had twelve to twenty mice, young and old, in the nest; they all slept together, and it was certainly a curious sight to see father, mothers, and children of all ages and sizes in the nest, the young of different ages suckling the same mother at the same time, and the mothers appearing to suckle each other's young indiscriminately. They also seemed to have no cessation of suckling; but on this point I will not speak confidently. So fast did the young attach themselves that the females could scarcely move without pulling two or three after them.
>
> The young were reared in the small box, but the mothers had a care over their movements outside, and carried them back to the nest until they reached the age of three weeks. They were not caught at the back of the neck, as is usual with dogs and cats when carrying their young, but generally by the side of the belly, midway between the fore and hind legs; the mother then raised the young one completely off the ground, and with head erect conveyed it to the nest. Sometimes the parental authority was attempted to be exercised on an 'old' young one, and a species of dragging was then resorted to. The entrance to the breeding-box was narrow, and it was not possible to carry the young through it. This the mothers soon learned, and they overcame the difficulty by dropping the young one at the entrance and then, going in themselves, they turned round and dragged it in head foremost.

Modern research on mammals often takes the form of a population study. Obviously it is more satisfactory to investigate a population as a whole than to look at a few individuals. The results are bound to be more representative and one can only

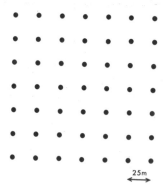

25m

Fig. 26 A typical arrangement of trapping stations for grid-trapping a population of small rodents. Each station is indicated by a dot.

obtain data on birth-rate, death-rate, emigration, immigration and overall age distribution in this way. Such information is essential in measuring the effects of a mammalian species on its environment and in formulating any management policy for it.

Populations of field mice and voles can most easily be monitored by regular grid-trapping, a method which has been used extensively for this purpose. The following is a brief and simplified outline. It cannot be emphasized too strongly that anyone contemplating a survey of this nature should consult someone conversant with the procedure and read some of the voluminous literature on the subject. Otherwise any results may be quite useless, and through faulty technique, mice may be injured or die.

The basic idea is uncomplicated and entails laying out a grid of equidistant points in the area under investigation, as shown in Fig. 26, which are then used as trapping stations. This can be done either with surveying equipment or, more simply, with lines of synthetic cord of some kind; dampness causes most natural fibre to contract. The performance is easy enough in open country but more difficult in a wood where trees get in the way. Trapping sessions are then carried out for a given number of nights every few weeks. Too frequent trapping will disturb behaviour patterns besides providing free meals. I usually operate for three consecutive nights every four weeks with two traps at each point. Box traps, catching the animals alive, are used, the most familiar in the British Isles being the Longworth, which is illustrated in Fig. 27. It consists of a tunnel section, containing a trip mechanism allowing the door to fall, and a nest box, which is baited to keep the captive alive during its sojourn. Mice will enter unbaited traps but perish without food. The tunnel can be detached from the nest box for removing the catch, and can be placed inside it for compactness in transport.

Each morning of the session the mice are removed, individually marked, weighed and the sex and breeding condition noted. They are then released. This is repeated on each session, mice marked previously being carefully recorded. By knowing the number of animals marked already and the proportion of marked to unmarked in the catch, one can work out the approximate total numbers of mice in the population. The basic concept in calculating absolute numbers is therefore quite simple but, in practice, there are usually mathematical refinements to allow for the various adjustments and errors, and these can be quite involved. The annual cycle of

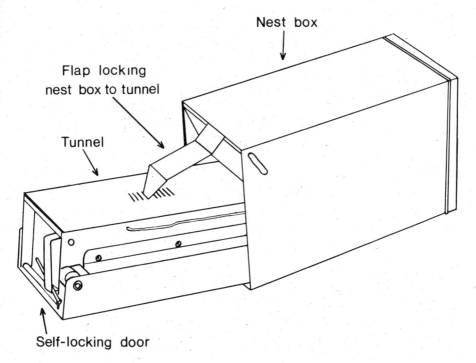

Nest box

Flap locking nest box to tunnel

Tunnel

Self-locking door

Fig. 27   Longworth small mammal trap with door in 'closed' position. The tunnel is separated from the nest box when removing a captive.

reproductive activity is easily deduced and so are the birth and death rates. As few mice normally reach full size before death, the weight can be taken as a fairish index of age. Movements and the normal ranges of individuals will be apparent from the particular stations which they visit. It is also easy to ascertain the types of cover most frequented by the animals.

In the three studies I have undertaken in Ireland (one yet unpublished), all of them in mixed woodland,[64, 87] the population density fluctuated between 15 and 50 mice per hectare (6 to 20 per acre). Normally, although breeding starts in spring, there is very little recruitment of young into the population until July or August. Clearly their survival is poor but the reason for this is unknown. In Britain it has been mooted that it may be due to aggressive behaviour by the old males.[202] Minimum density is reached by June or July. There is then a rise in numbers and a rapid turnover so that, by October, few of the mice which had overwintered are still alive. The maximum life-span of a field mouse in the wild is about a year and the mean expectancy half this, though they will live in captivity for well over two. I have kept them for two myself. Breeding usually ceases in October, but the peak trappable population is not reached until November or December, for the final young of the season must leave the nest before they can enter a trap. While I have caught a specimen of 7g in a Longworth, one does not catch many under 10g. Usually the males move greater distances during the breeding season and are more active than in winter. The average breadth of the range of a field mouse is about 50–70m for males and 30–55m for females but some move over much smaller distances and, at the other extreme, I have recorded individual movements of over 300m.

The Longworth trap, though convenient in operation, is bulky and expensive, over £2.00 at the time of writing. The tyro may feel that the possession of a few is essential to confer a professional aura, but home-made live traps will do just as well. The mechanism of the domestic 'snap' or 'break-back' mouse traps can be used to actuate the mechanism in a home-made box trap—not to kill the mouse but to shut the door. If it does not matter whether specimens are dead or not, then a break-back is often better and a shelter in the form of a tin or jar will prevent the specimen becoming wet. The 'Selfset' metal snap-trap is the most efficient of all.

5 The Irish Stoat

This little animal has more spirit than body, and its courage supplying the deficiency of its strength, with a great heart actuating a slender frame, it is vindictive and relentless in its wrath.

Topographica Hibernica   Giraldus Cambrensis

In Great Britain there are two weasel-like mammals: the weasel itself and the stoat. Both have red-brown coats with whitish under-sides, long sinuous bodies, short legs, rounded ears and heads which are both tapered and flattened. Both are intelligent, inquisitive and aggressive. Nevertheless they are easy to tell apart. Stoats are bigger animals and, although measurements of the adults of both species are highly variable, the following approximate figures will serve to illustrate this point.

		Weight in g	Length in mm of	
			Head and body	Tail
Stoat	Male	220-445	275-312	95-127
	Female	140-280	242-292	95-140
Weasel	Male	70-170	175-220	40-75
	Female	35-90	165-190	40-65

It will also be apparent from the above dimensions that the females are in both cases markedly smaller than the males.

Unlike the weasel, the stoat has a black tuft of hairs at the end of its tail, an absolutely characteristic feature. The chestnut fur on its back is somewhat duller than that of the weasel and the underside tends to cream, rather than the white of its lesser relative. In extreme instances it is an unmistakeable pale lemon-yellow. A further way to distinguish dead specimens would be to lay them down, chest-up, and look at the demarcation line between the dark and light fur. This line, while clear-cut and almost straight on stoats, is most uneven on weasels, the brown encroaching irregularly on to the throat, chest and belly and even occasionally joining to form a band across them. A few isolated brown flecks on the underside are to be expected too. The upper surface of the feet can also be partly white. Besides these differences there are a few others which are rather technical and much less completely diagnostic.

There are no weasels, definitely no weasels, in Ireland. The Irish stoat is, however, an endemic subspecies, *Mustela erminea hibernica*, found elsewhere only on the Isle of Man. The British mainland form is *Mustela erminea stabilis,* but there is another race, the Islay stoat, *Mustela erminea ricinae,* restricted to the Scottish islands of Islay and Jura. The main differences between the Irish and mainland British forms are in size and colouration, typical dimensions of the Irish subspecies being as follows:

	Weight in g	Length in mm of	
		Head and body	Tail
Male	196-284	240-283	72-117
Female	95-161	184-260	57-81

Obviously the Irish stoat is the smaller of the two. It is interesting to note that, of the individuals measured so far, those from the south tend to be larger than those from the north. But information in this respect is astonishingly limited, no weights at all having been put into print until 1971, so more data are required before much can be said with any degree of certainty.[76]

On the Irish stoat the border between the white and chestnut areas of the coat is like the weasel's—irregular, probably even more so, and two brown bands beneath are not unknown. This lack of uniformity means that it is often possible to iden- individuals from their undersurfaces if they can be examined at close quarters. Such a procedure is not recommended unless the animal concerned is either tame, anaes- thetized, enclosed in a glass-sided box, or dead. One is liable to be bitten quite a number of times before one realizes what has happened. Even with gloves the best to be hoped for is to keep a firm hold of the beast. Manipulation of a wriggling stoat is well nigh impossible. By the way, I have been informed that even an escaping stoat may bite the handler, in passing as it were.

Whereas *stabilis* has white hair on the upper lip, *hibernica* has brown with, very rarely, small patches of white. Again the British form has a white edging to the ear which is lacking in the Irish.

It was Barrett-Hamilton together with the distinguished English mammalogist, Oldfield Thomas, who first realized that the Irish race was, in fact, a distinct one and they published their findings in 1895.[198] When defining a new species or sub- species it is obligatory to select a specimen as a representative type, a tangible exam- ple to complement the written word. The type specimen of the Irish stoat, now in the British Museum, was from Enniskillen, Co. Fermanagh, and was supplied by the ubiquitous J.E. Harting.

One other feature of the coat remains to be mentioned. Moulting occurs twice a year, in spring and autumn. In the northern parts of the stoat's range, which ex- tends into the arctic in Europe, Asia and America, the winter fur is entirely white apart from the black tail-tip. The advantages thus conferred in latitudes where snow lies throughout the winter need not be elaborated upon. Further south winter whiten- ing becomes progressively less common. In the north of Scotland nearly all stoats whiten in autumn, whereas in southern England there is usually no change or only a partial one.

The stoat is often given the alternative name of 'ermine', particularly when in winter pelage, and ermine fur has been highly esteemed since early times. In medi- eval Europe fur was a luxury. It was forbidden by the Church to all but the highest ecclesiastics, while among the laity its use was regulated by frequent and often severe

Fig. 28　Irish stoat.

74

sumptuary laws. Sumptuary legislation in Britain was most extensive and detailed, its main purpose being to favour the aristocracy and assist the sale of English products. In the reign of Edward III the wearing of ermine was allowable only to members of the royal family and higher nobility. Sable, marten and genet were similarly restricted, the lowest orders having to make do with the skins of rabbits and cats. A man's social importance could be gauged by the amount and nature of the fur he wore. Traces of this may still be seen. For example, an earl's robe of state is characterized by three bars of ermine on the cape and a judge's ermine is a mark of office. Incidentally, the black tail was used to ornament the pure white fur.

Completely white Irish stoats are exceedingly rare and there appears to be only one such instance on record. The animal in question was originally in Barrington's personal collection and its present whereabouts are uncertain, but there are specimens in the National Museum in Dublin which are partly white. One has the dark colour only on the upper part of the head and neck; others show the change in having cream patches on the back and flanks. Whitening in a country where snow rarely lies for long would seem to be of little value in concealment. An interesting note on piebald stoats by G.H. Kinahan (an active and famous member of the Geological Survey but no relation of J.R. Kinahan) appeared in the *Zoologist* in 1892.[130]

I have seen albino Stoats, but never a true white one. Piebald Stoats are, however, not very uncommon. Years ago my brother had a remarkably large piebald buck stoat that was killed in a rat-trap in our house, in the Co. Dublin. About the same time a smaller one was caught in a trap set in a rabbit-run. I shot a piebald Stoat at Portraine, Co. Dublin, and I saw a very white one chasing a rabbit in Coole Park, Co. Galway. Others that I have seen were in the Burren, Co. Clare, and in the crags of Galway, Mayo &c. In general, when you see anything of the kind you have not got a gun, and anyone who has tried to catch a Stoat in an old wall knows what a task he has. Years ago, near the N.E. end of Lough Graney, Co. Clare, there was a farmer who used regularly to feed the Stoats, as he said if he gave them their meal of milk they never went near the hen-roosts. Besides, he said that they kept strangers away, and that the bucks used to get as 'white as snow in the winter'. This latter assertion, however, I will not vouch for, as I have often heard of a hare 'as white as snow' that did not answer my expectations when I shot it.

There is, in fact, a genuine albino Irish stoat in the National Museum. Albinism is a heritable condition in which the pigment melanin is absent from the body. Melanin is normally present in hair, skin and in a dark layer within the eye, where its chief function is to limit the reflection of light. Typical albinos have white hair, unpigmented skin and pinkish eyes.

In 1883 a rather curious letter was printed in the *Field*,[33] perhaps of questionable authenticity.

I saw, many years ago, a very curious variety of stoat. It was black and white, the former taking the place of the usual chestnut. I tried to kill it with a stick, but, though I got several chances at him as he thrust his head out of a rabbit hole, I missed him.

We must now return to expand on an earlier statement—that there are no weasels in Ireland. This is unquestionably true but, just the same, the Irish stoat is usually known as 'the weasel', the word 'stoat' being almost unknown in country districts. However, in some rural areas in the north the usual name is 'whithred' or 'whitterick', almost certainly corruptions of the apt 'white throat'. There have been many assertions that weasels are present as well, but, in proof, an example has yet to be produced. The literature is scattered with such statements and dissident correspondence on the subject, of the "'Tis, 'tisn't" variety, appeared in the *Field* and the *Zoologist* during the last century. Representative samples are given below. The first letter is from an English visitor.[20]

Observing by your editorial note . . . that there is some doubt whether the Weasel is found in Ireland, I write to say that on 5th November last . . . I saw a Weasel one afternoon hunting about a stone wall at Currawn, near Achill Sound, and as I watched it for some time at the distance of only a few yards, I could not possibly have been mistaken as to the species. I know the Stoat and Weasel too well to mistake the one for the other, and had I been aware at the time of the existence of any doubt on the subject, I could easily have shot and forwarded the specimen.

A more convincing narrative[111] reads

I see there is still a doubt as to whether the Weasel occurs in Ireland. I think both the Weasel and the Stoat exist there. I lived in the County Cork from 1851 to 1867, and with my terrier I came across several Weasels, as I thought, and one Stoat. The weasels were light brown, but the Stoat was chocolate colour with a black tip to its tail. I also saw what I considered a Weasel at Ballina, on the top of a wall, as I was riding one day. The Stoat I killed with terriers after a tremendous hunt. Friends of mine have also considered they killed Weasels in the Co. Cork.

However, the ease with which the Irish stoat may be confused with its smaller cousin is brought out by the following.[111]

I am aware that it is the right thing to say that we have no Weasels in Ireland; *certes*, I never saw an animal of the sort without the black tip to the tail. Many of them,–I may say most of them,–however, are so small, that a man who does not profess to be a naturalist is left in doubt whether he is not looking at a Weasel with a black tip. I have one before me now, an old bitch, giving suck,–whose size is exactly that given by Bewick as that of the Weasel,–7½in. from nose to tail; tail 2in., brush ¾in. I do not remember ever seeing any so small in England, though common enough here, as well as the larger size.

The matter is settled by a refreshingly sceptical correspondent.[48]

It is a pity that the folk who believe in the existence of the Weasel in Ireland have never been able to produce an Irish specimen. Some years ago a friend of mine made it known that he would give £5 to anyone who would bring him such an animal; yet up to the present time not one has been produced.

I cannot say, from personal experience, whether *hibernica* at a distance more closely resembles a weasel or a British stoat, for I must confess that I have never seen a living example of the latter animal. However, a few years ago, an English mammalogist of some standing enthusiastically informed me that he had definitely seen a weasel in Co. Galway. Having pointed out to him the peculiarities in size and in the coat of the native stoat, he was prepared to retract his claim.

A possible explanation for this curious reversal of terms will now be becoming apparent. When Irish was the universal language in the country there was probably more than one name but no confusion, for there was only one weasel-like animal to refer to. The arrival of English brought two alternatives and it was to be expected that the most applicable would come into general usage, and probably the Irish stoat looks more like a weasel. But the reason may be simpler still. The word 'weasel' is of ancient origin and similar sounding terms abound in other European languages. The earliest surviving English manuscript including it is dated *circa* 725 A.D., where 'uueosule' is used, and there is another instance for the year 1000. 'Stoat', used in the modern sense, cannot be traced further back than 1460. The Anglo-Saxon 'stoat' or 'stot' applied to an animal implied a larger, more pushing one and is derived from the Scandinavian and Low German root represented by the Gothic *stauten* = to push. 'Stoat' was formerly applied to a bull, stallion or maybe any male mammal and one can see here the origin of 'stud'. Stoats were originally called 'stoat-weasels', meaning the larger, more energetic weasels. It is therefore clear that 'weasel' arrived in Ireland well ahead of 'stoat' and that the first name has persisted, aided no doubt by the Irish stoat's resemblance to the weasel. The word 'weasel' is still erroneously used in parts of England for the stoat.

A useless but amusing fragment of information concerns the reading of a paper to the Zoological Society of London in 1863, namely 'Remarks on the date of extinction of the mole and weasel in Ireland'. It is regrettable that only the title was published. As there is no evidence that either mammal ever was native it must have included at least a few gems of absurdity.

Nearly every list of mammals compiled for Ireland, whether local or general, gives the stoat as abundant, including that of Giraldus Cambrensis. But, though stoats hunt at night, they are also commonly abroad during the day. Compared with, say, foxes they are much less fearful of man and are thus more frequently seen. A stoat which takes cover at one's approach will often reappear if the intruder will only stay still. A modicum of squeaking by the observer sometimes helps matters. There is something almost uncanny about the lack of fear in such a small beast, particularly in a stone pile where the animal may come into the open, then disappear only to peep and peer at you through the spaces in the pile a moment later. The effect is heightened by a realization of its ferocity and unrelenting endeavour when hunting down prey much larger than itself. Moffat[152] recalled walking *abreast* of a stoat carrying a rat some distance down a lane, and a geologist of my acquaintance told me of one which, after an initial retreat, ignored him completely in its efforts to trail a dead rabbit over a wall.

Cases of a familiarity too extreme for comfort are not unknown, as Pentland recounted.[169]

A few days ago, one of the ladies of my family saw a Stoat which had just killed a full-grown Rabbit, and was eating it. She sat down to watch it. At first, being intent on its meal, it did not perceive her, but presently it looked up, saw her and retired into a rabbit hole. She sat still and watched. It came out again, looked at her and disappeared again. She still waited. Presently she was startled by a shrill cry at her back, and turning saw the Stoat at the mouth of a hole about two feet from her. It snarled and squeaked at her. She picked up a stick and made a thrust at the Stoat which retreated for a moment, but reappeared again at once, defying the stick and offering such an angry and menacing appearance that she fairly dropped her stick and ran away, leaving the gallant Stoat master of the field and the rabbit. Stoats have increased in number here lately to my great pleasure. There is no more useful creature (outside the poultry yard).

The normal mode of progression, as with the Mustelidae (or weasel family) generally, is by bounding and the animal's suppleness in motion and surefooted agility is impressive, especially around a dry-stone wall. One can easily tell a stoat from a rat at a distance when it is crossing a road. A rat scuttles and maintains an inflexible profile; a stoat bounds and its long undulating outline is almost instantly recognizable.

Stoats ascend trees with ease, Moffat[154] remarking on more than one occasion that he had seen one scale a tree-trunk faster than a squirrel. In this context it is noteworthy that the usual name in Irish is *Easog*, which is often mistakenly applied to squirrels. An interesting observation was communicated to the *Field* on the subject in 1894 from Co. Cork.[205]

I have on two occasions shot stoats . . . in the act of ascending or descending trees viz. a crab-apple and a hawthorn. On the last occasion it was observed that the stoat had only one fore-foot. It had evidently lost the other one some time previously.

Stoats are also good swimmers and Thompson stated that

In proof of the swimming powers of the stoat, I may mention an anecdote which I have learned from a trustworthy source:—A respectable farmer, when crossing in his boat over an arm of the sea, about one mile [1.6km] in breadth, which separates a portion of Islandmagee (a penin sula near Larne, County Antrim) from the mainland, observed a ripple proceeding from some animal in the water; and, on rowing up, found that it was a 'weasel', which, he had no doubt, was going in a direct line from the shore; and it had reached the distance of a quarter of a mile, when overtaken. The poor animal was cruelly killed, though its gallant swimming might have pleaded in favour of its life.

Man and the elements are not the only adversities to be faced in water, as shown by a letter in the *Field* in 1901.[134] 'One of my men, a few days ago, caught a pike in the Blackwater weighing 5½ pounds [2.6kg] which had recently swallowed a full grown stoat'. That pike (*Esox lucius*) will swallow rats is well known, which seems the main reason why these fish, which are good eating and excellent when smoked, rarely reach the table in Ireland. So this tale is not improbable.

All that the stoat requires in the way of habitat is cover, whether in the form of low vegetation, hedges, dry stone walls, or heather and scree on mountain sides. I have seen one in a pile of stones a few yards from the sea at the Giant's Causeway Co. Antrim, another in heather on the Sperrin Mountains, Co. Tyrone, and a third at the top of the sea-cliffs of Sleay Head, Co. Kerry, besides many in walls, hedgerows and woodland. Life as a small but fearsome carnivore, with an ability to kill animals several times one's own size, presents few problems as far as a food supply is concerned. Nevertheless, it leaves one open to being preyed upon by larger predacious birds, mammals and even fish, as has already been mentioned. Cover is therefore necessary and is also important in sheltering from man, the chief enemy, on such occasions as the animal chooses to shelter.

No bird or mammal eats stoats as a staple item of diet but any predator big enough will be likely to kill one when the opportunity arises, especially a young one. The barn owl (*Tyto alba*) which is resident throughout the British Isles, is known to kill weasels in Britain and there is at least one record of a short-eared owl (*Asio flammeus*), a regular winter migrant to Ireland, killing a stoat in Scotland.[141] There is also an instance of a dead Irish stoat found amongst other food remains at the entrance to a fox's earth. C.D. Deane described how a gamekeeper at Baronscourt, Co. Tyrone,[40] told him of seeing a 'killy-hawk', a kestrel, seizing something heavy and attempting to fly away with it. After labouring upwards to a goodish height the kestrel spun down to earth again. The keeper watched as a stoat unfastened itself from the dead bird and ran off. This is pure hearsay. On the other hand Deane told me that the keeper was a reliable informant and the story is by no means impossible. Mr. H.G. Hurrell, the Devonshire naturalist,[121] witnessed a fight on the ground between a weasel and a kestrel in which the mammal was the victor, in which case a stoat would have even fewer problems.

Domestic pets seem quite capable of seeing to a stoat. Thompson mentioned that a cat dispatched a full-grown one at Holywood, Co. Down, in 1850 and brought the body to her kittens, which ate freely of it. A similar incident was observed at Powerscourt, Co. Wicklow, in 1936.[165]

A killing by terriers has already been alluded to, but the powerful smell produced by the glands around the stoat's anus would possibly deter some dogs. The late A.W. Stelfox told me of a ferreting expedition he accompanied, an important member being a collie dog which was stationed at what seemed a likely egress for a startled rabbit. Evidently the collie had some previous experience and had learned to bite first and find out what it had caught afterwards. Unfortunately it was not a rabbit which bolted but a stoat, which the dog promptly seized in its jaws on emergence and, a few seconds later, equally promptly, released. For the following hour the unhappy dog crept about with its tail down, licking its lips, casting reproachful glances at its owners and with every appearance of having a nasty taste in its mouth.

While the scent produced by the anal glands is undoubtedly strong—having accidentally squirted the contents of such a gland on my face while dissecting a dead specimen I have a close acquaintance of the fact—a light whiff is not unpleasant. The smell is particularly noticeable when the animal is alarmed. Its function is uncertain but it may be used to mark the limits of the stoat's range, and work in Scotland[141] has shown that the males can hold territories. That is to say an individual male may hold a particular bit of country as his own and chase off intruders. A female may live on his pitch, but at his pleasure. It was also found that not all males possessed holdings of their own. When a territorial male died his property was quickly taken over by one or more of these transients or by neighbouring residents extending their boundaries. It is quite possible that the laying of urine or droppings may be used to mark territory instead of or as well as scent. We do not know. Other carnivores and, moreover, many mammals use one or more of these three methods of delineating their ranges, in some way analogous to the business card. In this respect it is remarkable that the behaviour we consider most antisocial in, for example, dogs is probably, for them, of major social significance.

A note entitled 'The Stoat' was included in Patterson's *Ulster Nature Notes* and describes a fight between two of them.

> . . . a rustling among some underwood attracted my attention. Going towards the spot, I saw two Stoats fighting. They did not appear to observe me. One of them was covered in blood . . . while the other was comparatively free from blood, and appeared quite vigorous.

If this description is accurate, it seems that territorial disputes may at times involve a degree of violence.

Notwithstanding all of this, large numbers of stoats are sometimes seen together, usually in autumn, as is clear from a brief note in the *Irish Naturalists' Journal* of 1928 from Mallow, Co. Cork.[142]

> A pack of Stoats—thirty to forty strong—was seen here a few days ago (early in May) apparently wandering in an uncertain direction. The farmer's dog killed two of them. I have never before heard of stoats 'packing'.

Such groups are generally thought to be made up of a few family parties, each composed of an adult female and the offspring of the season. There may be old males as well, for adult males have sometimes been seen associating with their families. A stoat pack is not to be trifled with. Such reservations as individuals show in the presence of man are, on occasion at least, completely lacking. Moffat[154] remarked of this fact that

> It is well known that in autumn, when several families of Stoats have united (probably for hunting purposes) they sometimes make determined attacks on boys or men who have provoked them. Perhaps it is generally the English Stoat—which is slightly the larger animal—that figures in the stories told of these attacks; but I certainly heard of one instance in Co. Wexford when a country woman was fiercely set on by a number of Stoats that must have been of the Irish species, and had considerable difficulty in freeing herself from her pertinacious little assailants. An equally unprovoked attack on a tethered goat by a party of so-called 'weasels', in the wilds of Donegal, was quite lately the subject of paragraphs in several local papers.

In several newspapers in the early 'sixties appeared an account of an attack by a pack of stoats on a woman and her collie dog near Burtonport in Co. Donegal. Whether the dog provoked the stoats was not clear, but the woman fled to a nearby house. The collie was killed.

Small groups of stoats are sometimes seen playing together. I am ashamed to say that I have seen this only on film, and film shot in Devonshire, but the participants do give an astounding display, leaping, charging, counter-charging and turning somersaults, sometimes moving faster than the eye can follow. Moffat treated the readers of the Dublin *Daily Express* (date untraced) to a description of 'A Play of Stoats' he had watched. The extracts below emphasize his acute powers of observation.

One part of the play is particularly characteristic. Two stoats sit facing each other in kangaroo-like attitudes; suddenly, with a signal-cry, both rush forward, spring high into the air, and there cannon against each other, then, falling to the ground, rush on and occupy each other's original places, whence they immediately repeat the performance 'vice versa'—each from their opposite viewpoint. Mere ecstasy of high spirits, and nothing else, seems to actuate these gambols, and the wild guttural 'kroo-kroo-kroo' which forms their accompaniment is as unlike as possible from the notes uttered by the same creatures under more serious circumstances . . . the spot chosen for the manoeuvres is usually a clear space, a cart-track through the wood, or a lane skirting its edge.

Quite recently a student in one of my classes mentioned having seen such a play at Fenit, Co. Kerry, and mentioned, in particular, their charging at one another and then springing in the air. Moffat witnessed such play more than once, for he described a smaller 'show' elsewhere.[152]

The day had been wet, and in walking out—about 8 in the evening—I came quite suddenly on a group of three Stoats engaged in a great game of play on the road: they had a hole, or at any rate a niche, among the stones of the fence on each side, and retired for a moment on discovering an intruder, for they caught sight of me at the same instant as I did of them; but apparently they have just as great an objection to be baulked of their play as their victuals, for they almost immediately returned and, as I remained perfectly quiet a few yards away, the game was resumed, and proved extremely lively. From their behaviour I suppose the animals were young, but they seemed full grown: two of them (males I should think) were longer and redder than the third. A curious crowing sort of note—'curoo, curoo, curoo,' uttered very quickly—was frequently uttered, and invariably when they ran at full speed. Great part of the game consisted in all three animals careering across the road again and again, frequently crossing each other, when they sometimes sprang high in the air and cannoned against one another, all evidently in the height of fun. Then there was a ceremony which I could not quite understand, of pressing their noses on the bare ground and running along for a foot or so making a slight grating noise. I do not know how: they all did this. Then they would play with one another like kittens, one chasing another, knocking it down, and running off crying 'curoo, curoo', to be knocked down in its turn. And *one* of the three could turn as perfect a somersault as any boy I have seen, doing it moreover, in exactly the same way,— placing his head very deliberately on the ground as the first step, and then turning quite gracefully over, and righting itself just in time to avoid falling on its back, or standing erect on its hind legs. It did this several times but as far as I could make out it was always the same one.

For all this stoats are usually solitary and hunt alone. In the early stages of stalking they keep to cover but, when the quarry is located, will readily be tempted into the open. They follow their prey largely by scent, but sight is important in closing with it.

The stoat's skull consists of a comparatively short facial region and a long cranium, bespeaking a disproportionately large brain for a mammal of this size and, by inference, a comparatively high degree of intelligence. The four canine teeth are well developed for stabbing and gripping, and the cheek-teeth are knife-edge ridges, shearing past each other and thus well adapted to slicing flesh. The Irish stoat is therefore, not surprisingly, almost entirely carnivorous, the food consisting largely of rabbits, rodents and birds, which it pursues with a ferocity, relentlessness and craft astonishing in such a small mammal. Giraldus caught the impression a hunting stoat imparts perfectly in the quotation at the beginning of this chapter. He adds '. . . it is the tyrant of the larger sorts of mice. It preys also on hares and rabbits.'

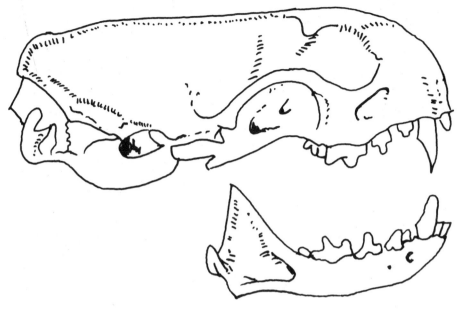

Fig. 29   Skull of stoat.

Mammals are dispatched by biting in the region of the neck. With small prey, such as mice, death may therefore be instantaneous, the sharp canines penetrating the more vulnerable regions of the brain almost immediately. Whenever the prey is larger, the process is liable to be more protracted and repeated attacks to the throat will be necessary before the hapless victim is rendered lifeless. It is, indeed, only due to its blood-thirsty perseverance that the stoat succeeds in killing animals bigger than itself. The prolonged attentions of the stoat to the throat and the amount of bleeding have given rise to the mistaken notion that the stoat actually derives its sustenance by sucking blood.

The stoat's climbing capabilities render it a redoubtable adversary of the feathered tribes and several encounters with birds are set down in the literature. Thompson wrote that

> On 2nd September, 1851, the gamekeeper at Tollymore Park (County Down) showed me a Portugal laurel, bordering on a walk in the pleasure-ground, near the house, on the exposed side of which he was attracted, some years ago, by the loud cries of a song-thrush [*Turdus ericetorum*] ; and on going near the scene, he saw a stoat descending the tree with a young bird. He instantly shot the depredator; and on examining the nest, found that the stoat had killed a couple of the young, and partly demolished the nest. Two other young ones were, however, still safe, and he had no doubt that they were brought to full maturity by their parents. The site of the nest—about eight feet [2.4m] from the ground—was pointed out to me.

From the *Irish Naturalists' Journal*[27] of 1933 comes the following, from Ballycastle, Co. Antrim.

> On the 24th of May I was watching some gulls from a rugged headland, some 600 feet [180m] high, when my attention was arrested by some sharp 'squeaks' and almost at once a female stoat appeared to take survey of her position. After a few seconds she gave a queer little purring sound, and, as if from the earth, three small stoats appeared; pretty little brown fellows

with black shining eyes. The mother, after sniffing around, bounded over to some rocks, and immediately two rock pipits [*Anthus spinoletta*] tried to attack her, diving at her, and all the while uttering piercing cries of alarm. The stoat disappeared behind a rock, and in a few seconds appeared with a young pipit, almost half fledged; this she took to her young, only some five or six yards from where I was sitting. The young stoats fell upon the luckless nestling and quickly devoured it. The mother made three more journeys, each time with a young bird. The parent birds kept up their cries and attack, and it was not until the stoat made a flying leap in the air and nearly caught one of them that they took their departure.

Stoats may well bring down birds by springing up and catching them. The British stoat can leap 1m vertically and so, presumably, can the Irish. A note in the above periodical of 1926 is also relevant.[168]

One fine day in July last, when on Lady Mabel Annesley's beautiful lake at Castlewellan, fishing from the boat close to the shore, we watched for some time the graceful movements of a stoat in pursuit of its mid-day meal. The creature was evidently much interested in a family of young dab-chicks [*Podiceps ruficollis*], swimming about the water's edge, accompanied by their proud parent. Several times the stoat made for them, causing much commotion in the family party. Eventually, our boat having drifted in closer to the shore, the raider gave up the attempt and disappeared from view among the thick growth of ferns and brambles.

Having landed for lunch, we were returning to the boat when we saw that our boatman, who had remained on board, was much excited, and eager to impart some news, which was to the effect that the stoat had just made another attack, and had succeeded in carrying off one of the youngsters. We were in time to see the mother and children—the latter now reduced by one of the their number—and to hear their lamentations.

Weasels are known to attack birds under the wing, at its attachment to the body, where the massive pectoral vein is close to the surface. While I have no information in this respect on Irish stoats, they may well proceed in the same way.

In October 1974 I was driving along the road outside Tulla, Co. Clare, when I saw something ahead which, by its movement, I concluded could only be a stoat. The animal was bounding after a wagtail (*Motacilla alba*) which escaped each time by flying a few m ahead and settling again. As I drew up and turned off the ignition the stoat disappeared into the bank on the roadside. The bird stood its ground, and, after a few moments, the stoat came out again to continue the chase, springing forward or jumping after the wagtail which avoided it nicely each time. A car passed, the stoat retired once more, only to emerge and to renew its efforts again. Finally a tractor came by and both participants left. The whole performance lasted about two minutes.

A note published in the *Field*[122] for 1896 shows that birds or fledglings need not always be the attraction.

While walking with friends close to the house a woodpigeon flew out of an ash tree covered with ivy. Suspecting a nest we went to look and were surprised to see first one egg and then a second fall to the ground. On looking up we saw a Weasel sitting in the nest . . . about 25 feet from the ground.

(As the incident was in Ireland the usual rules of nomenclature apply.) Eggs are a welcome addition to the bill of fare and if purloined from a nest on the ground can be transported intact for some distance. The egg is placed under the chin and manipulated with the fore-feet while the hind feet provide the propulsion for trundling the booty.

Rabbits are a favoured food and there are two extraordinary but well documented aspects of the stoat's dealings with them. First a stoat may play close by them without their retiring. Presumably, and there is no way of being certain, this is to arouse their curiosity and so avoid precipitating a hasty withdrawal. In any case the silly rabbits are usually fascinated by the performance. (Moreover, it has been noticed that a single rabbit may be followed through a group of its fellows, while they continue to feed, and that stoats have been known to live in rabbit warrens.) Yet another item from the columns of the *Field*, of 1887, illustrates the point.[44]

> While shooting rabbits the other day, I was much amused at watching the antics of a stoat on the sunny side of a wall, in the midst of a number of rabbits grazing and sitting up on all sides of it, apparently quite unconcerned, though they must have seen it. Although I watched it for more than a quarter of an hour, I could not perceive that it had any intention of attacking the rabbits; but its motions were most surprising for rapidity and activity, apparently without any object, unless perhaps for sport. Moving in a zig-zag direction it constantly turned a somersault in the air, and would then continue its zig-zag journey, which was not continuous but up and down the fence, through the midst of the rabbits and occasionally into the wall. I would have remained watching it but was disturbed by the arrival of the party with whom I was shooting, which soon sent the rabbits and the stoat to their places of concealment.

Whether, on this occasion, the stoat had any designs on the rabbits will never be known.

The second curious fact is the lack of resistance induced in a rabbit with a stoat in pursuit. Its efforts to escape seem at most half-hearted and it may appear paralysed with fright or lie squealing, panic-stricken at the approach of its mortal enemy. The contribution to Patterson's *Ulster Nature Notes* already referred to, includes the following observation.

> I was once walking through a thinly wooded portion of a park when I heard a strange noise as of an animal in great pain. On making my way through the underwood to the place from whence the sound proceeded I found that a Stoat had seized a rabbit by the side of the neck, but, seeing me, it instantly relinquished its hold and darted away, leaving the Rabbit lying as if dead. When, however, I put forth my hand to lift it the Rabbit jumped up and scampered nimbly away in the direction opposite to that taken by the Stoat. I then sought the path but it was not long before I heard again the same painful cry I had previously heard. Again I made my way to the spot and drove the stoat from the Rabbit, which it seized a second time.

The remainder of a note already quoted above is also significant.

> Stoats seem to be very plentiful in the Castlewellan demesne. On two occasions this year we came across rabbits terribly injured by these creatures, and in a dying condition. A rabbit must be pretty helpless when pounced upon by this enemy. The wounds on the dying rabbit we saw—and put out of pain—were at the back of the head and neck, and very deep, the bones being exposed.

Juvenile rabbits are eaten too. At Adare, Co. Limerick, in 1974, a student at University College, Galway, who was specializing in mammalogy, saw a rabbit break cover from the edge of a wood. A moment later a stoat appeared carrying a very young rabbit—practically hairless in fact. The stoat dropped its burden a few m from from her but, as she remained still, it returned and made off with it. Two further trips were made to the wood and on each of these it was also carrying something. While she could not be certain, as the action was several m away, she surmised that this was in each case another juvenile. The incident suggests that a nest had been raided. There are, however, cases on record in Britain of a doe rabbit with a litter seeing a weasel or stoat off the premises in no uncertain way.[112]

Moffat thought that rats might be stupefied in the same way by the approach of a stoat but, if this does happen, it is by no means inevitable. An account in the *Irish Naturalist* of the animals killed by keepers on the Curraghmore Estate in Co. Waterford, in 1912,[98] describes a confrontation between a rat and a stoat in which the latter was not long in delivering the characteristic *coup de grâce*.

A few months since I was a spectator of a fight between a Stoat and a Rat; I watched it from only a very short distance. The rat had no chance against its relentless assailant. Until I had witnessed the fight, I had no idea of the extraordinary ferocity and marvellous quickness and agility of a stoat. In a trice it killed its prey by a bite at the back of the neck. It then carried the Rat (a very large one) from one side of the road to the other. I interfered for a moment, and the Stoat left the Rat, but in a few seconds it appeared from a mass of briars, dashed out, collared its dinner, and was out of sight in a few seconds. It was a wonderful display of determination, adriotness and skill.

Thompson wrote of the stoat's food:

The gamekeeper at Tollymore Park (County Down) informed me, in June 1938, that he had on two occasions seen nests of this species. In one were about a dozen mice—a young rabbit and a young hare—also all the feathers and tail of a young woodcock [*Scolopax rusticola*]. In the other he found six or seven mice, in addition to other things. They were packed regularly on top of each other—'all laid the one way'—in beautiful arrangement.

Mice are certainly a regular item on the menu and young hares would present no problem. Whether an Irish stoat could kill an adult hare, even given the opportunity, is uncertain, although its larger relative in Britain can. There is a painting by Sir Edward Landseer, who is best known perhaps for his pictures of dogs, of such an assault. One art critic remarked of it, 'We do not consider this one of Mr Landseer's happiest efforts. We never saw a Rabbit so large nor a Ferret of this colour.'

Stoats are known to eat fish occasionally. Such an instance was recorded in the *Irish Naturalists' Journal* of 1936 by two ladies.[194]

We are anxious to know if you or any of your readers have knowledge of Stoats hunting and capturing fish, the reason we ask being because we saw a most interesting sight when walking along the seashore at Tawin, on Galway Bay, one day last June—six or eight Stoats carrying something in their mouths, and hurrying across a stretch of grass towards a loose stone wall. Beyond the grass is a low, broken cliff leading down to a rocky shore where pools are left by the receding tide, and when we were there the tide was some way out. The Stoats, on seeing us, ran into the wall, two of them dropping their prey which to our astonishment, we discovered to be young Mullet.

We kept quiet so as to observe what would happen, and in a moment or two one Stoat came out from the wall and retrieved a fish. The other fish, which was live and unharmed, we picked up and returned to a pool on the shore.

It has been suggested that the animals were young Otters and not Stoats, but we were within a few yards of them and are convinced that we are not mistaken in identity. The animals obviously were returning from a fishing expedition, and must have been swimming for they were very wet and the fish were freshly caught.

It is quite possible that the fish may have been marooned, maybe in a pool, by the tide. To me a misidentification also seems unlikely. One of the observers wrote other notes for the *Journal* and had thus more than a passing interest in natural history. A weaned otter is very much larger than a stoat and, as otters have litters of two or three, the presence of six together is unusual. Although stoats tend to hunt alone, such association is not unknown. If the animals had been otters they would have made for the sea rather than the stone wall, whereas this is exactly what a stoat would run for. Finally, otters would not have returned 'in a moment or two', whereas this could be expected of stoats.

Systematic analyses of the contents of the stomachs and intestines of large numbers of weasels and stoats in Great Britain[35] show that small rodents, lagomorphs (i.e. rabbits and hares) and birds are about equally important food sources for stoats. On the other hand, rodents form nearly half the food of weasels. This is not altogether surprising as the modest proportion of the latter predator enable it to follow voles and mice down their holes. The greater girth of the stoat makes this impossible, but its heavier build renders it fitter to attack rabbits and birds. Since size is of such significance, naturally the females of both species of predator take slightly more rodents than do the males. It has sometimes been suggested that the intermediate dimensions of the Irish stoat are a sort of compromise and may enable it to make the best of both trades, but there is no evidence to support this notion at all.

Very little quantitative work has been done in Ireland. I have examined about eighty dead stoats[76] but unfortunately, for a number of reasons, only twenty-nine contained recognizable food remains. Of these, fourteen were acquired from 1963 to 1966 from widespread localities in Northern Ireland, except one which was from Co. Cork. The remaining fifteen were supplied by the gamekeeper at Clandeboye, Co. Down, from 1968 to 1970. As it was impossible to tell rabbit remains from those of hares, I have for simplicity regarded all such as rabbit, which is more likely anyway. The numbers of stomachs in which the various foods occurred were as follows:

	Rabbit	Rat	Field mouse	House mouse	Birds	Eggs
First Series	1	0	1	3	9	—
Second Series	9	1	1	—	2	2

The discrepancies between the two are easily accounted for. As far as is known rabbits were scarce or localized in Northern Ireland in the early 'sixties. At the end of the decade they were numerous at Clandeboye. Even on this slim evidence, and it is little enough to go on, rabbit can be seen to be important food when available. Stoats underwent a marked decrease in Britain after myxomatosis all but wiped out the rabbit population in 1953 and 1954. I believe that much the same thing happened in Ireland. My main reason is, I confess, that every gamekeeper I discussed it with was of this opinion. However, gamekeepers kill stoats regularly and are in a position to judge. Another tentative deduction is that rodents may be of less importance as food in Ireland. The explanation is that field voles are the rodents most frequently eaten in Britain. These are relatively easy to catch but are absent from Ireland.

Of peripheral interest is the fact that the bones of a stoat have been found in close association with those of lemmings and field mice in excavations in the caves at Kesh, in Co. Sligo.[171] While this may be fortuitous, it could represent another and very ancient example of the stoat providing itself with a larder. No doubt stoats were the scourge of lemmings in Ireland in glacial times, as they are in the Arctic today.

In certain other parts of the stoat's enormous range in the northern hemisphere, insectivores (shrews, moles and their allies) and insects sometimes form large parts of the diet. Reptiles and earthworms are also eaten. In a study in the Kola Peninsula in the U.S.S.R.,[189] berries, especially juniper berries, were said to form 71% of the food, which is most irregular. Presumably our knowledge even of the range of foods Irish stoats will eat is, therefore, incomplete.

The subject of reproduction has received a great deal of careful study in England. I have looked at over fifty reproductive tracts in Ireland[76] and see no reason to suppose that there are any differences in this respect between the two subspecies. It is often stated that the Irish form differs in having five or six pairs of teats compared with the normal four. This is quite wrong and dates back to an assessment on insufficient material. Both Irish and British stoats can have from four to six pairs.

Males are fecund from March well into the summer and females, apparently, over most of the year, but mating only takes place during late spring and early summer. After fertilization the embryos proceed to develop only to an early stage, the *blastocyst.* Further development is halted and the blastocysts, which are minute, remain in the uterus unattached until the following spring. They then continue to grow, attaching to the uterus as in nearly every other mammal including man, and the litter is born three or four weeks later. This curious phenomenon is called *delayed implantation* and it happens in certain other species, including the badger and pine marten. Strangely enough, there is no delayed implantation in the weasel.

The usual litter size for the Irish stoat is not known for certain, but the only results ever published, from dissections of three pregnant females,[76, 180] are two of nine young and one of six. In twelve pregnant stoats examined in England, the number varied from six to thirteen and averaged nine.[189]

Whereas the male stoat does not become mature until the year after his birth, females are ready to mate in their first summer, a few months after birth.

The female shelters her offspring in her den, perhaps a burrow appropriated from some other mammal, a hollow tree or in a stone pile, but there is not much precise information on this for Ireland. One would naturally expect her to be a courageous mother. Moffat stated that she greets intruders on her nursery premises with a high-pitched, monosyllabic cry of 'cherk', which is intended as a warning.[154] Some years ago two labourers described to me how a stoat moved her family, one by one, from a site they had disturbed. They watched the proceedings with considerable but impersonal interest, for they killed the poor animal on her fourth or fifth trip.

The tenacity with which a female stoat will look after her young is shown in a letter to the *Field*[42] in 1874 from a reader in Moycullen, Co. Galway.

A short time since, while passing through a wood, I heard strange sounds proceeding from some masses of bramble lining the wall at a little distance from me. Presently, on top of the wall, coming towards me, a stoat made its appearance carrying some large object in its mouth. On seeing me it left the wall, sought the roots of an old hollow tree close to the opposite side of it, in front of my position, deposited its charge and then returned to reconnoitre. It kept changing its position with startling vivacity, so as to view the enemy from all parts. It would turn up here and there and everywhere—now peeping out of the old tree, now from one part of the wall, now from another. It next mounted the wall, and having looked at me full in the face, turned away with a satisfied air, as if it thought me an honest man and one to be depended on. Upon reappearance the burden had been resumed which proved to be a young one. It passed so close to me as I leaned over the low wall to observe, that I reached out my hand to take the young one, which was immediately dropped . . . and he gave tongue most vigorously, when handled . . . The old stoat now threw off all fear, her great object evidently being to get at the young one and carry it away regardless of consequences. At last I presented it to her as she stood on top of the wall when she forthwith seized it by the head and I held her dangling for some time before she dropped. The performance was several times repeated but at last I relented.

The stoat conflicts with man's interests normally only in one respect, namely in its depredations on stocks of game fowl. It will take eggs, chicks and attack sitting hen birds, given the chance. It is therefore considered necessary to trap them where pheasants are preserved and reared for shooting. In the early years of this century, when game preservation was more extensive in Ireland, the number of stoats killed by gamekeepers must have been considerable, but few figures are available. Twenty-nine were killed on the Curraghmore Estate, Co. Waterford, in 1912[98] and at the Headborough Estate,[200] also in Co. Waterford, 470 were accounted for in the twelve years from 1868 to 1879. In spite of this persecution there was never any suggestion that they became scarcer as a result.

Stoats were, of course, considered vermin from much earlier times and when forests began to be cut down, various laws were enacted to compass their destruction and that of other wild animals. Details are given in Chapter 10.

Often regarded as 'vermin' by hunting and shooting men, stoats have in fact been followed as beasts of the chase themselves. In Co. Cork about eighty years ago there flourished a pack of dogs known as the 'Cork Weasel Hounds', which may have been unique as a sporting institution. The 'weasels' were hunted on foot from April to October and were an agreeable diversion at a time when there was no fox-hunting. Reports of this unconventional activity appeared in the columns of the contemporary newspaper, the *Irish Sportsman*. As far as can be gathered, small dogs of the beagle or foxhound type were used and training them presented problems. The sport was strenuous with long fast runs and often ended in the stoat climbing a tree, disappearing into a thatched roof or going to ground in a burrow or pipe. As far as I can determine, there never seems to have been a kill. Weasel-hunting was therefore a bloodless blood-sport. The following report is typical.

Met at Grange at eight A.M. A lovely morning, the rain had come down in torrents on Monday night, there was a heavy dew, so scent was much improved. Struck the drag of a weasel at Grange, found directly afterwards; they ran away with a burst of music and ran very hard up Clifton's and Lynam's to Ferguson's screen. He turned here and a slight check occurred, but one of the hounds hit it off along the top of a stone wall, which he ran for a field, then led by one of the white Irish foxhounds they raced down the hill at a great pace to Frankfield. The weasel turned here, on being hard pressed tried dodging tactics again, running along the top of a wall, and slipping from one side to the other through various gullies, but the pack proved equal to the occasion, and unravelled all the doubles, and finally forcing him away from this they raced him across the Kinsale Road and past Colonel Heard's place on to Schenagh, when the sun becoming hot scent failed, and the weasel beat them fairly. Distance about six miles all in the open, most of it fast.

Stoats can make engaging pets if taken at an extremely early age and hand-reared but I do not recommend trying it. Thompson wrote an entertaining note on a tame stoat.

In 1845 a stoat was brought to Mr. Davis of Clonmel, which he gave to a friend, in whose house it became quite domesticated, and was greatly admired for the extreme light-ness and elegance of its movements, and also for its ceaseless activity. At first it was kept in a cage, whence it escaped, and murdered a jay [*Garrulus glanderius*] in the same room; after this it was not confined, but ranged at will through a large shop, a cellar, and two ware rooms, and never evinced any wish to leave them. Here it became quite tame, and obviously preferred some members of the family to others. Its frolics in the shop were very amusing. Sometimes it would scamper along the counter; at others, run up a lady's back until it reached her bonnet; but its greatest delight seemed to be giving battle to two old stuffed magpies [*Pica pica*], twining round their necks, pulling out their feathers, and occasionally tumbling with one from the shelf on which they were kept.

There is a deal of folklore concerning stoats in Ireland though much of this never seems to have been put in print. In some country districts they are held in great respect by the local people, a respect which is much more of a dis-trustful regard than affection. To many there must be something baleful in the appearance of a stoat contemplating them, and its lack of fear is disturbing to those who are used to seeing all other wild beasts flee before them. A parallel could be drawn between the pertinacity of a stoat following its prey and the devil relentlessly pursuing a lost soul. At any rate, the stoat is traditionally regarded as a witch in animal form in some areas. *'Beanín uasal'* is a name used in Connemara, 'the noble little woman', perhaps an oblique and ironic reference to one of these infernal old ladies. It may be pure coincidence but 'uasal' resembles the old English 'uueosule', meaning a weasel. They are also considered by some to be 'the Danes' cats'. There is no further explanation, but it is evidently sufficient reason for being wary of them.

A notion, the origin of which is obscure, is that a 'weasel' can spit poison. One story concerns reapers cutting a field of barley. During their exertions the weasel watches, and should they destroy her nest and kill her young ones, she will go to the bucket of buttermilk, kept for refreshment on the job, and spit poison into it.

A very widespread tale is that of the weasel's funeral. Usually the story-teller admits that someone told him, but one old forestry worker in Co. Tyrone assured me he had witnessed the rites himself. It is said that when the weasel dies, its friends and relatives all come to the funeral. The procession is led by two who carry the corpse, one at each end holding on with their teeth, and they are followed by the rest of the mourners. There are a few possible starting points for this one and stoats are, after all, seen together in large groups on the move. The mother stoat carrying one of its infants may have something to do with it. Stelfox told me that Moffat believed that stoats inspected the corpses of their fellows with great interest, which again may be relevant.

The packing of stoats has probably led to the belief, widespread in the north at least, that a 'weasel' summons his friends to his aid by putting the tip of his tail between his teeth and whistling, much in the enviable way that some human beings can whistle on fingers placed in the mouth.

G.H. Kinahan's musings on piebald stoats, quoted earlier, refer to a further superstition.

In my boyish days a Stoat-Skin or, as they were nearly universally called in Ireland, 'a Weasel-skin' purse was considered lucky, while a piebald Weasel-skin purse was the height of good luck.

In parts of Scotland there was, at the end of the last century anyway, a similar tradition, which is explained by the following translation of a poem in Scots gaelic.

Little yellow hole-frequenting weasel,
From gold is derived the colour of thy coat of fur,
Get it for a purse, to be tied with its thong,
And thou shalt not be without a coin, white, yellow or brown,
From Christmas till Rood-day, from
Rood-day till the feast of St. Brian.

6 Irish Owls and their Prey

Thy note that forth so freely rolls,
With shrill command the mouse controls,
And sings a dirge for dying souls,
Te whit, te whoo, te whit, te whit

Sweet Suffolk Owl   Anon

Dyed-in-the-wool mammalogists 'take' to owls rather better than to other birds simply because many species eat small mammals in large quantities. Thus owls have a marked and very final affect on the lives of millions of individual rodents and insectivores, even if not usually any permanent impact on the populations as a whole. As will be seen later, quite frequently the easiest method of recording the presence of small mammal species in a district is to investigate the food of the resident owls, and often even more can be deduced about the local mammal fauna from this source.

The eyes of owls are set facing forward, unlike those of most other birds, and the area around each eye is flattened into a concave disc bounded by a ruff of stiff radiating feathers capable of movement. Together with the bill they result in a startling resemblance to a human face. Whether this and the owl's upright posture at rest strike some deep psychological chord of response in the mammalogist I do not know, but these features do seem to endear owls to children. One very distinguished mammal-man, addressing an audience of mammal-men on owls, rather drolly admitted that he thought of them as mammals anyway.

The 'face', which (depending on the species) can appear friendly or menacing, the nocturnal habits and ominous hooting, have led to the association of owls with the occult and the supernatural. For the ancients the appearance of one was an infallible portent of disaster, and, because of their supposed ability to presage events, owls became symbolic of intelligence. The concept of the 'wise old owl' is thus largely rooted in superstition and superficial appearance and has nothing at all to do with cranial capacity. Nevertheless owls do have brains above average in size, for birds.

While the other raptorial birds (the hawks, harriers, falcons and eagles) are largely diurnal, most but not all owls work mainly on a night shift. When given due consideration, it is remarkable that an owl is able to catch such small animals as mice and shrews in the dark, even if we set aside the keen senses, alertness and agility of the quarry and the availability of cover.

Owls are beautifully adapted to noiseless, nocturnal predation. At first glance an owl appears to have no neck and, for a bird, a head that is disproportionately large. This is far from the truth, the effect being produced by the very thick layer of soft feathers enveloping the body and even the legs and feet, which are naked in most other birds. The plumage effectively muffles any sound made in flight and this is important for two reasons. First, it is essential that the prey should not be forewarned of the imminence of attack. Secondly, as the sounds which the prey themselves make are often used in locating them, the minimum amount of background noise is desirable. Anyone who has witnessed a barn owl in flight will have been impressed by the almost uncanny silence of the performance.

There is abundant anatomical evidence that the ears of owls are larger and more sensitive than those of other birds, especially to high pitched sounds. There can be little doubt that their excellent hearing is turned to good account in searching for victims: in listening for the rustlings made by mice in the course of their movements as well as their squeaks. The long, crescentic opening of each ear lies just behind the edge of the facial disc, hidden by the feathers. While owls do not possess external ear flaps as mammals do, some species, including all three Irish ones, appear to have an analogous structure arising *in front of* each ear-hole and covering it over. It has been suggested that the flap can be raised to form a sort of ear-trumpet for assessing the direction of the sound or to increase its resonance. Long and short-eared owls have particularly complex ears and the mechanisms on the left and right show marked differences in size and shape. Such asymmetry enables these birds to determine the exact position of the source of a sound. In effect two different bearings are taken on a luckless mouse.

Acute hearing is not the only means of pinpointing prey. The eyes are comparatively large and the retina, the area at the back on which the visual image is focused, is capable, in common with those of most other birds, of detecting far more detail than that of a mammal. The light-sensitive cells of the retina are mainly rods, cells concerned with intensity of light and used in conditions of poor lighting, rather than cones, which are used in colour vision. It is fairly certain, therefore, that owls do not see colours. The lens of an owl's eye is relatively enormous, even for a bird's. Readers with an interest in photography need not be told that a large lens makes pictures possible in poor illumination. In much the same way owls are thus enabled to see in extremely low light intensities. In daylight the pupils, which are the apertures through which light enters the eyes, shrink to a very small diameter, for the owl's retina is incapable of coping with such bright light. At night they dilate and the full light-gathering power of the lens can be brought into operation. Furthermore, it is quite plain that some species are uncomfortable with their sensitive eyes fully open in broad daylight and, under such conditions, keep them at least partially closed.

Some interesting experiments were carried out in the United States in the mid-'forties on the efficiency of the predation by barn owls[46] on different colour varieties of the American deer mouse (*Peromyscus maniculatus*). The work was conducted in an experimental room with a variable light source. Since initial study showed that in the absence of cover the owls could catch the mice in total darkness using hearing alone, shelter was provided in the form of a lattice-work of sticks about 20cm from the floor. This forced the owls to make use of their sight. The floor of the room was divided in two and each half covered with a soil either matching the coat colour of the particular mice used or contrasting with it. If an owl caught significantly more mice on the contrasting soil, it was obviously using its sight and this was the case down to a light intensity of 0.000,000,79 millilamberts at just under 2m, an illumination far below what is apparently total darkness to the human eye.

The owl's enormous lenses result in the eyes being fixed almost immovably in their sockets, but this is compensated by the extraordinary mobility and rapid reflex action of the neck, which allows the head to swivel to practically any position in an instant. An owl enjoys all-round vision, for it can turn its head through nearly 180° on each side. Any reader who has watched one at rest will have noticed how it keeps him continually in view simply by moving its head. This ability has led to the myth that an owl is capable of wringing its own neck. An unkind attempt to precipitate such a self-inflicted injury by continually walking round the bird will certainly fail: there is always an instantaneous reversal at the half-way point.

As both eyes face forward, true stereoscopic vision is possible over a wide field of view and it has already been stressed how necessary it is for such implacable, aerial foes of mice to judge distances precisely. It is also important that the thick coat of feathers should not obscure the view and hence the flattened discs around the eyes.

The eyes and ears of owls, together with the parts of the brain associated with them, take up a large part of the skull.

Owls are well equipped with offensive weapons which comprise a hooked bill and an appalling arsenal of talons. The latter are employed mainly in seizing the prey. They are widely spread as the owl pounces, which allows for any last minute movement of the victim before they close. The beak is used in dispatching it. Mice must die almost immediately as the rear part of the cranium is sheared off the moment the owl strikes.

The wings of owls are relatively large and the wing loading—the body weight per unit area—is low. This is rather like having a large under-stressed engine in a motor car. High speed is not necessarily always the result but effortless power at low velocity is assured. The owl is therefore certain of greater manoeuvreability and does not stall at low speeds, which is essential to enable it to drop accurately on prey. The wings are rounded and not long and pointed, a reliable sign of a slow-flyer. Long, narrow, pointed wings are used for rapid flight and will stall if speed is reduced.

Ireland can, in truth, boast of only three species of owl, the barn owl (*Tyto alba*) and the long-eared owl (*Asio otus*), which are resident, and the migrant short-eared owl (*Asio flammeus*). They are all about the same size, around 35cm long. Three other species have been recorded as vagrants: the scops owl (*Otus scops*—nine times), the little owl (*Athene noctua*—three times) and the snowy owl (*Nyctea scandiaca*—fifty-one times), but they are too rare to merit further consideration here. Moreover, nothing is known of their food in Ireland. There have been some unsuccessful attempts to introduce the tawny owl (*Strix aluco*).

The barn owl is chiefly seen on the wing as a ghostly white form at twilight, but though it hunts mainly at night, it is occasionally abroad during the day in winter or when feeding young. The flight is wavering but buoyant with occasional pounces on unfortunate small mammals. It quarters the ground along regular beats. It has a white face and underparts and pale golden-buff, finely speckled upper parts. The eyes are a dark brown, giving the face a solemn but amiable look and the discs around them are not discrete but continuous in a heart-shaped 'mask', the base of which extends around the beak. The legs are long and the bird perches upright. Partly because of its handsome appearance, partly because of a Victorian partiality for taxidermy and partly because of a contemporary national inclination to shoot any strange-looking bird, a stuffed specimen was almost a conventional ornament in some parts of Ireland towards the end of the last century.

Barn owls hunt over fairly open country, fields, around farms, park-land (especially with old timber) and light scrub, but not actually in dense woodland. They are the most closely associated with man of all the owls and often roost in ruins, barns, church-towers and dove-cotes but also far from human habitation in hollow trees, woods, thickets and in cliff-fissures. An individual was once discovered asleep in a crack in the rocks at Malin Head, Co. Donegal. Barn owls are also established on remote islands like Aran, Co. Galway, and Rathlin, Co. Antrim.

Fig. 30 Barn owl.

A roosting site I have found particularly favoured is a lime tree in an open field, the branches of which are enmeshed with that dense mass of twigs usually referred to as a 'witch's broom' and which is a pathological effect of a parasitic fungus.

Barn owls nest in unoccupied buildings and ruins (notably in the chimneys), hollow trees, crevices in cliffs and sometimes in old jackdaw (*Corvus monedula*) nests. They do not trouble with nesting material. The eggs, usually four to seven, are laid in April or the beginning of May (though sometimes much earlier or later). The hen incubates them for four to five weeks and the young fly when nine to thirteen weeks old.

A variety of sounds can be made from a hair-raising screech to a peaceful snoring noise. The latter may account for many of the ghosts heard in ruins.

In 1968 it was rumoured that a 'something' was snoring at night in the remains of Masserene Castle at Antrim. Hints appeared in the press that the ruin might be haunted. I visited it one evening to be greeted, as expected, with the stertorous 'song' of a barn owl. Thompson wrote

Fig. 31   Long-eared owl.

The family at Castle Warren, near Cork, were much alarmed on one occasion by hearing a loud snoring noise, like that made by a man after a day's hard labour, proceeding from one of the chimneys, and all apprehension was not dispelled until owls of this species, which had a nest there, were discovered to be the snorers.

To my mind the owl's hellish screaming is much more alarming. One of the most unearthly spectacles I have witnessed was in the long, luminous dusk of a summer evening at a derelict castle on the River Corrib—a family of barn owls shrieking at each other, flying about the ruin and back and forth into the darkness of the surrounding fields and hedgerows.

The barn owl is widely distributed in Ireland but from about 1950 a decrease in numbers was noticed, which has accelerated since 1960. It is easy enough to attribute a reduction in the numbers of any bird of prey to toxic pesticides and seed dressings. However, there is no hard evidence one way or the other and glib talk will not help matters. Extensive felling of old timber is another possible factor but, in any event, there is no reason to assume that the cause should be immediately apparent.

Long-eared owls are almost exclusively nocturnal and are easily recognized by the tufts of feathers, one on each side of the head, from which the name is derived. These are not, of course, ears at all and are laid back flat on the head in flight. The body feathers are freckled, and mottled buff and brownish grey on the back and upper surfaces of the wings, while below they are buff marked with grey-brown streaks and fine cross-barring. The eyes, like those of the short-eared owl, are yellow and give the bird a malevolent look. This species is mostly associated with conifers and it hunts in coniferous woodland and open country. The roosting places are nearly always in conifers or other evergreens and even when the resting-place is in mixed woodland, a deciduous tree is rarely chosen. During the day it perches upright on a branch close to the tree-trunk, hidden in the foliage, and it issues forth at night in search of food. The flight is similar to that of the barn owl.

Long-eared owls lay their eggs, three to eight in number, in the disused nests of other birds or sometimes those of squirrels, but in some tree-less areas will nest on the ground. The eggs are laid in March or early April, or exceptionally, earlier. Incubation lasts about four weeks and in a further three the chicks are ready to fly. An aid to finding a nest is the call of the young, a piercing mew, like an authentic imitation of a rusty old iron gate being opened. Adults make a sort of cooing groan, a low, protracted 'oo, oo, oo', rather than a hoot. It is heard mostly in spring.

The long-eared is the commonest Irish owl and is believed to have increased in numbers with the spread of forestry. It may be an entirely subjective assessment, but I have found roosts more often in the north-east than elsewhere in Ireland. In winter these owls are sometimes seen in groups.

The short-eared owl is similar in colouration to the long-eared but tawnier and lacking the cross-banding beneath and freckling above. These differences are not always easy to make out in the field and the distinctive feature is the ear tufts which, unlike those of the long-eared owl, are short and, at a distance, scarcely visible. Short-eared owls in Ireland are found in open country, usually on marshes, bogs or sand-dunes and, most frequently, near the coast. For many years a favourite haunt has been the North Bull Island in Dublin Bay and they often winter in the harbour area of Belfast, notably on the waste ground at the seaward end of Duncrue Street and formerly on the East Twin Island, before the enormous dry dock was built there in the mid-'sixties. In 1836 Major-General

Fig. 32   Short-eared owl.

Joseph Portlock,[170] an esteemed member of the Irish Ordnance Survey, remarked that these birds were regular autumnal visitors to a rabbit-warren at Magilligan, Co. 'Derry. Curious to relate, they were making use of the burrows for shelter, retiring into them when disturbed. Some were shot emerging from the holes, sad to say, and one was caught in a trap sited at an entrance.

Short-eared owls are usually seen in parties of two to six in Ireland. The flight is slow, wavering and rolling and usually, but not always, low down. The owl wheels and glides regularly and often settles on the ground, but will make use of any tree, bush or post to perch on. At rest the body is not held vertically but rather at a slant to the perpendicular. The bird is generally silent but emits a sneezing bark, 'kee-awk', as a warning and the song is a hollow 'boo-boo-boo'.

The short-eared owl is a winter migrant, though there are a few records of its presence in summer and it is known to have bred in Ireland once. It is irregularly distributed and its numbers fluctuate very much from year to year.

Many birds regurgitate the indigestible parts of their food in the form of pellets or castings. While we may not particularly admire this aptitude from the point of view of table-manners, it has an advantage. Material of no food value is ejected quickly from the digestive tract and does not make the longer journey to its far end. Our feathered friends, just like any other flying-machines, can well do without any unnecessary load and so the shorter the time that the excess baggage is aboard, the better. The retention of such waste would not only act as dead weight but also, as it were, take up valuable fuel space.

The typical owl pellet consists of a neat rounded packet of all the feathers, fur, bones and hard parts of insects in the food. A careful examination of the contents will therefore reveal what the bird in question had been eating at the time. Regular collections of pellets will shed a lot of light on its food-habits.

There have, from time to time, been experiments to check how well owl-pellets reflect the actual diet. Most of these have consisted simply of feeding known numbers of small mammals and birds to captive owls, collecting the castings, and comparing the figures from them with the numbers of the food items originally provided. The results of these experiments are reassuring. Although owls do not always eat every part of the animals they catch and, in a few instances, they digest some skulls slightly more than others, we have adequate confirmation that this method of studying the food of owls is, in general, a reliable one.

Castings are most easily obtained at roosting or nesting places. If they are found accidentally, the nature of the sites should give a clue to the species which produced them. Short-eared owls are often in the vicinity of their pellets and a walk about the area may raise them. Barn owl roosts can be watched at twilight for the birds to show themselves. Although sometimes there is a bout of snoring before an appearance is made, constant vigilance is imperative for the emergence itself is usually completely silent. It is somewhat more difficult to catch a glimpse of a long-eared owl in the same way if it spends the day in a wood or copse, but one can try.

The characteristics of the pellets of the three species are noteworthy and illustrations of them are given in Fig. 33. It is hard to mistake those of the barn owl as they are covered in a smooth black crust which gives them the appearance of having been varnished. They vary in shape from approximately spherical to cylindrical with rounded ends. The former may be as small as 25mm in diameter but the latter sometimes reach over 80mm in length and are usually between 25 and 30mm wide. Long-eared owl pellets are greyish in colour, friable and round in section, 22 to 62mm long and around 20mm in diameter. Those of the short-eared owl are similar but are frequently longer, over 80mm in some instances, and the outline is often more irregular. Finally, on the subject of recognition, many objects have been mistaken for owl-pellets. I have, more than once, been presented with fox-droppings by an enthusiastic, would-be owl-pellet hunter, bursting with achievement. The unwelcome enlightenment must be broken gently. Much confusion can be avoided by remembering that the droppings of mammals and castings of other birds of prey never have the very high content of relatively intact mouse-bones that owl pellets do.

There is, of course, no guarantee that one will be able to obtain all the material an owl ejects by visiting the nest, regular roost or perch. Other castings may be regurgitated elsewhere, on the wing or at occasional perching places. But the collection *will* give a very good idea of the nature of the food and the relative proportions of the various species taken.

In an analysis the bones must first be separated from the hair and feathers packed around them. Not only is it quicker to identify bones, but they will give absolute numbers of the animals consumed, which the packing cannot. The easiest way to sort out the hard parts is to dry the pellets in an oven, or some-

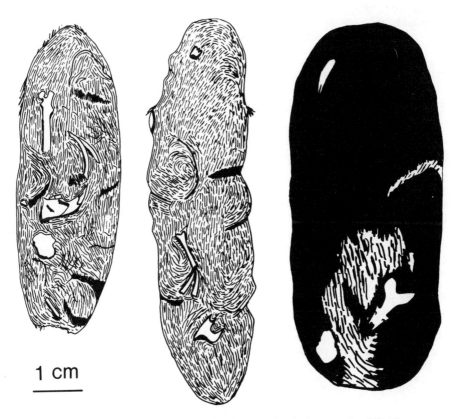

1 cm

Fig. 33   Typical pellets of (from left to right) long-eared owl, short-eared owl and barn owl.

where else where it is hot and dry, and break them up with the fingers. Occasionally a tiny bone splinter may lodge itself in one's skin but this is practically painless and, once removed, I have never known such a wound to fester. Forceps (tweezers) are also useful in teasing out small but important items. Some people soak the pellets in water before dissecting them but this is messy and not recommended.

By far the most important bits to look for, as far as mammals are concerned, are the skulls and their lower jaws. Other bones from time to time give supplementary information but they are harder to assign to a particular species, never indicate more individuals than the skulls and are normally not worth keeping. Personally I have found it unnecessary to retain even the skulls, the total numbers of right or left jaw-bones alone never giving a smaller count. Skulls are made up of a number of bones which tend to separate when dried out in the castings. The process is hastened by the owl's habit of twisting off the hind end with its bill in the act of killing the mammal. In contrast the left and right jaw bones of mammals are each composed of a single bone, the *dentary*, which rarely fragments and is easy to spot. Incidentally, a jaw bone composed of a single unit is one of the less well-known features which are absolutely diagnostic of mammals.

There being far fewer mammal species in Ireland than Great Britain, recognition of the dentaries is a relatively simple matter, and the drawings in Fig. 34 will help in showing that this is true. As the structure of the teeth is usually important in identification, they may need a little extra cleaning before the significant parts can be picked out under a strong hand lens or low-power microscope. In the latter case the specimen can be supported on a blob of plasticine on a glass slide.

Most of the lower jaws encountered in the pellets of Irish owls—those of rodents—have the characteristic form shown in Fig. 34, and have a diastema—a wide gap between the incisors at the front and the cheek teeth. Rabbit jaws are similar in form, but larger, and so an individual dentary of 35mm long or longer is almost certainly that of a young rabbit. Confirmation is easy, for there will be five cheek teeth, and not three as in rats, mice and voles. Moreover, the cheek teeth of rabbits have a recognizable pattern on the grinding surface, an oval outline and a line within bisecting it on its long axis.

Really large adult rats are rarely captured and most of those taken by owls are young animals. Even so, their dentaries are readily distinguished from those of lesser rodents on size alone. Those of rats are always more than 20mm long, whereas they rarely exceed 15mm in mice and bank voles. The teeth of voles are quite characteristic and, even when they fall out, so are the sockets. Looking directly down on them, the teeth can be seen to be made up of a series of triangles, which, in combination, look for all the world like a Christmas Tree.

The most difficult task is to tell apart the jaw bones of house mice and field mice. Generally those of the latter are longer, but there is considerable overlap in this respect. Fortunately the arrangement of the cusps on the tooth surface is diagnostic, as can be seen in the drawing in Fig. 34. The field mouse has several extra cusps, and the first inner cusp of the first cheek tooth of the house mouse is disproportionately large. If the teeth are missing things become even trickier, but the problem is not insoluble. The rooting of the third cheek teeth, those nearest the back of the jaw, is diagnostic. In the field mouse there are two distinct roots leaving two discrete pits on the jaw. There is only one hole on the jaw of the house mouse for the third tooth, though it divides into two *below the surface.*

Pigmy shrew skulls have no diastema, the upper and lower jaws having a full complement of teeth which, as explained in Chapter 1, are armed with tiny, sharp cusps tipped with enamel which is unmistakeably red. The skull itself is minute and the lower jaw does not exceed fractionally more that 8mm in length. Bats sometimes turn up in the pellets, and their teeth resemble those of shrews, but *lack the red enamel.* The bat skull is usually rather bigger than a pigmy shrew's, but never greater in size than that of a mouse. The identification of the species of bat is better left to a mammal specialist. In the case of shrews and bats it is best to retain skulls as well as dentaries.

The remains of birds are readily detected. Numbers can be estimated by picking out the bony halves of the bill, which withstand digestion, unlike their horny covering. The *humerus,* the first bone in the wing next to the body, can also be picked out from a background of mammal bones, for one end is greatly expanded.

Frog skulls are invariably shattered beyond recognition and to try to collect the pieces is a formidable task. However, the right and left halves of the

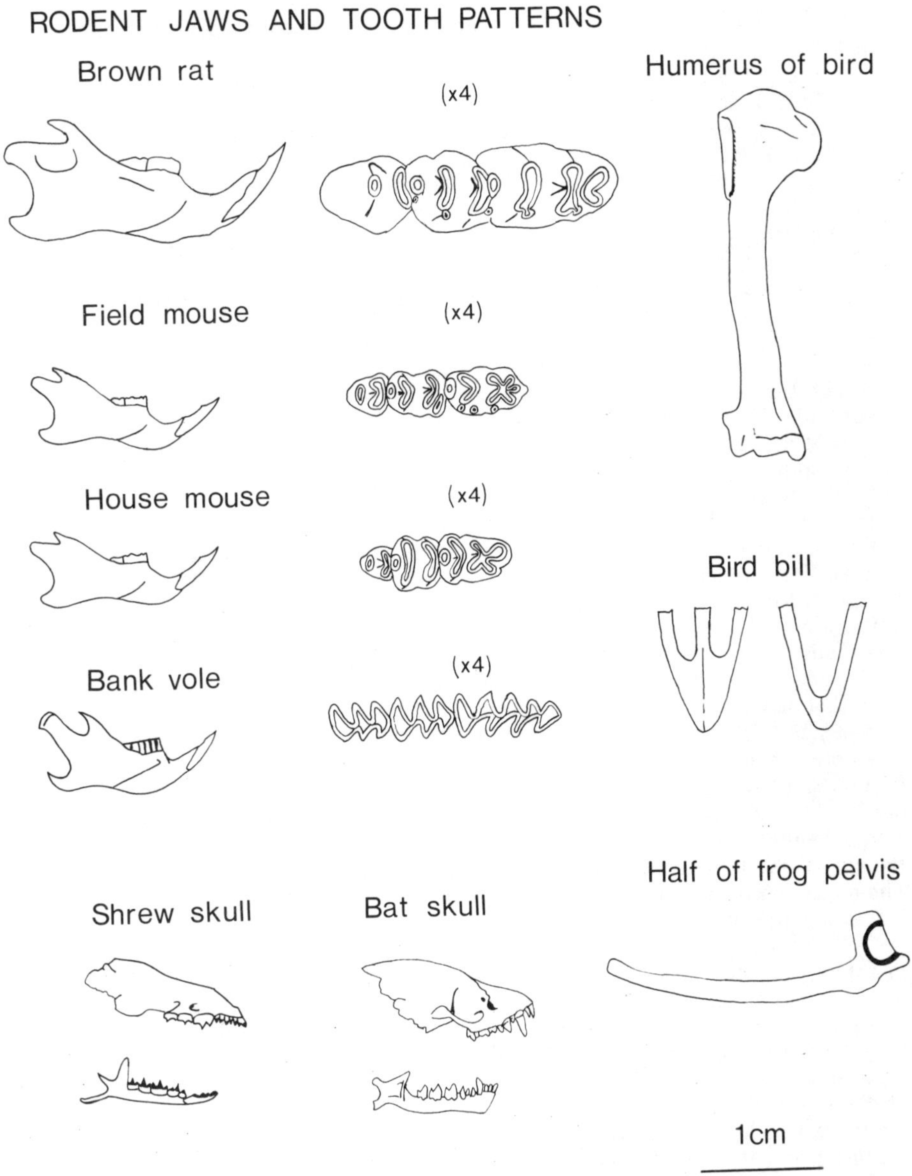

RODENT JAWS AND TOOTH PATTERNS

Brown rat
(x4)

Humerus of bird

Field mouse
(x4)

House mouse
(x4)

Bank vole
(x4)

Bird bill

Shrew skull

Bat skull

Half of frog pelvis

1cm

Fig. 34   Diagnostic items in the pellets of Irish owls. All drawings are to scale, apart from the grinding patterns on the rodent teeth which are x4.

frog's pelvis, shown in Fig. 34, are easily seen, and quite unlike anything else encountered in the castings. They can be used to determine the precise numbers of frogs devoured. The only other remains will be those of insects, mostly beetles, and if a precise identification is required an entomologist should be consulted.

Having sorted out all these bits and pieces, an estimate of food can be made. Rodents and rabbits are given by the number of right or left dentaries, whichever is greater, and for shrews and bats the skull count should also be considered. The total number of frogs is determined from the halves of the pelvis. Birds can be counted from available bones, but time will be saved by concentrating on the bill and humeri. If there is much of a discrepancy between right and left parts, then some may have been missed and dissected pellets may usefully be combed further.

After analysis one must assess the significance of the data obtained and here there is a slight problem, perhaps best illustrated by an example. Supposing one found that a batch of castings yielded the remains of 100 pigmy shrews, 30 mice and 10 rats. The shrews taken might have a mean weight of about 4g, the mice around 20g and the rats, which would not be full-grown, about 100g. The owl therefore consumed 400g of shrew, 600g of mouse and 1,000g of rat. It would therefore be quite misleading to say that the diet was one of ten parts shrew to three of mouse and one of rat, as might be suggested by a cursory glance at the initial results. To avoid giving this mistaken impression, a system of correction factors have been devised, originally for the tawny owl[188] in England, to allow for the differences in weight between the several prey species. They are based on a theoretical 'standard' small rodent of 20g. Thus the factor for mice and voles (and birds and frogs) is x1, for rats x5, for rabbits x10, for pigmy shrews x0.2 and bats x0.25. Our original hypothetical figures, after multiplication, would thus read: shrews 20, mice 30 and rats 50 prey units or, in percentages, 20%, 30% and 50% respectively of the total prey units. It is plain that half of the food in the theoretical example was rat.

When I first became interested in the food of owls I was surprised to find that only one analysis of pellets had ever been carried out in Ireland. This was by Lionel Adams, a prominent English conchologist, while on an excursion to northern Co. Antrim in company with other English naturalists. They came across the material in pine woods near Ballycastle and a vigorous, narrative account of the activities of the party appears in the *Irish Naturalist* of 1897.[190] The remaining work mentioned below is therefore my own or produced in conjunction with colleagues.

The results from most of the Irish barn owl pellets examined are shown in Table III. Besides the items listed, remains of beetles, especially dor beetles, were fairly commonly encountered as, indeed, they are in the castings of long-eared owls. It is immediately apparent from the table that the chief quarry of barn owls, over most of Ireland, are field mice and rats. House mice and very many shrews are also taken, but the latter tiny beasts comprise only a fraction of the total bulk. Birds and bats are only occasionally caught. At Adare in Co. Limerick, which was the only site investigated within the range of the bank vole, the latter rodent was also important, which is surprising for, as already stressed in Chapter 1, bank voles usually stick strictly to areas of heavy cover and would consequently be the more troublesome to capture. A point worth stressing is the large contribution made by rats and house mice to the pellets from Castleward, probably due to the extensive old farm outhouses in the vicinity.

The overall results differ markedly from those obtained in Great Britain where, as will be recalled from Table I, there are several small mammals which are absent from Ireland. Thus the field vole, normally found in grassland and

Table III

The results of analyses of some Irish barn owl pellets. For an explanation of the term 'prey units' see text

Date	Locality	Terrain	Total prey units excluding insects	Percentage of total prey units					
				Field mouse	House mouse	Brown rat	Bank vole	Pigmy shrew	Bird
1964-65	Castleward, 57 Co. Down	Parkland and woodland strips. Farm buildings.	650	51	15	30	–	4	<1
*April 1966	Castlecauldwell, 88 Co. Fermanagh	Well wooded area with lake	225.6	53	1	40	–	5	1
May 1970	Glenmalure, 91 Co. Wicklow	Glen with agricultural land and woodland	330.8	77	9	11	–	2	<1
August 1970	Menlough Castle, 83 Co. Galway	Agricultural land, river and marsh	360	72	7	19	–	1	<1
August-September 1973*	Adare Manor, 89 Co. Limerick	Grazing and woodland	94	34	–	32	33	1	–

*and one Natterer's bat.

easy to kill, is the major prey there. The amount in the diet varies but averages around 46%. Common shrews also make up, on average, around 25%.[103] Thus normally over half the food consists of species not found in Ireland, where it appears that the owl compounds for the missing dishes by more intense but proportionate predation on those small mammals which are available, as we might well expect.

Whilst the findings so far are instructive, they represent, to a large extent, random observations. One is not in a position to compare possible local and seasonal differences in the availability of rodents and insectivores and so attempt to explain the discrepancies between the various sets of figures. It is preferable to collect material regularly from a single roost over a period of time and to become familiar with or even to monitor local conditions, if only in a simple way. The fruits of such a study are shown in Table IV from castings collected at Menlough Castle, Co. Galway, from September 1970 to August 1971.[85]

Before attempting an interpretation of the table, it would be wise to bear in mind that chance plays a greater or lesser part in the apparent rises and falls in the results, more so in months when few castings were found. It is therefore rash to interpret small changes from month to month as of any significance and doubly so when there is only a modicum of material to go on. Fortunately, there are statistical tests which can be applied to the figures to show precisely how much reliance can be placed on the observed differences, and these have been used in the present case. A detailed explanation is unnecessary and, in any case, is outside the scope of this book.

The peak consumption of field mice was in autumn and early winter, which is not surprising as populations are highest at that time of year. There is no effective change in the numbers of house mice over the entire period. The quantity of rats appears to change but it must be remembered that the original numbers were multiplied by a conversion factor of x5, and so rather less importance should be attached to differing percentages from month to month. However, there can be no disputing that comparatively more rats were devoured in August. The explanation is almost certainly the harvesting of a field of barley beside the castle, no doubt suddenly depriving the rats previously living there of sustenance and shelter, obliging them to forage in the open or in terrain foreign to them, and exposing them to the owls' attentions.

The most puzzling set of figures is for the pigmy shrew, where there are some spectacular increases and decreases; it is as well to remember that even these have been somewhat reduced by the correction factors. Little is known of the seasonal changes in population density of these animals but irregular fluctuations have been noticed in England. No satisfactory explanation is available in the present instance.

That substantially more birds were eaten in January, February and May than at other times is easier to explain. In the former months winter migrants arrived, naturally unfamiliar with the country and in poorer condition than residents. They probably fell easy victims to the owls. The high percentage in May might reflect an abundance of newly-fledged young and, presumably because the winter of 1971 was a mild one in the Galway district, many birds had nested early.

Over most of the year frogs were taken in small numbers, even during the winter months. Although they usually hibernate, this is intermittent if the weather is not severe. They may appear on warmer days and disappear again

Table IV.

The results of analyses of barn owl pellets collected each month from September 1970 to August 1971 at Menlough Castle, Co. Galway. For an explanation of the term 'prey units' see text.

Month	Total prey units excluding insects	Percentage of total prey units					
		Field mouse	House mouse	Brown rat	Pigmy shrew	Bird	Frog
September	138.2	67	10	18	3	1	1
October	214.6	58	9	23	6	–	4
November	53.4	52	9	28	5	4	2
December	84.8	57	9	30	2	1	1
*January	42.6	54	5	12	13	14	2
February	31.6	41	13	15	12	19	–
March	49.8	36	22	–	16	4	22
April	18.0	39	28	–	22	6	6
May	17.2	41	6	–	7	29	17
June	51.8	46	12	37	2	2	–
*July	34.2	50	9	29	12	–	–
*August	62.4	16	11	64	4	–	5

*and one bat in each case (January: Long-eared; July: Natterer's; August: unidentified).

when it grows colder. Frogs come out of hibernation to breed *en masse* in late February or early March and, until the seasonal increase in vegetation for cover in May, would be readily available to the owls in large quantities in marshy areas. This is quite obvious from the table, the low value in April perhaps being due to sampling error.

Thompson's observations on the prey of the barn owl are in fairly close agreement with the conclusions drawn here. He and his associates noted the remains of food at nests, analysed the contents of a few stomachs and even some pellets but, sadly, gave no absolute numbers. Mice were the most common item from all sources, followed by rats and beetles. He and his colleagues rarely came across any bird remains

The information from the two analyses of the pellets of Irish long-eared owls are summarized in Table V. My own collection comprised thirty-three batches from sixteen different roosts,[59]nine of which were in coniferous woodland and most of the remainder in mixed woodland strips.

The conclusions to be drawn from both studies are very similar. Fieldmice are a staple food with rats definitely in second place. House mice and birds form a minor part in the owl's regimen, and pigmy shrews and bats are seldom taken. Judging from this and results in Britain, which support the impression of the extreme unimportance of shrews, the senses of the long-eared owl are not as finely tuned to locate minute mammals as those of the barn owl. The lesser numbers of rats and house mice in the diet are perhaps an indication of the tendency to hunt in localities not in such close proximity to the dwellings of man, where these two rodents are commonest.

A comparison with the surprisingly scanty data from Great Britain is interesting.[187,199] English long-eared owls, depending on the terrain, have been shown to include on their menu around 25% field vole, 25 to 50% field mouse, up to 25% rat and around 15% bird. Again, the absence of voles from most of Ireland readily accounts for the discrepancies between the English and Irish information.

Although regular collections were not made at any one point, the data can be divided to give some idea of seasonal changes in the prey, as shown in Table VI. As the fractions of birds and house mice are small, their variation can hardly be regarded as of any consequence. The two major prey species—field mice and brown rats—do show marked and significant fluctuations. The percentage occurrences of the field mouse for the first three periods are substantially the same. The April-May figures admittedly differ slightly, but due to an unusually high proportion of house mice in one of the batches of pellets, which was most irregular and almost certainly related to some entirely local happening. In summer the proportion of rats is low, while in autumn it is higher than at any other time. These differences are not correlated with numbers of field mice, since the latter are most numerous in autumn and scarcest in summer. They are

Table V.

The results of analyses of Irish long-eared owl pellets. For an explanation of the term 'prey units' see text.

Date	Total prey units	Locality	Terrain	Percentage of total prey units				
				Field mouse	House mouse	Brown rat	Pigmy shrew	Bird
*May 1897	508	Glenshesk, Ballycastle, Co. Antrim	Pine wood	70	1	22	‹1	6
1963-64	1157	Sixteen localities in north-east Ireland	Mainly coniferous woodland or woodland strips	70	6	20	‹1	4

* And three bats.

Table VI

Seasonal fluctuations of the main foods in the pellets of Irish long-eared owls. For an explanation of the term 'prey units' see text.

Period	Total prey units	Percentage prey units			
		Field mouse	House mouse	Brown rat	Birds
December—January	388	79	6	12	3
February—March	375	74	4	16	6
April—May	230	66	9	22	3
June—August	158	84	6	6	4
October—November	189	43	5	50	2

probably related to the availability of rats, for even a small increase in numbers will be reflected in the owl's diet simply because the average rat will provide about five times as much food as the average-sized mouse.

A tentative explanation of the seasonal variation is as follows. During the summer there is heavy cover available for the rats, both from crops and uncultivated vegetation. In autumn, when crops are cut and herbage dies down, food and cover become scarcer. Rats, unfamiliar with their surroundings, move over strange terrain in search of food and towards farm buildings, where some take up residence. During this time they must be particularly vulnerable to attack from owls. By the end of the year the feral and farm rat populations will be more or less stable, with the former minimal. The numbers in the open, and therefore available to owls, increase as the weather improves and as those in buildings move out to the fields. After the massive seasonal growth of cover in May, the rats presumably will become more difficult to catch.

Thompson's remarks on the food may profitably be quoted here

The nest contained . . . a dead field mouse . . . With respect to food, the stomachs of three . . . contained:- One, a sparrow almost whole; the second, portions of a large coleopterous insect [a beetle] ; the third, the remains of three buntings. The stomach of a long-eared owl, shot at Killaloe, contained part of a rat, the skull of a mouse and the heads of two sparrows.

Dr J.D. Marshall, of Belfast, informs me that for five or six years, when he lived in High-street, opposite St. George's Church, he kept long and short-eared owls instead of cats, and found them to be much more effective killers of rats and mice. Their patience was extraordinary. At the entrance to one rat-hole, which happened frequently to come under his view, one of these birds was always stationed until it succeeded in killing the whole of the inmates, consisting of a pair of old, and nine well-grown young ones. They were invariably seized with its foot by the back of the neck, so that the bird never suffered the slightest injury. Living rats too . . . let out of the cage trap, and a fair start given to them, were always captured by these owls . . . These owls had free access to the dwelling-house and cleared it completely of mice; as they did the yard and store, of rats. They were great pets and very fond of having their ears rubbed.

Ussher and Warren, in *The Birds of Ireland,* state that long-eared owls have been repeatedly observed to catch bats and have been seen hunting for them over the surface of a pond.

I have managed to collect comparatively few castings of the short-eared owl, mainly from five localities in 1964 and 1965. The resultant total of 178.2 units was composed of prey in the following proportions:[56] field mouse 9%, house mouse 3%, rat 76%, pigmy shrew (recorded once only), rabbit 6% and birds 6%. Obviously short-eared owls exist largely on rats in Ireland. All of the localities where the pellets were gathered were either coastal or boggy and undoubtedly had high rat populations, even though it was winter. The scarcity of field mice on damp ground and their nocturnal habits, in contrast to those of this largely diurnal owl, go far to explain the small numbers consumed.

In Great Britain and on the continent, the food is mainly voles, in southern Europe field voles and, in the north, lemmings (which are also, technically speaking, voles). Nevertheless other rodents and even birds may be important in a few areas. Both as a resident breeder and a migrant the numbers of short-eared owls vary considerably in any particular region and may be suddenly augmented when the vole populations reach plague proportions. In the strict sense many of these owls are not migratory, but nomadic. There are two reasons for this. Firstly, the numbers of field voles and lemmings fluctuate more violently than other rodents and these changes are frequently localised. A vagrant bird is therefore able to utilize such high concentrations. Secondly, on the bog, grassland or tundra over which short-eared owls operate, knowledge of the ground is rather less important than in woodland, scrub or other less homogeneous habitats. So, when provender is scarce, the owls have a better chance of survival if they move on in search of more fruitful hunting grounds. It is interesting, in this context, that in the winter of 1907-8, when according to Barrington[128] rats were particularly numerous in Ireland, short-eared owls were unusually plentiful and well dispersed throughout the land.

Barn owls, on the continent, sometimes show a comparable wanderlust in years when rodents are particularly scarce. On such occasions in time past they may have presented a windfall for taxidermists.

There is one final aspect of owls' predation which is worth discussing, even if inconclusively. There is manifestly no question of owls conflicting with man's interests. While this may sound close to damning the poor birds with faint praise, it is really all that can be said with any degree of certainty. Whether they actually keep rodents down is an entirely different matter and, as it is quite clear that all three species are far from being truly abundant in Ireland, there is no question of them doing this in a general sense. It is conceivable that they *might* limit mouse or rat numbers locally, but of proof there is none. The reproductive rate of rodents is proverbial and they usually breed up quickly to the limit of their resources when unmolested. Where owls are commonest, it is much more likely that rodent density is dependent, in the long term at least, on other factors such as food, extent of suitable habitats and aggression within the various species.

7 The North-eastern Fox . . .

The fox has been celebrated from the earliest antiquity for the cunning and ingenuity which it manifests, whether in obtaining its food or in eluding pursuit. The general expression of its features, the obliquity and quickness of the eye, the sharp shrewd-looking muzzle, and the erect ears, afford the most unequivocal indications of that mingled acuteness and fraud which have long rendered it a byword and a proverb; for it is well known that the character of its physiognomy is not falsified by the animal's real propensities and habits.

British Quadrupeds   Thomas Bell

  The fox, besides being the most celebrated of the Irish beasts (it was Oscar Wilde who described fox-hunting as the 'unspeakable in pursuit of the uneatable'), is the easiest of them all to recognise. When someone confides to having seen one, you can be reasonably sure that he has. The diagnostic features are too familiar and distinctive for any error to be made. This may sound superfluous, but it is wonderful how often the points for accurate identification are normally overlooked in the excitement of an unexpected sighting of any other wild mammal.

  In appearance the fox is unmistakeably dog-like, but it is more slender than most dogs and the muzzle finer and sharper, giving it that sly expression which, as Bell declares, is no libel on its character. From extensive series of measurements it is apparent that the foxes of north-east Ireland—the only part where ample data have been collected—are, like Scottish foxes, somewhat larger than English ones. Those in Northern Ireland have shorter tails than those in Britain.[132] In Scotland and England tails average about 60% of the length of head and body combined. In Ireland the figure is only 50%.

  The dog fox is generally larger than the vixen, respective averages for over two hundred specimens of each sex being 6.9kg and 5.8kg.[73] He has also a thicker muzzle. At close quarters, one is often, but by no means always, able to distinguish the sexes on this basis. In the field it is not normally possible, though some experienced fox-shooters can tell dog from vixen at a distance with a remarkable degree of accuracy. Whether they do this on appearance or behaviour

Fig. 35 *Fox—on the investigation.*

I do not know. Most people who talk about seeing 'a big dog fox' (for some reason it is nearly *always* a big dog fox) could just as well be talking about a medium-sized representative of the opposite sex.

The fox's coat, like that of most other mammals, is composed of two types of hair, a dense, short underfur and the long guard hairs which overlie it. The general colour is reddish-brown but varies from yellowish to a rich chestnut, the back and tail being rather darker than the flanks. In fact a guard hair is not of uniform hue and each has a series of coloured bands: the tip (about 2mm) is black, beneath which is about 4mm of red, followed by 6mm of yellow. The remaining 10–15mm is again black. Thus small differences in the lengths of the upper bands can produce marked overall effects. The underside of the body and the inner surfaces of the limbs are grey-white; actually the guard hairs are white, the underfur grey. During the summer, when foxes moult, the underfur is more exposed as the longer hairs fall out, and so the animal appears darker beneath. Similarly, as the guard hairs on the back are gradually lost, more of their underlying colours are exposed and the fox looks more yellowish.

Black guard hairs are distributed to a greater or lesser extent through the 'red' ones and occasionally they may also be found on the chest and belly, sometimes to such a degree as to render the underside charcoal-coloured. One black-bellied fox which arrived at the Natural History Museum in Dublin in 1896 led Scharff to maintain that there was a distinct race of fox in Ireland with this character.[178] The backs of the fox's ears and the feet are always black, though I have seen two specimens with some white patches on the hind feet. There is also a sable streak extending from the eye to the mouth on each side, but the lips themselves are white. The brush always has a white tip, or at least it had on the thousand or so foxes I looked at. But sometimes this 'tag' is minute.

The curious title of this chapter is explained by our scanty knowledge of the species in other parts of Ireland. True, there has been a plethora of ink spilt on the joys of traditional fox-hunting, horns, hounds, red-jackets and all. Much of this is ephemeral, for most popular sports induce what amounts to a *cacoethes scribendi* in some of their followers. Where such literary activities truly apply to the fox itself, they are, at best, subjective accounts of the animal under abnormal conditions, and deal with only a small segments of its activities. The only substantial scientific work completed on Irish foxes was undertaken by myself, from 1966 to 1968 in Northern Ireland, and this chiefly in the counties of Antrim and Down.

It is manifestly clear from Arthur Stringer's book (1714) that the fox was ubiquitous in Co. Antrim in his time. This was almost certainly true throughout the eighteenth century, for Robert Patterson (the younger) wrote in 1900[167] of an old 'Court Leet' book of the Manor of Glenarm which yielded plentiful evidence of the former abundance of foxes in the county. The Manor of Glenarm, about 132 sq miles (342 sq km) in area, lay on the east coast and extended north from the town of Larne to the Glendun River. The courts were held twice a year and the records in the volume Patterson examined dealt with the years 1765 to 1812. There were a host of entries of the following kind.

17th day of November, 1765.
We psent the Sum of one pound four shills to be levyd off the inhabitants of the parish of Ardilenish and paid to Daniel Mc Vicar for killing twelve foxes of prey . . . We psent the sum of two Shillings to be Levyed off the inhabitants of Carncastle and paid to Thomas Palerr for killing one old fox.

Thus, two shillings (10p) a head was the reward whether the animal was a 'fox of prey' or merely 'an old fox'. From 1865 to 1781 an average of forty-six foxes were produced for a bounty annually, and although there were changes in the value of the bonus and of the responsibility for funding it, a total of 1,462 such premiums were shelled-out between 1765 and 1812 in this small part of the county, with no perceptible effect on the fox nuisance.

Thompson, in the middle of the last century, remarked that the fox was 'still to be found throughout the island, wherever it can remain in spite of man', suggestive of a thinning of the population, and this is corroborated in 1874 by a passage from the Belfast Naturalists' Field Club *Guide to Belfast,* compiled for the meeting of the British Association in the city during that year: 'Foxes are frequently met with, but seem to be rapidly decreasing before the gamekeeper's gun and shepherd's trap.' Whether man was responsible for a diminution in the density of foxes we do not know but, by the end of the century, they were rare enough for Patterson to speak of their disappearance from Co. Antrim.

Lord Antrim informs me that the only Fox he ever heard of in the two Baronies was killed in his deer-park about the year 1870 . . . Even this one is supposed to have been 'turned down' . . . Mr Sheals, the well-known Belfast taxidermist, informs me he cannot remember having received Foxes from Co. Antrim.

Finally in the whole of Ulster there is not one pack of Foxhounds, although there are two packs of Stag-hounds, and eleven packs of Harriers, to satisfy the hunting proclivities of the Northern gentry, who would doubtless hunt Foxes if there were Foxes to hunt.

I have discussed foxes with many of the older country people and have been repeatedly told of a time when there were no foxes. Closer questioning usually reveals that they began to appear again between 1920 and 1930. Letters in the *Irish Naturalist* and the *Irish Naturalists' Journal* suggest that there were local increases at least, in the early 'twenties. They were probably still scarce in 1917 when Nevin Foster, an active naturalist of the period, in a lecture on the Mourne Mountains to the Belfast Naturalists' Field Club, commented that 'in the recesses of these mountains the fox and badger still lurk'—a statement surely indicative of their rarity elsewhere. As mentioned in Chapter 1, the badger too was scarcer in Ireland seventy years ago than it is today and, in the north-east anyhow, was localised.

During the 'thirties foxes came to be regarded more and more as a pest and several 'vermin' destruction societies were formed to deal with them. ('Vermin', by the way, is a catch-all word, replete with tautological overtones, which can be used to slander any animals you do not happen to like. It is never used objectively.) Eventually an official bounty system was introduced in 1943, with regular subventions for those who produced the bodies, or merely the heads, at police stations, the tongues being excised as a precaution against repeated presentations of the same animal. The money was raised in individual counties. Finally the system was taken over completely in 1960 by the Ministry of Agriculture. By 1970 over 200,000 bounties had been paid with no noticeable benefit as a result. The Northern Ireland scheme, like almost every other bounty programme throughout the world, was a failure.

It is the opinion of all wildlife biologists that bounties are a wicked waste of time and money. At best they are mere political expedients to appease wishful-thinkers. The histories of these fanciful extermination schemes tend to follow a universal pattern. They are commonly started locally by groups of farmers or by gun clubs because some objectionable species seems impossible to control. After appropriate wrangling, reproach or cajolery they are supported, wholly or partially, by local authority. If they do not founder at an earlier stage, they eventually become the responsibility of the national government, which soon finds that it has a political fly-paper on its hands. The trouble is that the initial payments must be large enough to produce more deaths than natural mortality factors in the first year of operation. The enormous outlay necessary frightens the officialdom concerned so that they seldom are. After this the incentives must be increased, for hunting smaller numbers requires greater effort. Even if this is possible financially—and, as authorities shrink from enlarged expenditure, they are browbeaten into it belatedly if at all—all manner of fraud is the result. For example, Red Indians have skilfully dyed ground squirrel (*Citellus* sp.) skins and passed them off as coyote (*Canis latrans*) cubs. When the bounty is sufficiently higher in Northern Ireland than in the Republic, there is reputedly a brisk trade in foxheads across the Border.

The bounty in Northern Ireland is to be abolished in March 1977.

In 1966 I was happily financed to research on foxes in Northern Ireland for three years by the Ministry of Agriculture, and to make recommendations as to official policy. During this time I was able to observe foxes in the field, to obtain from bounty-hunters a sample of about a thousand bodies for dissection, and to ear-tag some 120 cubs and adults. The tags were smaller versions of those used to mark cattle, and each bore an address and the promise of a reward for its return. The animals were always released where they were captured, after marking. By these methods, and by discreet enquiries into the fox's depredations, I was enabled to build up a dossier on the north-eastern fox, a digest of which forms the remainder of this chapter, and the following one.

Since 1954 there have never been less than 9,000 bounties bestowed by a bountiful government upon the fox's foes each year. Vulpicide, in one form or another, is thus a traditional amusement, and I propose to outline the more common techniques employed to compass Reynard's destruction.[65]

The vast majority of those who lay claim to expertise in fox hunting use terriers to locate the animals in suitable earths. Hunters prefer the foxes to bolt so that they can shoot them. If the animals are cornered below ground they have to be dug out which, though often possible, requires considerable labour. A few people rely entirely on digging, in which case any extra entrances may have to be stopped and this, together with the proximity of the hunter to the earth, discourages bolting. Terriers sometimes succeed in killing the victim below ground and this is especially true of cubs, vixens in late pregnancy or suckling young, and mangy adults generally, all of which are inclined to stay put. Although the dogs are rarely given any formal training, some become remarkably proficient. During the summer, when many foxes are to be found in cover above ground, the terriers are employed in raising them. Alternatively the vegetation may be beaten. Older foxes are much less easily startled than the young and will often lie still until a dog or beater is practically upon them. Moreover adults are adept at using anything available to screen themselves and can pass through vegetation 24cm high quite unnoticed. Cubs, even those three-quarters grown, on the other hand, may run into the open when there is adequate herbage to shield their escape.

Shooting foxes can be humane when the hunters are experienced, though inferior marksmen may merely wing them; but when a fox is killed below ground this can, on occasion, be a lengthy and savage business for both fox and dogs. Adult foxes suffer in silence but, where cubs are tackled, screaming may last for

110

several minutes.

An analysis of bounty figures for one year[67] revealed that a quarter of all rewards were claimed by people killing only one or two foxes. None of the claimants can have had any special skills in fox destruction, and it seems highly probable that the bulk of the animals thus dispatched were shot on chance encounters or dug out after having been observed to enter earths. The latter is particularly true of those individuals guilty of raids on poultry, or of cubs which had been seen playing outside their homes.

While I was working on foxes, gin traps were a permitted means of catching them (with certain unenforceable restrictions). From the beginning of 1969 this type of trap has been illegal in Northern Ireland. Generally speaking, proficient vulpicides only used them in special circumstances, if at all: for example, when a marauding individual cannot be dug out a trap may be set near the entrance to the earth. A few hunters, however, specialised in their use. One gamekeeper I knew claimed to catch a hundred animals annually in this way. As he was collecting about 200 bounties each year, there was no reason to disbelieve him. As far as I am concerned it is good riddance to the gin trap, an indisputable cruel and indiscriminate engine which will catch badgers just as easily. I need not appal readers with accounts of broken limbs and feet chewed off by captives in their efforts to escape. The use of gin traps is illegal in the Republic. In spite of this, one can still buy them!

Foxes are sometimes caught with heavy-gauge wire snares which can be laid at fences and hedges, where they are supposed to be less conspicuous to the intended victims. Strangulation of a mammal the size of a fox can hardly be regarded as humane and takes time to work, during which the animal will damage itself in efforts to escape. It is no more selective than gin trapping either.

Relatively few foxes are dispatched with poison and most experienced hunters avoid it because of the undoubted danger to their dogs. Trapping, snaring and poisoning all require experience as foxes are conservative and suspicious of unfamiliar objects. The gassing of earths, though necessitating no particular skill, results in relatively few deaths, although actual numbers cannot be estimated as the bodies are not recovered. Unless dogs are used to determine if a fox is in residence, this method is haphazard and inefficient.

Traditional fox-hunting on horseback accounts for only a minute fraction of the total annual kill, and activities of this kind do not affect the fox population as a whole in Northern Ireland for good or ill. It is a sport and not a method of control.

The best and most humane way of killing foxes remains shooting, where necessary with the use of terriers, and local shooting is necessary. Persons who are in favour of introducing legislation to preserve the lives of all foxes must remember that farmers who lose poultry, and those who rear game birds, have, at least, a legitimate right to protect their property. By the same token, those who are likely to be horrified by the extensive use of corpses in my research should remember that, whether I had dissected them or not, the animals would have been killed anyway. No matter how shocking it may seem to a few animal-lovers, some of the information on wildlife can only be obtained from dead bodies.

Foxes are to be found in practically every type of terrain, except entirely urban areas.[66] Nevertheless they are well established in several suburban districts of Belfast and many a city-dweller has been taken aback by one strolling unconcernedly through his garden. They are common on cultivated land, where earths are established on any patch of rough ground, in hedge banks, or even in open fields. This is also true of woodland and they abound in scrub. Much the same can be said of moorland and mountain, where they often seek shelter in holes between rocks. I have even found them frequenting the old iron mine workings at the head of Glenariff in Co. Antrim. On the coast they live almost anywhere, from sand dunes to sea cliffs, and it is not widely appreciated just how sure-footed foxes are, for they regularly make use of narrow paths on precipitous crags.

The notion that Forestry plantations harbour foxes is true, but irrelevant in any campaign to reduce their numbers. As will be explained later, adult foxes restrict operations to a surprisingly small area and therefore the depredations of those living in forests are of importance only in the immediate district. As the animals are about as common there as anywhere else and forests occupy only a small fraction of Ireland, it seems unfair to single them out as a particularly significant haven.

Foxes are primarily nocturnal, which fact is testified to by the pupil of the eye which is eliptical, like that of a cat, allowing greater accommodation for a wider range of illumination than a round one. In daytime the pupil is a vertical slit, but it opens wide at night. Just the same, foxes are not uncommonly at large during the day. In early summer, when bringing up cubs, they can be seen quite often in the two hours after dawn. During this season at least they are creatures of habit and several instances have been described to me of their crossing roads or gardens at about the same time each morning, or calling punctually at dustbins and refuse tips in the outskirts of Belfast. The most convincing instances of Reynard's routine I encountered in company with Mr Sidney McAvoy of Dunmurray, Co. Antrim, to my mind the most knowledgeable and effective amateur fox hunter in the land, who spends part of his time just watching foxes. On one morning he drove with me to a spot and predicted not only the early arrival of a fox, but where it would appear and the path it would follow. He also brought to my notice the value of the alarm calls of birds, particularly blackbirds (*Turdus merula*) and magpies in detecting the presence of a fox and in tracing its movements. Magpies often 'scold' a fox and even fly down and follow it. One can thus sometimes deduce where it is likely to appear, and scan the likely spot with binoculars. Needless to say, the would-be observer must remain out of sight. One morning, in company with him, I watched no fewer than five of these birds swooping down on a long stand of bracken, making their displeasure known in no uncertain terms. Eventually a couple of foxes emerged.

Foxes usually go about their business at a trot, with frequent pauses to investigate anything which takes their fancy: but they are quite up to galloping long distances. When moving at speed the brush is stretched out horizontally behind and a fox on the run is a magnificent sight. As any Master of foxhounds knows, his quarry is adept at all manner of evasion and subterfuge, and is a fine swimmer, which it seems to do purposefully to confuse its pursuers. Although I have only witnessed it once, it is widely known that a fox may 'play dead', and so further its ends in one way or another. It is also a well attested fact that foxes can climb trees.

For most of their travels foxes have established runs which may be common property with badgers, rabbits or hares, but are sometimes entirely their own. Paths used exclusively are much less marked than those of other Irish mammals, tend to be fragmentary and cannot, indeed, always be recognised as fox-runs on sight. There is a strong tendency for routes to lie along topographical features such as hedges, ridges or glades. Characteristically feathers or fur from kills may be shed on them and droppings deposited here and there. The latter, even without handling, can usually be seen to contain hair, feathers and bone fragments. Fox droppings are generally smaller than those of dogs and smell quite different, though usually only enthusiasts care to prove this for themselves.

A strong foxy effluvium is sometimes scented in the countryside and doubtless betokens the recent presence of a fox. Occasionally it is noticeable where a run crosses a lane or ride and it is no doubt a form of range marking. The fox is well provided with scent glands. There is one under the tail, two by the anus, and probably one associated with the urinary tract.[30] The precise social functions of the glands are uncertain and it is not clear which produces the typical odour. Territory marking is believed to be done with urine, which would suggest the last one. The smell, which is an accompaniment to all adults, is detectable stronger when the animal is frightened. For all this foxes seem remarkably tolerant of each other over most of the year and there is no doubt that ranges overlap considerably. While I have read of fighting and do not doubt that it occurs (because one of the writers is an outstanding naturalist)[121] I have never come across it myself, and none of the vulpicides I talked to, some of many years standing, had ever seen it. It is probably limited to the breeding season. It is perhaps worth adding that I have heard two veteran hunters correctly divine the presence of a vixen in late pregnancy in an earth by her smell.

An adult fox spends its time in a fairly small area—I except occasions when one is hunted from horseback. This conclusion I reached from the tagging experiments.[67] Tags from twenty adults were returned and over 300 days elapsed in nine of these cases between tagging and death; one animal had been at large for nearly three years. The greatest distance moved was 5.4km (3.3 miles) but fifteen of the movements were less than 1km (0.6 miles), results surely suggestive of a smallish sphere of activities.

The word 'earth', used of the fox's subterranean dwelling, gives a quite false impression of restricted ownership. 'Earths' are quite often the former residences of badgers, and both species may be found in the same tunnel system, where the insanitary habits of the fox may be a trial to the fastidious badger. Rabbit holes are also commandeered and, in fact, though perfectly capable of the work, foxes rarely excavate their own burrows. The only evidence I have seen in this direction personally is the enlargement of existing accommodation or the reopening of earths which have been filled in.

An extremely widespread and quite erroneous notion is that foxes spend most of the day in their earths. It cannot be emphasized too strongly that, with the exception of pregnant vixens, they can be raised above ground in all seasons. Herbaceous cover is not even necessary, though surprisingly small amounts can be utilized: heather, bramble, bushes, hedges, ditches and stone-piles can all afford concealment. With the abundance of such suitable sites in Ireland, the fox's proven ability to make use of them, its thick insulating coat of hair and the mild climate, it is small wonder that the habit is so prevalent. The idea that foxes hunt at night and sleep in burrows during the day is a gross oversimplification.

The mating season begins early in the New Year and both sexes can reproduce in their first winter. While only a few dog foxes are capable of breeding in October, virtually all are in condition in December.[73] By then it is by no means unusual for hunters to raise a dog and vixen together, but there is no real sexual activity and the couples are 'just good friends'. The marital status of the fox has been a subject of some controversy but it is agreed generally that monogamy is the rule, for the season anyway. True, there have been reports of a lady fox with more than one suitor following her and one cannot preclude polyandry or polygamy on a small scale, but those who have bred silver foxes, which sometimes involves mating the best males with more than one female, do not doubt the monogamous tendencies of the animal.[121] Silver foxes are mutant strains ('sports') of the American red fox (which is now considered to be the same species as the European) and are bred commercially for fur. Nevertheless, as nearly all Irish vixens whelp each year, and there is a rapid turnover in population, it is unlikely that most marriages last long after the cubs of the union have dispersed. By January most of the population have paired off and, as the numbers of each sex are approximately equal, there are comparatively few spinsters and bachelors.

Foxes, though usually silent, have an unexpected vocabulary of weird noises. These are normally only heard during the mating season and doubtless help in pairing off. The commonest sounds are a sharp bark, often triple, and an answering scream. While the first is often attributed to the male and the second to the female, there is no reason for such an assumption. Both may well be made by either sex.

Vixens are receptive to their mates over three weeks but are only capable of being fertilized over three days.[196] The mating season as a whole can, in fact, be delimited indirectly with varying degrees of accuracy, but to explain the techniques involved it is first necessary to say a little about the reproductive tract of the female mammal. The female sex cells, the eggs, are produced in a pair of ovaries, which lie, one on each side, near the kidneys. As the eggs mature, each becomes surrounded by a fluid filled cavity or follicle which enlarges until eventually, when the egg is ready, it bursts. The eggs are washed into a funnel at the top of a narrow tube, one for each of the ovaries, where they are fertilized. They then pass to the uterus where the developing embryos become attached and obtain their nourishment from the mother. Immediately after the eggs leave the follicles, the cells lining the latter begin to grow and soon each of the original spaces becomes filled with a mass of yellowish cells called a *corpus luteum* (which is Latin for 'yellow body'). These cells produce a hormone which passes in the blood-stream to the uterus causing it to prepare for the reception of the embryos. In many mammals, including vixens, these yellow bodies are large and easily seen. If, therefore, one can examine a steady supply of dead foxes with information as to times of death, one can date the beginning of the mating season from when the yellow bodies first appear. The last vixens to acquire them will indicate the close of the season. There is also corroborative evidence of various kinds. I obtained vixens about to shed their eggs, with greatly enlarged follicles, and sometimes was able to detect male sex cells (sperm) in the female tract, an indisputable sign of recent sexual activity. In addition there is an enlargement of the penis associated with coupling which I observed in some of the carcases of dog foxes.

There is a second and rather oblique approach. From studies on a colony of captive foxes in Germany[196] and from observations on silver foxes, it is known that the gestation period is about fifty-one to fifty-three days, exceptionally a little longer. If the unborn young from the carcass of a pregnant vixen are examined, it is possible to determine the approximate age of those of about eighteen days or more from their degree of development. Again, knowing the day on which the mother was killed, one can easily, by subtraction, obtain the approximate date of fertilization.

Having accumulated data of this sort over three winters it was plain that practically all conceptions were from 4th January to 15th February and the vast majority between 7th January and 8th February,[73] in other words over a period of one month. Judging from the information available, this is a week or two earlier

114

than in England and Wales. In Scotland the season is later still.

During February, and even late in January, the expectant parents prepare nurseries for the approaching happy event. Freshly turned-out soil can be seen scattered around the mouths of burrows, marked with footprints and perhaps droppings. Quite small holes, unoccupied at other times, show these tokens of activity, but some earths, which would seem to be more satisfactory, are unoccupied. Foxes presumably know their own business best. Arthur Stringer, who knew a lot about foxes, observed that

> The place in which they commonly have their young, is an old badger's hole, or under a rock, or in a tree-root, or sometimes they scour a rabbit-hole, and have their young there. They do not so much matter a strong hole at first, but when the young . . . are a month or six weeks old, they do commonly remove them to a stronger earth . . .

In February and March the adults stink more strongly than at any other time. This is not only remarked by hunters, but was more than obvious at close quarters whilst I was dissecting. When handling animals during tagging, too, they were noticeably restless and more difficult to manage at this time than was usual. All of this would tend to suggest some sort of heightened aggressive and probably territorial behaviour.

As the vixen nears term she remains below ground and during the day the dog fox lies out in cover nearby or, less frequently, in the mouth of the burrow. There is often a cache of provisions in the hole and there is little doubt that the dog fox hunts and carries food to his wife in her confinement.

Just as the time of mating can be determined from post mortem examination of vixens, so can the whelping season. This is again done from the estimated ages of the embryos, this time by extrapolating *forward* to the hypothetical dates when the cubs would have been born. These results I supplemented from the appearance of vixens, among the animals I was dissecting, which had had cubs. Cubbing extends from the last few days in February to the first week in April, with the large majority of births in March. At birth the mother's mammae and their teats enlarge rapidly and enormously, and most of the hair on her underside is lost, leaving only a fine covering which is an unmistakeable shade of pink.

Now for a few vital statistics on the birth rate.[73] There was an overall mean of 5.4 embryos in the pregnant animals I looked at, with no differences between the years 1966, 1967 and 1968. However, as the young develop, some die before birth and are reabsorbed, as happens in many other mammals (for example, the field mouse and rabbit, as described in Chapter 4). So at birth the figure is about 4.5. Of the vixens a calculated 90.2% produce young. This gives, effectively, a figure of almost exactly four cubs per vixen, slightly higher than available figures from Britain. Since the sex ration is unity, there is therefore a triplication of numbers every spring. For, on balance, each two adults produce four cubs, increasing numbers in the family from two to six. The litter size in practice varies between one and eight.

The cubs are tiny and helpless when born and covered with dark, chocolate-coloured fur, though the tail-tip already has the distinctive white tag. But the muzzle is foreshortened and rounded, and the appearance in general is far from foxy. Like many new-born mammals, they have no teeth and their eyes are closed. During the first few weeks of life their mother spends a large part of her time with them and the father continues as the breadwinner. In this context it is significant that, though there is no shortage of food, dog foxes lose weight from January to May. The cubs increase in size steadily. By June they are half grown, and by

Fig. 36   Fox cub about seven weeks old.

September are becoming difficult to distinguish from their elders on size alone.

From April the slaughter of foxes increases apace in Northern Ireland and nearly half of the total annual kill is accounted for in May and June, most of it cubs. With a plentiful supply of bodies to work on, it was a simple matter to follow development. As the whelping season lasts over a month, there is a difference of an identical period between the ages of the oldest and youngest cubs in a season, and consequent overlap in the extent of development at any given time. The times and durations of the various changes in the cub population as a whole are shown in Fig. 37. From this data it was also possible to deduce how old cubs are as the various stages are reached.

Suckling lasts about thirty-eight to forty-three days and, in the last week or so, the young cut their first set of teeth. At about seventeen weeks the permanent dentition begins to replace the milk teeth and it is complete in a further five to six weeks. When the cubs are six weeks or so old they begin to moult, and in around seventeen days the chocolate fur is entirely replaced by a juvenile coat, much more like that of the full-grown fox, but paler. The underside is not white but a buffy reddish-brown. At the same time the muzzle elongates and endows the cub with an unmistakeably vulpine physiognomy. At about eighteen weeks the young fox begins to acquire the typical adult pelage, a more gradual process. It is not at all widely appreciated, by the way, that there are two moults before maturity. After the first there is an ominous change in the reaction to handling. Before, though the cub may bite, it simply looks bewildered when grasped by the scruff of the neck, the safest way to hold a fox. After the moult the mouth is opened wide in readiness, the invariable reaction of an old fox. There is, indeed, nothing quite so baleful-looking as a captive fox.

The adult's hair is also replaced during the summer, but the process is prolonged from late spring to autumn, and the new underfur in both young and adult is not fully grown until winter approaches. The loss of fur during warm weather is

116

no disadvantage. Because of this extended moult, fox skins are regarded as being practically worthless in spring and summer.

The litters first venture above ground when around a month old but keep close to the earth, staggering about as if their little legs will hardly carry them. By May many cubs are playing outside their homes and the grass round about is often rolled flat or worn away with their antics. With care a litter at play can be sighted in broad daylight, usually in early morning or during the evening. Playing consists of mock battle, the cubs rolling over each other, pretending to bite, somewhat like dogs disporting themselves, with periods of rest after temporary exhaustion. Some of the fun is much more cat-like, with stealthy stalking of real or imaginary objects. Adult foxes are known to play too, though I have never seen it myself. Mr McAvoy told me of two playing with a ball in the grounds of a school in the outskirts of Belfast and the fox's interest in balls is well known in England. On one links in London, golf balls were regularly purloined by foxes and caches of as many as eight were found, all severely chewed.[195]

Both parents attend to the needs of their offspring assiduously, bringing all manner of prey in surfeit to the earth. As a result the immediate area around it may become littered with carcases at all stages of dismemberment and decomposition. The amount of cadavers is a fairish index of length of tenure of the residence. Supplies usually arrive at dusk and dawn, and so vulpicides often lie in wait then to shoot the old ones. However, the latter are exceedingly wary and, taking the most circuitous routes, approach by stealth, undetected. Besides, like all the dog family, the fox has an extremely good nose and can detect any enemies up-wind.

Any sort of human disturbance will have one inevitable result—the cubs will

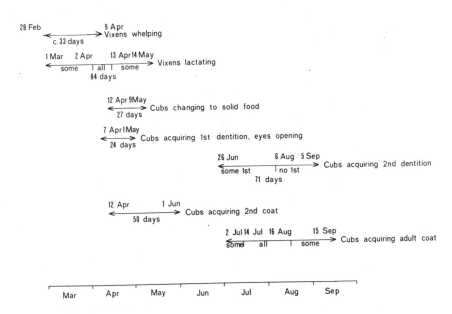

Fig. 37 *Times and durations of the various stages in the development of fox cubs in Northern Ireland.*

117

be removed to a new earth for certain. It is quite possible that they may be moved occasionally anyway and one can easily think of advantages to be derived from regular flitting. For example the parents may strike a particularly favourable hunting ground and shift the family to be nearer it. This is, of course, mere speculation. Stringer comments that ' . . . if they find the least annoyance at the earth where the cubs are, they will infallibly remove them the night following' and even walking by the mouth of a burrow is sufficient to precipitate matters. I am convinced that in some cases one of the parents, hidden in cover close at hand, may actually see the interfering human. This has been put to me by hunters on more than one occasion, and I was once in company with two in early summer, digging at an earth, when it was suddenly realized that a fox was sitting on a dry-stone wall close by, watching their exertions. In the flurry of dropped spades and grabbing for guns, the onlooker made good its escape. Even when the vixen is shot, the dog will continue caring for the litter.

A quite unexpected phenomenon, described to me more than once, is that of two litters being raised together in the same home. Such 'communal denning' is well attested for the American red fox and has been reported in Devonshire too.[121] I was only fortunate enough to come across it once. As one of the litters was quite obviously a few weeks older that the other, going on size and coat colour, there was no doubt in my mind that there were indeed two families in the earth.

Reported independently by a number of hunters, but never heard personally, was a sort of guttural wheezing bark, used by a parent to summon the cubs or send them below ground. The cubs themselves are quite vocal and yelp, whine and 'wuffle'. I have even heard a pet make a sort of whinnying sound.

The keeping of cubs as pets is not recommended. They usually form no attachment, except to the person who feeds them, and grow wilder as summer progresses. They are not to be house-trained, which, considering the state of some earths, is hardly surprising. Neither do they appreciate correction and tend to vindictiveness. The only truly tame fox I ever saw was a full-grown male in England, but that one had 'had the operation'.

It is probable that the dog and vixen take their family hunting but, by mid-June, some of the young are operating on their own account, and by the middle of July all are fending for themselves. Onwards from mid-June too, the litters begin to split up although, even in August, four or five young may still be found together.

During the summer adults spend their time almost entirely above ground, lying up in the greatly increased cover available during the day, and hunting at night. From mid-July the young too begin to live more or less permanently out of the earths and by August few foxes are to be found below ground. All are also more strictly nocturnal than earlier in the season. The cubs will, however, still go to ground if attacked. Until October the young are more likely to be killed by hunters for this reason, because of their aforementioned inability to use cover to best advantage and, of course, because there are more of them.

Arthur Stringer, over two and a half centuries ago, was aware of the content of most of these last passages, and I make no excuses for quoting him at length.

When the cubs come to be three months old they begin to go abroad from the hole to seek prey, but on the least disturbance will run straight to the hole: when they are four months old, they begin to lie in rank fields of corn, or thickets of bushes, or such covert as is near them, to prey on any thing they can find for their purpose; and commonly in the month of August or September they leave their hole clearly, and then the old ones forsake them, and they are upon their own shifts to prey for themselves. It is certain that the dog doth provide prey for the cubs when young as well as the bitch; for if you find the earth or hole where the litter of cubs are and sit with your gun in the evening, you will be apt to kill the bitch first, but in a night or two (if the dog doth not remove the cubs) you will be sure to meet him; for though he doth not bring the prey to the very hole as the bitch doth (unless when the cubs are but two or three days old . . . yet he will not fail to bring his prey to some place near the hole, whence the bitch bringeth it to the cubs, or the cubs come out for it themselves . . .

While this account differs from my own in some details, it is an outstanding bit of observation for someone without facilities and working from scratch.

Stringer's statement that the cubs commonly 'leave the hole clearly' in August or September is a profound one, in view of the results I obtained from tagging them. With one exception, they were all tagged from May to July in 1966 and 1967, and there were thirty-seven returns in all. The latter fell into two groups. Of those which were retrieved from May to July of the same year, only one had moved more than 1km, and it had only covered 2.1km. Many were killed in the same area as they were released. The thirty-one killed from August onward, while some had apparently not shifted at all, generally travelled greater distances. The records were 19.7km, 30.7km, 37.1km and about 58km (36 miles), measured as the crow flies. The last, a minimum estimate, was from Ballynure, Co. Antrim, to Stewartstown, Co. Tyrone, and naturally assumes the wanderer did not swim Lough Neagh! Tagging studies in Europe, especially Denmark, and the U.S.A.[125] have produced quite comparable results for both cubs and adults. It is plain that a sizeable proportion of the young on dispersion move great distances before settling down to a restricted adult range. They 'leave the hole clearly' in no uncertain way. Such facts show that localized fox control must be carried out every year if it is to have any chance of success.

From late September to the end of the year, foxes are increasingly to be found at earth. The factors responsible are most likely the reduction in cover and the onset of colder weather. Certainly more kills seem to be made by hunters during a severe frost or snow-fall. Still, there always seem to be some animals resting above ground, and a fox will actually lie down in snow. In autumn foxes are mainly solitary and pairs are not noticeable until December. Just the same, hunters will occasionally bolt a brace from an earth in October and November, though not necessarily of opposite sexes. The ease with which foxes may be killed and the number of hunters killing them does not change much in the short-term, and so the total bounties paid annually gives a fairish index of fox numbers. As the figure changes comparatively little from year to year, we may assume that the population, in the end, does not increase or decrease much from one year to the next. Since the number of foxes is triplicated each spring, two-thirds of all foxes die one way or another to maintain a steady population. Infant mortality one might suspect of being high. It is therefore unfortunate that for much of the year it is not possible to monitor the ratio of cubs to adults in the population as a whole by reference to samples of the foxes killed by hunters. The reason is that, as mentioned above, cubs are much more easily killed. By October, however, young and old are normally outwardly indistinguishable, and have about equal chances of being shot. While one cannot then tell the difference between the males of different generations with any certainty, it is possible to distinguish the young females from the old ones by an examination of the reproductive tract.

At the end of the umbilical cord of an unborn mammal is a flattened pad, the placenta, which attaches the embryo to the wall of the uterus. After birth, the placenta leaves a scar. The scars in vixens are quite plain, heavily pigmented, and persist right up to the following January, when they fade at the beginning of the mating season. If, therefore, one looks at the uterus of a vixen up to early January, one can be sure that scars signify an old fox, and the lack of them in most cases (for less than 10% of vixens do not breed) a young one. Using such criteria and allowing for barren vixens, it was found that, from October until the scars disappear, consistently half of the females were young animals.[70] Since the sex ratio at birth is unity and is the same in the adult population, there is every justification for assuming the same fraction of young among dog foxes.

These facts are of great interest. For it follows that, from one whelping season to another, one out of every two adults die, and three out of every four cubs. One can further deduce that few foxes live more than four years, for theoretically half the population will consist of individuals of one year old or more, a quarter two years old or more, and so on. Another startling deduction is that, if the population is indeed equally divided into young and old in October, even if all of the adults survived the summer, half of the cubs must die during it. So, over the first six months of life, there is massive infant mortality, much more than half of the young dying by autumn.

What causes this high death rate amongst the young? It cannot be due to aggression within the species. The parents are especially solicitous of their children's welfare and foxes are remarkable tolerant of each other over most of the year. It is not primarily caused by their slaughter by man, extensive though it is. This, I admit to be a bald statement, and those who demand corroborative data must consult the original paper.[67] Briefly the conclusion is supported by various statistical treatments of the bounty figures, and by the simpler fact that the temporary suspension of the bounty in some counties does not seem to have had any beneficial effect on the population. Moreover, it is an astonishing coincidence if the numbers killed by man are *just* holding the population steady and not diminishing it or allowing it to increase. Further evidence comes from the tagging studies and, last of all, from the cold fact that fox-bounties have never worked anywhere else. Although on less firm ground, I do not believe that deaths from starvation are important. But this discussion I will leave to the next chapter.

It is my opinion (and I might be wrong) that infant mortality is mainly due to disease and to parasites.[143,173] During my research into this aspect of fox biology, I was fortunate in having the cooperation of Dr J.G. Ross and Dr W.J. McCaughey of the Northern Ireland Veterinary Research Division, who, in fact, did most of the work.

Of some importance is a disease known as leptospirosis, which often results in severe jaundice or kidney damage. It is caused by bacteria, and is better known as Weil's disease or spirochaetal jaundice. It is usually thought of in association with rats and is, on rare occasions, transmitted to man, where it can prove fatal. Foxes could pick it up by eating rodent carriers, or one fox might become infected through contamination with the urine of another.

We found seven species of parasitic worm in foxes' intestines. Four were tapeworms, occurring infrequently, and they are of little significance. Of the remaining three, two were roundworms and the other a hookworm. All three were common and sometimes constituted a heavy internal burden. In such large numbers they are very probably a serious danger to cubs, if one can expect effects comparable to those on puppies. The worms' eggs pass out with the droppings. To develop further those of the roundworms must be swallowed by another fox, and this is no doubt aided by the fox's slovenly habits, allowing contamination of its food. The eggs of the hookworm, on the other hand, hatch outside the body and

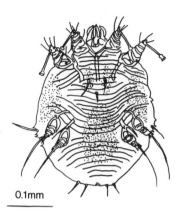

0.1mm

Fig. 38   Mange mite (Sarcoptes scabiei).

the larvae, which are highly susceptible to death from drying out, can penetrate the skin directly.

The mode of transference of the worms, and possibly of leptospirosis, is such that the denser the fox population, the better the chance of their spread. It is quite possible, therefore, that the more foxes there are, the greater the number of deaths from disease. In other words there may be a kind of negative feedback which tends to maintain the population roughly constant.

One other pathogen must be mentioned which, if not a serious debilitating factor in cubs, is a major source of discomfort, misery and death to the adults. This is mange, or scabies. Mange can infect other mammals, including man, but its association with foxes has been known for a long time: Dr Samuel Johnson's *Dictionary* lists *fox evil* as a disease in which the hair falls out. Mange is caused by a tiny mite, less than half a mm long (Fig. 38), by name *Sarcoptes scabiei,* which is picked up by close contact with an infected fox. Again, a dense fox population facilitates its spread. The female mite bores into the skin and lays eggs, giving rise to a second generation of mites which, in turn, reproduces to augment the numbers further. The burrows made by the parasites become inflamed and cause an overwhelming itch. Further damage is then done through the repeated scratching by the tormented host, which removes the hair and breaks the skin, often allowing secondary infections of one kind or another. Foxes with severe scabies are barely recognisable and a pitiful sight, almost hairless, covered with encrustations and scabs, and accompanied by a characteristic offensive smell. Such individuals lose weight, become moribund and eventually die, though there is evidence of recovery in lighter infections. A tenth of all the adults I saw, and a few cubs, were at least partly mangy. The actual fraction is higher, for such foxes are frequently, as already stated, disinclined to bolt, and are therefore not shot as often as healthy individuals. Moreover, as hunters were understandably reluctant to handle advanced cases, some of these, which I would have had if in good health, never reached me.

The north-eastern fox, though murdered and beset by pestilence, is still singularly successful, and this is in no small measure due to its dietary proclivities and sagacity in pursuing them. The fox is a gastronomic opportunist, and fulfils this role with a panache one cannot but admire. This I will endeavour to show in the next chapter.

8 ... and his Bill of Fare

When the fox turns preacher, the geese had better not go to night meetin's.

Sam Slick's Wise Saws and Modern Instances   T.C. Haliburton

The form and arrangement of the fox's teeth (Fig. 39), and of members of the dog tribe in general, have much in common with those of other flesh-eaters. The canines are large and the cheek teeth specialised for shearing, in other words for slicing up meat which is then 'wolfed' in chunks. There is none of the lateral action that is so demonstrably necessary when a cow or horse is grinding up its tough vegetable food. But whereas in the stoat and the domestic cat the teeth are adapted to a diet almost entirely of flesh, those of the dog family are not. The last pair of teeth on each side of both upper and lower jaws are flattened, bespeaking a more flexible regimen. Blackbacked jackals (*Canis mesomelas*), for example, have become a pest in parts of South Africa through their depredations on pineapples.[51]

Other features of the skull also relate to food and food-finding. The large cranium indicates a sizeable brain, pointing to the degree of intelligence which might be exercised in securing a dinner. The ridges on the cranium, one dividing it in half along the top lengthwise and the other at right-angles to it along the back edge, serve as anchorages for powerful jaw muscles. The long muzzle houses a capacious nasal cavity in which are situated the extensive, complex and delicate scroll bones, associated with a remarkable sense of smell, common to the dog family. This is in marked contrast to the foreshortened muzzle of the cat, with its

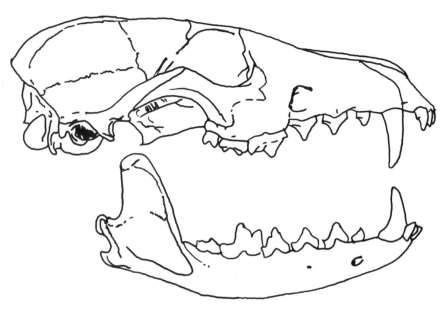

Fig. 39   Skull of fox.

122

relatively poor powers of scent. The fox has also keen hearing and the eyes face forward, giving it binocular vision. With few enemies besides man, sight is used primarily to look for food. Although binocular vision improves the quality of sight, the field of view is narrowed. This differs from that of, say, a mouse or rabbit which, with eyes at the sides of its head, has what approaches all-round visibility. But the latter is of much more importance to the hunted than to a hunter.

The food of the fox can be investigated, like that of other mammals, in four ways. First, one can observe it eating. This is not altogether satisfactory as foxes naturally disappear as soon as they are aware of man's presence. For this and other reasons it is also very time consuming. Nevertheless, the fox is common, quite large and there has been a fair amount of observation on its hunting habits. Other problems arise in assessing the foods quantitatively and in the definite possibility of not seeing it eat particular victuals. This is mostly true of smaller items, which one may never get close enough to identify.

A second approach is to look for remains of the food eaten. This may again take up considerable time and is thus impractical over much of the year. Furthermore, the results will always be incomplete. There will be no leftovers, for instance, from small prey, eaten whole.

Probably the most satisfactory method is the analysis of stomach contents. Sadly, this involves killing the owner of the stomach, but when I was researching, thousands of foxes were being slaughtered anyway and it was merely a question of tapping the supply. If an animal is killed shortly after its final meal, the food in the stomach will be quite easy to identify. Should it be dispatched later, the more digestible foods will be missing and a false impression may be gained. There is, however, comparatively little that the fox eats which does not leave some trace. Stomach contents are particularly suitable in a quantitative approach.

Finally, one can unscramble the fox's droppings. In such work they are usually referred to as 'scats', presumably because of the imprecise nature of the word 'droppings', and because other synonyms are not in polite usage. Unfortunately there is no evidence in scats of foods entirely broken down in the animal's gut; in the case of foxes, as already stated, this is not a major hindrance. A more serious objection, from a quantitative point of view, is that those items which contain a large proportion of indigestible matter, will bulk proportionately larger in the droppings. In fact a refined technique for correcting this has been developed from feeding experiments at the Edinburgh Zoo.[139]

I propose to look at the fox's bill of fare using results obtained from all four sources.

The fox's dealings with rabbits are a recurrent theme in many a nursery story and, when available, they are the single most important prey. The methods employed are well documented, and some of my fox-hunting acquaintances were aware of them from personal experience. I should, in honesty, state that I have never witnessed any of them, except on film. An adult rabbit is secured by a sudden, head-long charge, in which it is caught off guard. Beforehand the fox will make use of any cover available to narrow the distance, waiting until it judges the situation to be to its best advantage. The approach is therefore cat-like, as is the crouching and repositioning of the feet as it gathers itself for the rush. The similarity of behaviour of fox and cat was remarked to me more than once by hunters. A variation of the above is reminiscent of the stoat. The fox shows itself to a colony of bunnies, and, while a few of them may bolt, the bolder ones watch it, some of them sitting up on their hind legs for a better view. Meanwhile their adversary indulges in seemingly aimless activity, rolling about, playing with its brush or trotting in a circle. The fox seems simply to be amusing itself and to have no apparent designs on the on-lookers at all. But once they are reassured and begin feeding again, the wily beast is upon them instantly and has, as like as not, caught one. A variation was recorded on film in the New Forest by Mr Eric Ashby and was televised some years ago. In it a fox trots along mobbed by two lapwings (*Vanellus vanellus*) which, one would expect, would hold its attention. It draws level with a silly rabbit a few m away. With no warning, in a split second, it is on the rabbit and has killed it.

By far the most serious depredations are on young rabbits, sometimes at a very early age. While a doe rabbit may rest in the main tunnel complex of the warren, she often excavates a special short, blindly-ending 'stop' or 'scab' at some distance from it. At the bottom she makes a nest of dried grass and moss, lined with fur plucked from her own body. After the young are born she visits the stop to suckle them, usually at night, and seals the entrance with earth when leaving. Presumably this is to protect her litter from the infanticidal tendencies of the bucks. In any event, the arrangement suits the fox, which is adept at digging directly down to the nest, after apparently pin-pointing its position by ear. Before starting, some foxes have been observed with their heads cocked to one side, listening for activity below. In Finland, Dr. H. Osterholm made a special study of the operation with captive animals.[164] He concluded that both hearing and smell were used. As digging was in progress loud 'snufflings' were audible, suggesting maximum use of the powers of scent. Every so often the excavations were interrupted and the fox jumped in the air. This curious behaviour was not mere exuberance, but probably caused sufficient vibration to frighten the prey into activity, and thus make them betray their position.

Rabbits breed at a sufficiently high rate to render the predation of the fox of no long-term effect, that is if the bunnies are sufficiently plentiful. The same may not be true after an outbreak of myxomatosis. The main evidence for this comes from Australia, where a great deal of research has been done on the disease.[96] After the usual abrupt reduction in numbers, those rabbits in fenced experimental areas bred up to high densities fairly quickly. But the populations in the surrounding countryside stayed low. The sole mortality factor from which the animals in the enclosures were protected was predation, and it seemed certain that it was preventing a swift resurgence in density outside. The scientists inferred that feral cats and, especially, foxes were responsible. So foxes were probably controlling numbers at low density. Predation was likened to a poor hand-brake on a motor car, which prevents it from moving on a gentle slope, but becomes progressively less effective as the car starts moving and gains momentum. Taking into consideration the proverbial fecundity of the rabbit and its failure to recolonize with any rapidity after its numbers had been reduced in the British Isles, it is arguable that something similar was happening. If foxes thus assist in keeping numbers down for some time after an outbreak of the disease, it is to man's benefit. The rabbit is, on balance, indisputably a pest.

Foxes may stalk hares and birds in much the same way as rabbits. Mr McAvoy mentioned to me that he had once seen a hare watching, with rapt attention, a fox repeatedly rolling off a tree stump. Foxes will also leap into the air after birds and have splendid opportunities for this while being mobbed. A sitting bird, superfluous to state, is just that.

The killing of poultry and lambs are perhaps, from man's point of view, the blackest stains on the fox's escutcheon.[68] There is no question about it, foxes take all manner of unhoused domestic fowl, though with most economic egg-production now under cover it is less of a scourge than formerly. Although attacks on poultry are usually at night, I heard of many undertaken in daylight, often at dawn or dusk. I was sometimes able to view the battlefield after the action and, in one instance, no fewer than twelve hens had been dealt with in a single night. The farmer in question suffered repeated visits and two dozen birds were lost before the raider was shot. Although I have never seen it, I am sure that, should Reynard succeed in entering a hen-house, he would give a very good account of himself. Foxes are wantonly destructive and typically kill far more fowl than they carry off. I am tempted to think that having hens fluttering and squawking all around excites and encourages the marauder in prolonging the slaughter. Injuries are characteristic: either the head is bitten off the bird or a patch of feathers is missing from the head-end, the skin exposed bearing the marks of the assassin's canine teeth. The victims are probably dispatched with a shake and the action must be brief to allow the fox to kill so many birds in a short time. All of this applies to the rearing of game birds, and should a fox force its way into a pen of pheasant (*Phasianus colchinus*) poults, it may kill the lot before leaving. Gamekeepers in time past who had to stock pheasants and preserve foxes for hunting at the same time had an unenviable task. The attacker may return several times to the same farm, killing whatever he can each time. As foxes have set runs, they will likely begin to include a suitable farmyard on their itinerary once it has been located. Simultaneous raids by more than one animal have been reported. Nearly all the complaints I received of the latter were for May, June and July, which rather suggests family parties, possibly examples of parents giving their offspring a sound practical training.

There is an ancient myth to the effect that a fox will swing a murdered cock or goose over his back to carry it off. While fox-hunters scorn the idea, it is still believed in some quarters. It was mentioned by Chaucer in his *Nun's Priest's Tale* and there are many examples in medieval drawing and church carving. The subject is eruditely covered in Dr Kenneth Varty's *Reynard the Fox* (1967), which contains many amusing illustrations of carvings depicting foxes preaching to geese, going on pilgrimage or playing bagpipes etc.

Caching of food is a common occurrence and a mutilated hen, found buried, is to be suspected as the work of a fox. The bone-burying habit of dogs is a close parallel.

The question of predation on lambs and sheep is a knottier problem. I never met a hunter or farmer who knew of foxes killing adult sheep and, in fact, never came across any evidence of it at all. As farmers give Reynard a bad name, if there was any hint of it, it would hardly be kept secret. I have only come across one account in the literature of sheep-killing in Britain which was sufficiently documented by a reliable authority to be believed.[121] The deaths of adult sheep due to foxes are negligible.

A great deal of alleged lamb-killing is based on insufficient or even non-existent evidence. When interviewing farmers I found that, in some cases, a dead, unwounded animal or the mere disappearance of a lamb were attributed to the work of a fox. Unfortunately, actual attacks are rarely seen. As will be shown from the analyses of stomach contents, foxes will eat ovine carrion, and as they are fond of garbage from dustbins and refuse tips, it would be surprising if dead lambs and afterbirths were ignored. As dead lambs are not normally burned or buried in Ulster, lambing fields are frequently a good place for an opportunist like the fox to scrounge a meal. Remains at earths cannot, therefore, be taken as corroboration of killing, and neither can bodies with marks of feeding. To be certain a post-mortem must be undertaken to determine the cause of death.

In Australia, where the fox has been introduced, its effects on sheep-farming have received much scientific study. Post mortem examination has revealed that only a small fraction of the dead lambs mutilated by foxes are killed by them.[43,145] In South Australia intensive observations were made from a hide on the activities of foxes among a flock of Merino ewes.[4] These showed that the chief interest of the foxes was in carrion, and that some of them were actually intimidated by the ewes and even the lambs. However, one deliberate, unhesitating attack was witnessed, the fox killing a lamb and feeding upon it for about an hour. The conclusions drawn were that most foxes are merely scavengers, a few individuals doing most of the killing.

The injuries noted in Australia are similar to those observed in Britain and N. Ireland—crushed skulls, removal of jaws and heads, bitten throats and, less commonly, body wounds and the removal of tails. Direct comparison of predation on lambs in Australia with that in the British Isles is not entirely permissible since the breeds of sheep differ and the predator and prey do not breed concurrently, and thus the nutritional needs of the fox may not be as great. Just the same, it does not seem unreasonable to infer that many lambs in Ireland would suffer mutilation *after* death. It is, too, the opinion of many fox hunters that the damage is done by a few rogue individuals which (it has been suggested) acquire the trait through having been weaned on mutton. On the other hand the habit may be acquired much in the same way as a cat becomes a rabbiter or specializes on birds. It is interesting that on the Ravenglass Nature Reserve in England, where several foxes are known to live,[138] black-headed gulls (*Larus ridibundus*) were being killed on their nests. The killing of just one fox (apparently recognised by its peculiar footprint) caused the damage to cease, a clear instance of a peculiar dietary specialization.

Reliable data on lamb-killing I found difficult to accumulate, for one must have fresh bodies for a satisfactory post-mortem. In the end I only obtained two which had been made away with by foxes.[68] One had been savaged around the neck. The other had a cut in the throat, the tongue missing, and the skull and brain were penetrated. Their examination at the Northern Ireland Veterinary Research Laboratories showed them to be otherwise perfectly healthy. My overall conclusions were that while some lambs are slain by odd foxes with a taste for that sort of thing, the bulk of mutton devoured was mutton before the foxes set to work on it.

The fox's leavings can be quite illuminating. Over most of the year one must be content with the occasional scattering of fur or feathers, though sometimes one will find a fresh kill, perhaps a half-eaten hen lying far from the nearest hen-run. During spring and summer, however, the remnants at burrows are often exceedingly informative, and such material is around from the time vixens go to their confinement. One vixen in advanced pregnancy I saw dug out from an earth on Island Magee, Co. Antrim, had provisions in the shape of a complete fowl, a pullet and half a rabbit. On another occasion a terrier reappeared from old mine workings which foxes had been using at Glenariffe, in the same county, carrying a sheep's foot. The hunter I was with remarked that to him (the terrier) it was like a Paris bun, which is a delicacy regrettably confined to the north of Ireland.

Incidental to other field work, I was able to list the remains of food brought to cubs at twenty-three earths. Most of these I visited in company with hunters, for several of the tenants were believed to have taken poultry or game birds. Thus the latter items are probably better represented than is usual. There was often some uncertainty as to numbers of prey as much of the material was in pieces and in an

advanced state of putrefaction.
1. Feathers
2. Feathers and rabbits
3. Feathers, probably of hens
4. Numerous remains of rats
5. Turkey feathers and a turkey wing
6. Feathers
7. Poultry feathers and remains of rabbits
8. Two rabbits, a rat, and numerous feathers, some of pigeons (*Columba palumbus*) and others probably from hens
9. Wing and feathers of a magpie and a young hare
10. Poultry feathers
11. Wing of a hen pheasant and pigeon feathers
12. Fur from a rabbit or hare
13. Poultry and pheasant feathers
14. Young hares (possibly two), two or three rabbits, magpie and pheasant feathers, at least one rat
15. Feathers
16. A complete hen's leg, rats and rabbit or hare fur
17. Poultry feathers
18. Feathers
19. A pigeon and part of a hen pheasant
20. Remains of young hares and poultry feathers
21. An almost complete hen and remains of rabbits
22. Two young hares
23. Feathers

This list gives quite an insight into the larger prey. Rabbits, immature hares and rats are all common foods. So are poultry and game birds (though the bias here must be re-emphasized), magpies and pigeons. Young hares would probably present no more problem than rabbits and, when small enough to be confined to the form, are easy pickings. The magpies are no surprise either and put themselves at risk when flying down on a fox to scold it.

The most comprehensive picture of the fox's menu emerges from what was found in the stomachs, but before discussing the findings it may be of interest to readers to hear something of the techniques involved. Each stomach was removed, cut open and its contents washed with a little detergent on a sheet of perforated zinc. (Sieves are not recommended. Hair becomes entangled around the mesh, makes cleaning difficult and may contaminate following samples.) The washed material was then spread out and sorted on a white tray.

The mammals consumed can sometimes be established from bone fragments and nearly always from teeth, when they are present. Drawings of some of the teeth one is likely to come across are shown in Fig. 34. Feet and tails were sometimes swallowed and one can often deduce their owners almost immediately. Hair is in many cases easily recognised, notably the coarse pelage of rats, the soft buffy-brown, black-tipped guard hairs of rabbits and hares, and wool. Nevertheless, óne cannot always identify it confidently with the naked eye and sections were frequently cut, the nature of which must now be explained.

A single hair can sometimes be identified to some extent by its colouring, length and outline, but a positive determination usually requires the consideration of other points. The outer covering of a hair is scaly and the scales form distinctive patterns of several kinds, and these often provide a valuable clue as to the identity

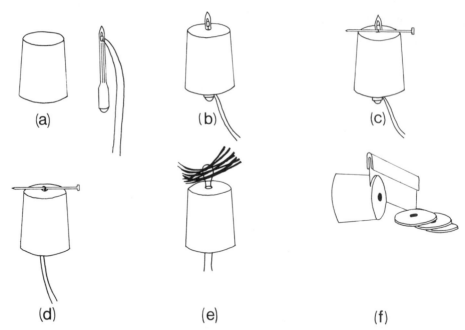

Fig. 40   A simple method of cutting cross-sections of hair. (a) Cork and threaded sewing-
machine needle. (b) The needle is pushed through the cork. (c) A pin is inserted
through the loop of thread passing through the eye of the needle. (d) The needle
is withdrawn leaving the thread secured in place by the pin. (e) The pin is removed
and a sample of hair placed in the loop of thread. It is then drawn into the cork
by pulling the threads at the opposite end. (f) Sections are cut with a razor blade.

of the species concerned. Under the microscope the surface of the hair itself is not
easy to view, because it is opaque and usually darkly coloured. However, an impression of the surface can be made on a warm smear of gelatine solution on a glass slide
and, after the gelatine has dried and the hair stripped off, it shows the form of the
scales quite plainly.

    A cross-section of a guard hair is particularly useful and the details often quite
characteristic. Because the number of mammalian species in Ireland is so small, a
section alone was sufficient to identify the hair of any wild mammal the fox is likely
to eat in Northern Ireland. In fact I never needed to study scale patterns.

    The cutting of cross-sections can be carried out in several ways. Forensic labora-
tories use an instrument known as a Hardy microtome, and textile manufacturers
have gadgets for sectioning fibres which will do just as well for hair. The most primitive procedure, set out in Fig. 40, involves the use of a cork, a sewing-machine needle,
a pin, a length of thread and a razor blade. With practice it works well. Drawings of
some representative sections prepared in this way are shown in Fig. 41.

    Unfortunately it is not possible to distinguish between the fur of rabbits and
that of hares with any certainty. While there are distinct differences in the skulls,
it is not feasible to look for these for the skull is invariably crushed, assuming that
the fox even eats it. As leverets (young hares) are eaten, one cannot go on relative
bone-lengths either.

    Bird remains present a different problem. There is rarely anything diagnostic

0.1 mm

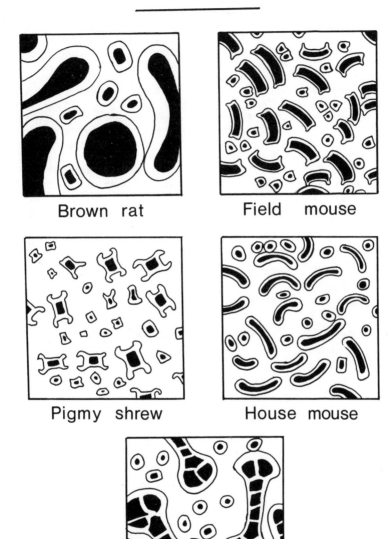

Brown rat   Field   mouse

Pigmy   shrew   House   mouse

Rabbit

Fig. 41   *Cross-sections of the hair of some Irish mammals (to scale).*

about the bits of their bones and so feathers present the best clues. The intricate structure of an intact feather enables the specialist to deduce the species of its owner with a high degree of accuracy. By the time it is recovered from a fox's stomach, it has not only been broken, but much of the fine structure has been digested. Nevertheless one can often still tell the Order to which the bird belongs from the *downy barbules*[34]—an Order being a major grouping. It is plain to the unaided eye that the vane on each side of a feather is made up of a series of narrow parallel strips or *barbs*, running out at an angle from the quill, each united to those on either side of it. The barbs are linked together because each has a series of fine branches or *barbules* on either side which interlock with those on adjoining barbs. At the base of the quill are a number of free barbs which closely resemble down, and it need hardly be said that their barbules are also free. These downy barbules are studded along their length with swellings or *nodes*, and the size, shape and spacing of the nodes are characteristic in most bird Orders in Ireland. Furthermore they will withstand considerable exposure to the juices secreted by the fox's stomach. Typical arrangements are shown in Fig. 42. All that needs to be done to determine the Order

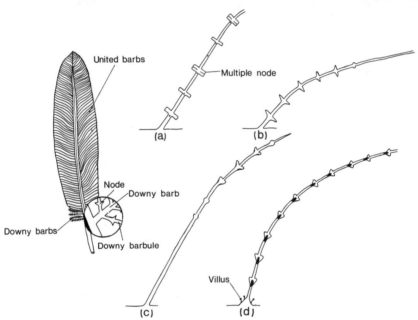

Fig. 42   *The structure and arrangement of the downy barbules on the feathers of some birds. Shown on the left is the position of the downy barbules on a flight feather. On the right are downy barbules from various avian Orders. Note the shape of the nodes in each case. (a) Order Galliniformes (poultry and game birds). The presence of multiple nodes is characteristic, and they may be composed of up to five individual nodes. (b) Order Columbiformes (pigeons). Nodes are often confined to the base of the barbules. (c) Order Anseriformes (ducks and geese). The nodes are heart-shaped and occur only at the tip of the barbule. (d) Order Passeriformes. Note the large pigment spot at each node and the villi at the base of the barbule. The downy barbules of the Order Charadriiformes (waders) are similar but lack villi.*

to which the feather's owner belongs is to cut off some downy barbs close to the quill and view them in water under a microscope. (The preparation is greatly improved by first washing in xylene and viewing in 70% alcohol if these are available.)

These techniques can also be applicable to droppings, which must be dried and broken up for analysis, but the downy barbules are frequently too damaged to permit identification.

All of the fox bodies I received were accompanied by a note of where and why they were killed. This allowed me to assess the influence on the final results of those animals shot for alleged depredations on livestock, and I was also thus aware of the sort of terrain over which foxes had been hunting. The foxes studied were all killed between February 1966 and March 1968. Of the stomachs I opened, those of 340 adults and 163 cubs contained food. For the purposes of the study the cubs were considered to be adults from the October after their birth. The frequencies with which the chief foods occurred are shown in Table VII. Thirty-six of the adults were supposed to have been killing sheep and, of these, 42% contained sheep remains, as opposed to 5% of the remainder. Of the forty-three alleged to have been taking domestic fowl, 30% had poultry remains in their stomachs, as compared with 14% of the others. There is, therefore, a slight bias in the overall results in favour of sheep and poultry.

Enlarging on the table, it may be added that many of the rabbits, and especially the rats, I judged to be immature, and it is likely that a full-grown rat presents a sufficiently tricky proposition to foxes for them to concentrate on smaller ones. In November 1966 and December 1967 over half the foxes examined contained rat remains, suggesting a regular abundance of rats in late autumn. Readers will recall a comparable peak in the consumption of rats by the long-eared owl at about the same time of year (Chapter 6) and the underlying causes are likely the same in both cases.

Field mice, though plentiful over most of the countryside, are not caught as often as one might expect, probably due to their deep burrowing habits and leaping abilities. Often it is no doubt a case of too much effort for too little reward to the fox.

Sheep are chiefly a seasonal food source, mostly in winter and spring, corresponding roughly to lambing time which extends, with negligible exceptions, from January to May. The earliest births are on low or sheltered ground and hill sheep reproduce last. Altogether thirty-eight foxes, both adults and cubs, I dissected had been eating sheep. Seven of these were killed outside the lambing season, and so the material eaten must have been carrion. Of the fifteen from January to March, eight were from high ground or sea cliffs where lambing had not begun, and these foxes too must be considered carrion-feeders. Last of all, two foxes killed on lambing grounds contained afterbirths, an unequivocal sign of scavenging. As mentioned earlier, a great deal of the mutton eaten is mutton through no agency of the fox.

As well as the mammalian food listed in the table, pieces of what was probably a small dog were discovered in one stomach, and the foot and part of the leg of, most likely, a kid in another. Pig's bristles were retrieved from the insides of four foxes as well. These remains probably indicate feeding from corpses too. Sir Harry Johnson in his *British Mammals* (1903) mentioned the inhabitants of Achill Island, Co. Mayo, complaining of the audacity of local foxes, which they accused of stealing geese, fowls, lambs and young pigs. One must take such anecdotes with a grain of salt. Presumably if piglets were kept in the open in large numbers it is not inconceivable that some fox might acquire a liking for them, but this is the

131

veriest conjecture. Much in the same category is the insistence by one of my correspondents that, 'If something is not done about foxes, they will eat all the young pigs'.

Part of a cat had been the final meal of one vixen which I saw bolted and shot. A partly-eaten, freshly-killed cat of the same ginger colour lay at the entrance of her earth. It seems to be widely acknowledged that foxes will kill cats though, judging by my own results and field-experience, this cannot happen often. The idea seems to have caught the rural imagination and, to hear a few countryfolk, one would think that foxes had a vendetta of long standing against the race of cats. A quite different suggestion is that the fox's overriding interest in pussy's remains is to roll on them, much in the way in which dogs delight in doing so on most things unspeakable and evil-smelling. There is also a notion that a dead cat is an infallible bait for foxes. I do not feel qualified to comment on any of these hypotheses.

Surprisingly, there was no evidence, in the stomachs, of shrews, house mice, squirrels or hedgehogs. As mentioned in Chapter 4, shrews possess scent glands which make them repellent to many potential mammalian predators. Some mammals may kill them, but apparently they rarely eat them. Predacious birds, on the other hand, have little sense of smell and some feed on them regularly. The unusual smell of house mice may also discourage the fox which should have ample opportunity to catch them in hedgerows, as they lack the agility of field mice. Squirrels are uncommon and localized in north-east Ireland, are arboreal and presumably rarely encountered by foxes. The absence of hedgehogs, on the other hand, is surprising for in Britain five turned up in the analysis of 420 stomachs.[137] Many natural history books recount how Reynard gets the best of a hedgehog in spite of its prickly shirt of mail, either by a smart bite on the soft underparts before the hedgehog has time to roll up completely, or by dropping it into water, thus forcing it to uncurl. Nevertheless no one reliable will admit to having actually witnessed either technique. The first seems feasible. The second would involve picking up or trundling the enrolled urchin—a painful business.

Fox hair, presumably derived from grooming activities, occurred fairly often in the stomachs, usually in those which were empty or almost empty. In only one case was there actual evidence of cannibalism.

Fortunately all the representatives of the avian Order Galliniformes in Ireland, which are easily identified from their downy barbules, are birds of economic importance: the hen, turkey, grouse (*Lagopus scotius*), pheasant, partridge and quail (*Coturnix coturnix*), the last two being rather scarce. Moreover, all the wild species have a great proportion of their feathers marked with horizontal stripes. One can therefore easily differentiate between remains of poultry and game birds. In only four instances were such banded feathers retrieved. The remainder were either red-brown, white or, less commonly, black, suggesting a high proportion of domestic fowl. While some of this may have been consumed as carrion, I have little doubt that much of it came from birds killed deliberately by the foxes themselves.

Passerine birds (belonging to the Order Passeriformes) include an enormous variety of (mostly) smallish species such as thrushes, sparrows, finches, crows and warblers. Sometimes the foxes had swallowed them whole. Besides the birds listed in Table VII, there were six instances of pigeon, three of ducks and one wader. Egg membranes were also detected thrice. The number of farmers who claimed the loss of ducks and the frequency of pigeon feathers at earths is at variance with the small fraction of stomachs in which remnants of these birds were found. Perhaps the necessary detail on the coarser feathers of the hen survives longer than on the finer plumage of other birds. Much of the latter may have been too far digested to identify and may account for a sizeable fraction of 'unidentified birds' in the table.

Insects were recovered from the stomachs in small numbers from April to September. Most of these were beetles, dor beetles and particularly ground beetles, known in Northern Ireland as 'clocks'. The fox's liking for them is well known among hunters. Other insects, rarely met with, included caterpillars and maggots. Earthworms and slugs were also found occasionally. Both of them, having entirely soft bodies, would be quickly broken down and are probably consumed more often than analyses would seem to indicate. Admittedly the minute bristles or *setae*, with which worms gain a purchase on the ground, are unharmed by gastric juices, but to examine all the washings from stomach contents for these is simply not worth the labour involved.

Grass had been eaten by many foxes in varying quantities. Whilst it might well be swallowed accidentally along with prey, it may be that foxes, like dogs, derive some medicinal benefit from it. Other vegetable matter included dead beech leaves, dock leaves, spruce needles, cereal grains, moss, twigs and blackberries. Fruit is known to be an important seasonal food in some countries and the same is true of some districts in Ireland. I found blackberry seeds in six out of fifteen groups of fox scats collected on the sand dunes at Dundrum, Co. Down, in November 1963.[54] An insight on how fussy Reynard may be about his fruit was given by scientists in south-east Iowa in the U.S.A., who found that while red foxes[182] dined on a range of fruits, they never took them until they were ripe. There are some very ancient references to foxes taking fruit. In the Song of Solomon are mentioned '. . . the little foxes that spoil the vines'. Aesop told of 'The fox and the grapes' and Theocritus alludes to the nuisance of foxes in vineyards. Whether such references are indeed to foxes or to some species of jackal is debatable.

Finally, various oddities found in the stomachs attest to the catholicity of the diet: pebbles, paper, polythene, string and, possibly, bran mash.

It is obvious from Table VII that there are marked discrepancies between the amounts of the various foods consumed by the adults and cubs. These are largely explained by the superior abilities of the adults both in hunting and in digesting prey. In April there were no signs of birds in any of the twenty-three cubs' stomachs containing foods other than milk, which accounts for the overall difference in total birds eaten by young and old. Probably the alimentary tract of cubs recently weaned is not well enough developed to deal with feathers, which are much coarser than fur. Similarly, the higher percentage of passerine birds and the lower one of unidentified birds may simply be because feathers withstand digestion better in cubs than in old foxes, and are therefore identified accurately more often. Experiments in Edinburgh showed that feathers survived better in a twelve-week-old fox than in adults.[139] Nevertheless, passerine fledglings, which would be most readily available in May, June and July, would present a very easily obtainable prey for cubs learning to hunt for themselves.

Having now sketched the fox's bill of fare in some detail, it is of interest to compare Arthur Stringer's thoughts on the subject, which are remarkably accurate.

133

A fox is certainly a very subtle creature, and is very ravenous, and will kill sheep, lambs, fawns, turkeys, geese, hens, ducks, wild or tame, pheasants, partridges, woodcocks, hares, rabbits &c. all of which he takes by policy in creeping under the wind so nigh them, before they can fly or run away that he leaps upon them; they take hares or rabbits, most by lying still till the hare or rabbit comes so near them, that he can reach them; a fox will, when hungry, run after a hare a mile or two, and if she happens to be a leveret, or big with young, or weak, will surely kill her; he preys very much on rats, mice, clocks, snails, small birds, and berries; he will also kill cats if he meets them from the house.

Note, That every fox doth not kill old sheep, but some chance fox that hath found a sheep lying and could not rise, or fast in briars, and yet alive, and by that means I believe the fox to learn to kill sheep, for they seldom do it but in a country where sheep are plenty, and commonly in a barren mountainy country where sheep are small.

I knew a fox in one night to kill nineteen hens and two cocks, which he took out of a roost in a little hen house, and hid them all in ploughed ground under trees, and in bushes within half a mile where he killed them.

A fox when he is too full will vomit it up, and hide it in a hole in ploughed ground, or any place where he scrapes with his feet, and so will cover it, and will find it again when he wants it, as also he will vomit it up to his cubs.

Whether a fox will regurgitate food to its young is not known, and no one else has ever claimed to see it. Just the same, it has been noted in other members of the dog family including the wolf, coyote, jackals and the African hunting dog (*Lycaon pictus*).[52] Stringer may yet be vindicated.

When myxomatosis decimated the rabbit population in Britain, the fox concentrated on its other sources of food, and field voles largely replaced rabbits on its menu.[137] There are no field voles in Ireland. A small investigation of stomach contents and scats I made in 1964 and early 1965[58] in areas where rabbits had been severely reduced by the disease, suggests that rats are the main alternative. Indeed they are a more common item on the diet in Ireland than in England even when rabbits are readily available. Perhaps, with the smaller fields and consequent additional cover in the form of hedgerows, rats are commoner, but they may merely be filling the 'gap' left by field voles in Ireland.

Do many foxes starve to death? I think it improbable. If adults starve it would surely be most likely in wintertime. To check this I examined the entire guts, stomachs and intestines of 203 animals dissected during the winter of 1967-68. Only twenty-two were empty or near empty.[73] As it is known that virtually all food is passed through the gut in two days in captive foxes, one must conclude that 89% of all the animals had had a meal less than forty-eight hours before death. There is no reason to believe that the remaining 11% were consistently without food for longer periods, and foxes should be able to stand several days fast in winter without loss of condition, especially with the fat reserves most of them have. It is my opinion that comparatively few cubs die from this cause either. In May, when all of them are fed by adults, about 40% of their stomachs were found to be empty. The explanation for the high figure is, however, that hunters tend to kill most foxes in the afternoon or evening in summer when, of course, a considerable time may have elapsed since the last meal. Later in the summer, when the young are fending for themselves and presumably lying up in daytime, the 40% level is apparently maintained, suggesting that they are doing fairly well for themselves. While it would be desirable to have more direct evidence of this, what there is indicates that, in general, they hunt sufficiently successfully to provide for their needs.

Finally, there is an intriguing assertion appearing in many writings on the fox and mentioned to me by some hunters. It is often stated that a fox using an earth close to a hen-run may never attack the birds. While there is no proof of this which I would like to accept and some certainly do kill poultry nearby, no less a naturalist than J.E. Harting believed it,[109] and the hunters of my acquaintance were not inclined to whitewash Reynard unnecessarily. That foxes will occupy the same tunnel complex as rabbits is well known and probably the bunnies keep to the tunnels which are too narrow to accommodate their dangerous fellow-lodger. However, it is frequently asserted that they are immune from attack, the fox going further afield to forage. While this, again, seems incredible, so many naturalists have repeated it and, quite independently, hunters remarked upon it, that perhaps there may be something in it. Considering the beast in question, it is difficult to set limits to its sagacity.

Table VII

Percentages of the stomachs of 340 adult foxes and 163 cubs containing various items of food

	ADULTS	CUBS
Rabbits and hares	45	59
Sheep	9	6
Rats	17	16
Field mouse	6	1
Poultry and game birds	16	15
Passerine birds	4	10
Unidentified birds	20	9

9 Irish Mammal Fleas

The butterfly has wings of gold,
The firefly wings of flame,
The little flea has no wings at all,
But he gets there, just the same.

It Ain't Gonna Rain No Mo'   Wendall Hall

The last two lines of the above, not-too-serious verse embody two remark-ably sound observations. For a flea is an insect which, like many of its parasitic allies—lice, louse flies and certain bugs, has lost its powers of flight the better to enjoy a more intimate relationship with its host. The latter term, by the way, is perfectly respectable zoological etymology, even though the host may be an unwilling or even, initially, an unwitting one. That the tormentor 'gets there just the same' is a statement sufficiently profound to make further comment at this juncture unnecessary. It is an animal remarkably capable of reaching its destination.

Fleas form a compact, homogeneous Order of insects known as the Siphonaptera (literally, 'a sucking tube—without wings') or Aphaniptera ('non-apparent—wings') which, because of their characteristic appearance, are practically impossible to confuse with other insects. Certainly zoologists can recognise their diagnostic build instantly, and the layman knows them as the elusive, tiny brown animals which leap so splendidly, if not for the irritation they can in-flict. Some years ago I made an appeal for fleas on television and subsequently received specimens from over 150 people. Only two of the gifts proved to be other insects, a signal tribute to the infamy and distinctive bearing of the flea.

Although there are not more than 100 scientists in the world today with more than a passing interest in fleas, the information on them is quite well documented and collated. This is in large measure due to the late Hon. N.C. Rothschild (1877-1923), son of the first Lord Rothschild. He too was con-cerned in the family banking business but in his spare time his tastes ran to entomology; he specialized on fleas. His collections, writings and enthusiasm gave a decided impetus to twentieth-century siphonapterology and the world flea-fauna is currently being covered in a superb monographic series of volumes based on his material.[116] Research on fleas has been stimulated too by the fact that some species spread disease, though Irish fleas are relatively innocent in this respect. As the vectors of plague, black rat fleas have had a shattering impact on the course of history. Strangely enough, the human flea (*Pulex irritans*—literally 'the irritating flea') has not had a sizeable share of study, probably as nobody, without good cause, will work on a parasite whose main host is man.

Siphonapterists are among the most grateful of all zoologists for specimens and are more ready than most to encourage the amateur. They tolerate the frivolous attitude of the public to their endeavours with a surprising degree of good humour and are noted for their drollery.

Fleas are exclusively associates of warm-blooded animals, the birds and mammals, so Dean Swift's oft-paraphrased verse on them is invalid.

So naturalists observe, a flea
Has smaller fleas that on him prey;
And these have smaller still to bite 'em
And so proceed *ad infinitum*.

In fact they are mammal specialists and hence their inclusion in this book. Of about two thousand forms only 6% are regular parasites of birds and many of these are closely related to species which feed on mammals. Indeed the diversification on to avian hosts probably came fairly late in siphonapteran evolution.

Fleas became parasites of mammals fairly shortly after the latter appeared on the earth, just under 200 million years ago. There are only four fossil fleas known. Two were discovered preserved in Baltic amber dating from 50-60 million years back and the remaining one, and a doubtful second specimen, are from Australia and presumably 110-125 million years old.[186] As all four closely resemble contemporary forms (assuming that they are indeed genuine relics), apparently quite modern fleas had evolved in the short space, geologically speaking, of 60-70 million years.

While adult fleas are entirely committed to a parasitic life, it is well known that they can pass freely from one source of food to another and, unlike lice, can spend long periods away from the host during which they must fast. This time is spent in the living-quarters of the host. In fact they only regularly parasitize animals which have at least a semi-permanent nest, where the insects pass a greater or lesser part of their lives depending on the species; it is here too that the flea grows to maturity. Thus, rodents have fleas but deer do not. Likewise, wild rabbits are usually infested but hares only pick them up occasionally. Monkeys, contrary to popular belief, are not troubled with them but man, who has a permanent 'nest', is.

Thirty-six species of fleas have been recorded in Ireland and of these fourteen are primarily bird parasites. While after the preceding remarks this may seem a large proportion, it must be remembered that, as birds can fly, their associates have much better facilities for dispersal than their earth-bound colleagues. Thus bird fleas tend to be more widespread in their distribution. Furthermore, to put things in perspective, there are ten times as many kinds of birds as there are mammals in Ireland. It is significant that, of the fourteen, half attend the house-martin (*Delichon urbica*) exclusively, a bird the interior of whose mud nest more clearly resembles the environment of a mammal's burrow than that of any other bird which breeds in Ireland.

Fleas vary in size from 1 to 8mm in length, females being usually somewhat larger than the males. Irish mammal fleas range from about 1.5mm up to the gigantic *Hystrichopsylla talpae,* females of which sometimes reach 6mm. Fortunately this monster never attacks man. A typical flea is shown in Fig. 43 and, like all insects, its body is divided into three parts, the head, thorax (bearing three pairs of legs) and abdomen. Each of these is subdivided into a number of segments, though such segmentation is not apparent on the head, and covered with overlapping plates of chitin, a hard nitrogenous substance. The latter material surrounds the otherwise soft bodies of all insects and acts as a stiffening structure, in other words a skeleton. We are used to thinking of animals having an internal skeleton, but insects and many other lesser forms of life carry theirs outside, where it may have an additional protective function. The chitin gives the flea its colour, which varies from almost black to a hue nearly matching that of golden syrup.

The siphonapteran external skeleton or *exoskeleton* is, comparatively speaking, especially stout, smooth and slippery. These features combine in making the insect particularly difficult to hold and to squash. The exoskeleton is covered with numerous bristles which point backwards and outwards at around 45^0 to the surface, and these, besides increasing the slipperiness of the animal, help in general streamlining and in adhering to the coat of the host. They may also facilitate the sense of touch. The flea thus flattened, streamlined and silken-smooth is enabled to glide through the fur of a mammal with consummate ease, the bristles warding off the hairs as the insect slides between them.

Sometimes a series of bristles are flattened and thickened into spines to form a comb. This commonly occurs round the back of the first segment of the thorax, and 80% of fleas possess such a structure there. About half of these also have one around the mouthparts. Some species have a series along the back of the abdomen as well. Combs are not limited to fleas, and other insects parasitic on birds or mammals may have similar accoutrements. There is some argument as to their function, but they are probably to protect vulnerable parts of the body.[186] The comb around the base of mouthparts is almost certainly to prevent damage to them, though it has been suggested that the flea may use it to make room between the hairs of the host in order to feed. The thoracic comb is thought to parry the hairs of the host, thus preventing them from abrading the exposed delicate joint between the first and second segments of the thorax. At this point the majority of lateral body movement takes place, which is so important in allowing the insect to insinuate itself unimpeded through the host's coat. Fleas without a thoracic comb have the joint guarded by a flange of chitin instead, but this does not permit the same degree of flexibility and presumably, in these forms, this is not so important.

Some flea-men have noticed that there is a degree of correlation between the breadth of the spaces in the comb and the diameter of the hairs of the host.

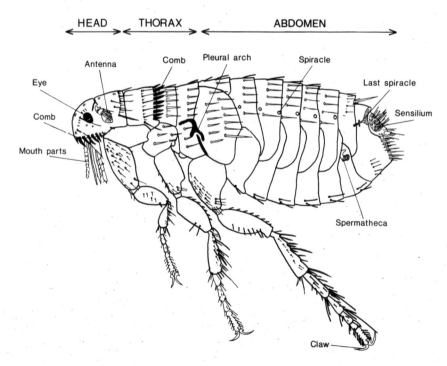

Fig. 43   Dog flea (Ctenocephalides canis) showing the more important features of fleas.

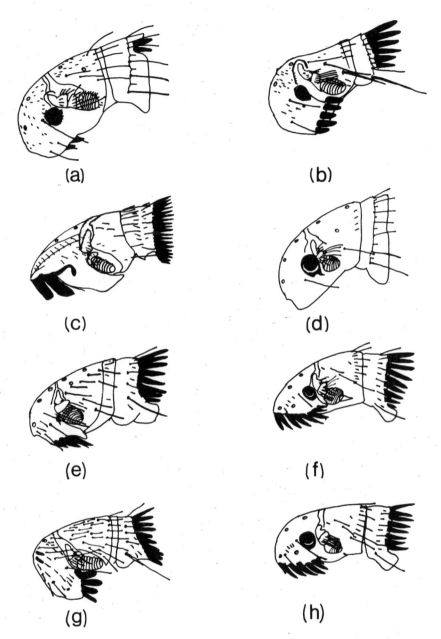

Fig. 44   Heads of (a) Hedgehog flea (Archeopsylla erinacei). (b) Rabbit flea (Spilopsyllus
cuniculi). (c) Bat flea (Ischnopsyllus hexactenus). (d) Human flea (Pulex irritans).
(e) Common field mouse flea (Ctenophthalmus nobilis). (f) Cat flea (Ctenocephalides
felis). (g) House mouse flea (Leptopsylla segnis) (h) Dog flea (Ctenocephalides
canis).

Such entomologists affirm that if the flea were to be dragged backwards through the fur, the hairs would lock into the slots between the teeth. Now it is argued that a mammal trying to dislodge a tormentor is most likely to seize it by the abdomen and attempt to pull it out of its coat backwards. The combs are thus supposed to prevent this, or at least to impede it. In practice there is no evidence that hairs are caught in this way. There is a great deal of variation in their thickness and no one ever seems to have found them sticking through the comb in the suggested manner.

Combs vary considerably in their shape, size, number and in the arrangement of the spines, so they are often useful in distinguishing one species of flea from another. A glance at the 'rogues' gallery' in Fig. 44 will confirm this.

The mouthparts of all insects have a basically similar plan, but they have been transformed in the various subgroups to suit particular modes of feeding. Fleas suck blood and theirs are therefore greatly modified for piercing and sucking, as shown in Fig. 45. The incision is made by two razor-sharp stylets or blades which are serrated, especially at their tips. These close on a central *epipharynx* to form a tube or food canal through which the blood is drawn up.

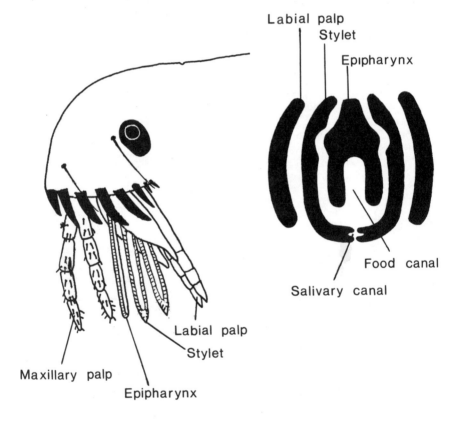

Fig. 45   Mouth parts of a flea.

The composite structure is sunk through the skin into one of the minute veins near the surface. It is protected and guided on to the skin surface by a pair of segmented *labial palps,* one on each side, which are probably sensory and are used to select a good spot into which to drive the stylets. All five parts form an apparatus which is extremely efficient in operation. In addition there are two other structures (*maxillae*), also provided with palps, which are probably sensory too.

While blood is being imbibed, the blades and epipharynx are fully embedded in the flesh and the first and sometimes the second pair of legs are either turned up above the body or tucked well back to keep them out of the way. The flea thus lies at an angle of at least 45° to the surface of the host's body while feeding.

The hind edges of the two stylets are grooved and when brought together they form a minute canal down which saliva is pumped into the wound. Blood would clot rapidly in such a tiny perforation, making the flea's trade impossible, if it were not for the anticoagulant properties of its saliva. It is the host's reaction to the injection of this foreign fluid which causes the itching so characteristic of the 'bite'. Otherwise one would not grudge the meal to anything like the same extent. It is quite apparent from the behaviour of mammals other than man that they suffer from flea bites in the same way. However, the susceptibility of individuals differs. A minority of people do not react, and feel nothing but a faint tickling as the parasite rambles over the surface of the skin. Most experience a degree of irritation which, in exceptional circumstances, can be quite severe. While fleas are a source of fun in the abstract, they are an annoyance in (or on) the flesh. Those persons who are forced to occupy infested premises can suffer considerable misery as a result.

The feeding behaviour depends on the species of flea. Some suck briefly and repeatedly, while others devour copious volumes of blood (for a flea) at greater intervals. One may bite shortly after its arrival on a host, while another may prowl about, loitering here and there before settling down to a meal. Flea bites never seem to come singly and, for such a small animal, a flea appears to have an enormous appetite. Much of the blood, indeed, passes through unchanged and is squirted from the flea's posterior end in a practically undigested state. This accounts for the characteristic spotting of blood on the clothes and bed linen of those who carry fleas.

The digestive tract includes a large stomach. Before this is a much smaller crop, the inside of which is lined with hundreds of tiny spinelets which serve to macerate the blood cells extracted from the host.

The majority of fleas are provided with a pair of eyes, one on each side of the head, usually protected by a row of 'hairs' standing just in front of it. The eyes are simple. That is to say they can distinguish between light and dark but do not form visual images as our own do. Also on each side of the head, set snugly in a groove, is an antenna. These antennae are quite unlike the 'feelers' of most other insects, are much reduced in length, and are club-shaped. Sometimes they are swung upwards and 'cocked' above the head. Their function is indeed not exploratory as in insects generally: they are used principally in mating.

The head has no obvious neck and is set closely on the thorax. The latter bears three pairs of legs, the first pair being the shortest and the third by far the longest. All are segmented and clad with numerous bristles. The terminal section of each is fringed with a row of spines on either side and furnished with a pair of robust claws which are often curved, and are important in gaining a hold on a host when landing from a jump. They are also, of course, used in hanging on, and their size and gripping ability are correlated with the texture and diameter of the host's hairs.

The legs supply motive force. While roving through the coat of the victim the second and third pairs propel the insect, but the first are held folded forward and are employed in pushing aside obstacles. When the ground is clear, however, all six legs are used. Incidentally, on a flat, smooth, open surface, without the supporting pelage of the host, fleas have a tendency to keel over on their sides, their tallness working against them. However on a rough surface they manage commendably well.

In leaping the third and biggest pair of legs are in action. Although the Siphonaptera are notorious for their vaulting abilities, this is the least frequent mode of progression, and it is not used to trek about the host. However, it is sometimes of paramount importance in reaching the latter and as a reaction to sudden stimuli, more of which later.

Jumping requires that the hind legs operate in a vertical plane which is facilitated by the insect being flattened in the way it is. The jump is a remarkable feat, the human flea being said to clear 30cm and reach an altitude of nearly 20cm in a single bound. Equivalent athletic achievements for a man would be a long jump of 137m and a high jump of 83m. Moreover the rabbit flea (*Spilopsyllus cuniculus*) has been shown to take off with the almost incredible acceleration of 135 gravities. It is mechanically impossible for muscles alone to give such a performance and so the answer must perforce lie in the storage and sudden release of mechanical energy. The main propulsion for the jump[18] is provided by the downward swing of the long third segments of the hind legs. Above these legs, on either side of the body, is a rounded depression facing downwards known as the *pleural arch.* Into this is inserted a rounded portion of the top of the leg. In the arch is a pad of *resilin,* a colourless protein of near perfect elasticity. The flea pulls the long segments up by muscular action, at the same time compressing the resilin, until the legs are fully cocked. There is naturally an efficient locking system to prevent accidental release. The mechanism is discharged by a small muscle which allows the resilin to expand suddenly, swinging the third segments down, pushing the legs violently against the surface on which the insect stands and hurling it forward faster than the eye can follow. A camera, specially designed to photograph the event, has shown that the flea cartwheels through the air with the second or third pair of legs reversed and sticking up above its back.[174] Thus, whether it lands right-way-up or upside-down, there will be at least one pair of legs with the claws ready to act as grappling irons on, with luck, a hirsute destination.

Mammal fleas which spend a large part of their adult life in nests, for example the apparently rare field mouse flea *Rhadinopsylla pentacantha,* have limited powers of saltation, for they feed on the host when it is in its nest and hitching a ride presents no serious problem. In these forms the pleural arches are apparently absent.

Along the sides of the body are a series of openings known as *spiracles.* These communicate with pits which in turn lead to a network of pipes which branch repeatedly and ultimately end in tiny blindly-ending tubes. The spiracles are opened and closed rhythmically corresponding with the inflation and deflation of the tubes, and in this way air is conducted to every part of the flea's body. The method of respiration employed by insects is clearly radically different from our own. The hind-most spiracles are especially large and the associated pits often have a characteristic shape, sometimes a useful diagnostic feature in determining the species of flea. There also appears to be some correlation between the size of the spiracles and humidity of the nest of the normal host. The pits are larger in forms which habitually make their home in humid conditions.

On the upper side of the hind-end of the abdomen is a curious structure resembling a pin-cushion. This is the *sensilium,* an oval plate densely clothed in short bristles and containing a number of sockets, each giving rise to a longer bristle. The sensilium is important in detecting air-currents, such as those set up by, the passage of a potential host. Its destruction renders the flea insensitive to such stimuli.

Male fleas may be distinguished from females by the rakish upward tilt of the abdomen, which is rounded in females. The sex organs of the female are fairly simple and include a prominent structure for storing the sperm from the male after copulation. This is shaped rather like an old-fashioned retort and is called the *spermatheca.* The male reproductive system is unbelievably intricate and comprises a staggering series of plates, rods, struts, lobes, spines, hooks, ducts and tendons. One might be inclined to doubt that so fantastic an apparatus would work at all, if it were not obvious that fleas are manifestly successful in reproducing themselves. There is, in fact, a great deal of specific variation in the genitalia of both sexes, and the peculiar features of each species are often used in its identification.

The lady flea may have a scent particularly attractive to the gentleman flea for sometimes he appears to zig-zag purposefully towards her, but nothing is known for certain. When they meet, the male's antennae are erected, and the female turns so that she faces away from him. Her consort then slowly crawls beneath her, supporting her body above his own with his antennae, which in many species bear adhesive organs on their inner sides. He then curls his abdomen upwards and, with his elaborate generative equipment, transfers sperm to his partner. It appears that the process is not only complex, involving a careful adjustment and serial alignment of the male's assorted bits and pieces, but a violent one. Serious injuries are often sustained by the female as a result. One suggested explanation for the paraphernalia of the male is that it prevents accidental cross-breeding between different species inhabiting the same nest. For it is thought that the complex steps of copulation could not take place with a female of the wrong type. Be that as it may, hybridization has been recorded between some species.

Many males die soon after mating, which must in some measure account for the preponderance of females found in any collection of Siphonaptera. The female lives on to produce eggs, up to a few hundred in her life span. Adult fleas can live for well over a year if well treated in captivity but, like other animals, they probably survive for much shorter periods in the wild.

Flea eggs are rounded or elliptical, soft, smooth, pearly white and slightly sticky when new-laid. They are, relative to the adult, rather large, about 0.5mm in diameter, and just visible to the naked eye. They are deposited either directly in the nest of the mammal parasitized or, in some cases, in its fur, notably in the case of the cat flea (*Ctenopcephalides felis*). The eggs fall out later, usually when the host is grooming or arranging itself for repose on its bed.

Eggs hatch in from two days to a fortnight of laying, depending on the temperature. In fact they and the larvae require closely defined ranges of temperature and humidity for their development. For example, the human flea will not develop outside the range 8°C to 34°C, whereas the common rat flea (*Nosopsyllus fasciatus*) can tolerate temperatures below freezing: -5°C to

20°C.[11] The warmer the environment, the greater the humidity necessary, for the earlier stages in the flea's existence are especially susceptible to drying out. It should be pointed out that the 'microclimate' in the nest or lair may be quite favourable when conditions in the open are lethal. Often nests are below ground and the interior is insulated by bedding. The host's sweat, the water-vapour in its breath and even its urine all contribute to the humidity.

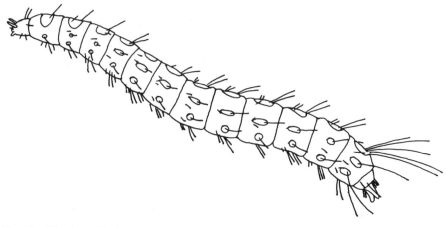

Fig. 46   Flea larva. The head is to the left hand side of the page.

The flea larva rends the egg-shell asunder with a spine on its head. It then crawls out—an unlovely, cylindrical, maggot-like creature, a few mm long, with a brownish head and dirty-white segmented body (See Fig. 46). It is sparsely covered with hairs, some species having more than others, but is both legless and eyeless. The larvae are none the less sensitive to light, and clearly prefer darkness, secreting themselves in the rubbish of which the nest is composed. They move actively, twisting and curling themselves in a horizontal plane so that one end overlies the other, giving the impression of a slack watch spring. They are provided with two projections at the tail end, a pair of short antennae and have biting mouthparts with strong jaws, in contrast to the suctorial mouthparts of the adults. The larvae are not, in fact, parasitic, but chew up organic debris of one kind or another. An extensive series of observations on the nature of this material has not been made, but it consists, in most cases, of flakes of dried skin, fragments of droppings, perhaps loose hairs of the host and other particulate matter. This unappetising fare alone appears adequate for some species. For instance the human flea larva develops in accumulations of dust in dark corners of our own dwellings with nothing more for sustenance than its substrate, which contains a proportion of organic matter. However, other larvae, such as those of the common rat flea, must have blood to grow to maturity. This is provided in the dried form from the undigested food which the adult squirts out as already described. It seems likely that dried blood is available in most mammal nests and it could regularly comprise part of the diet of many larvae. The tastes of the various species of flea larvae are thought to be fairly specific, and are fulfilled only in the nests of the hosts that the adults regularly parasitize. So immature stages are closely adapted to the microclimate and menu provided by a particular kind of nest. A species of flea is thus more closely attuned to a type of nest than to a particular host. The adult's choice of blood is often, but not always, varied and is usually of secondary importance. Mature fleas of many kinds can rub along on the blood of a mammal which is not of the preferred species, should fate decree their ending up in such an imperfect situation. Nevertheless adults are fitted to operate with most efficiency (with a few exceptions) on one or a few preferred species, and some fleas appear to be quite fastidious in this respect.

The larvae grow and shed their skins twice in order to accommodate their increasing bulk. The length of time the larval stage lasts is greatly dependent on the type of flea and conditions in the nest, but generally it is two or three weeks. When fully grown the animal spins a cocoon for itself with silk produced by the salivary glands. The fresh fabric is viscid, and so becomes festooned with the dust and other detritus which adhere to it. After a few days the cocoon loses its skin and, from being white in colour, gradually darkens. One can eventually recognize the features of the adult flea into which the larva has transformed itself, lying dormant within, its legs folded by its sides.

The adult flea needs a stimulus for it to burst from the cocoon, and without it can remain quiescent, in suspended animation, for over a year; but under optimal conditions some fleas hatch in as little as one or two weeks. The cocoon can, if necessary, thus tide the flea over an unfavourable period when no host is available. On suitable stimulation—the vibration caused by passing animal can be enough—emergence is almost instantaneous and the young adult so released is already ravenous. This explains why persons entering a house which has been vacant for some time may be assailed by innumerable fleas. On the other hand, fleas can survive for considerable periods without feeding and some species, newly emerged, will even copulate without a blood meal. Others require one first, and some must take theirs from the preferred host. All female fleas are obliged to feed before producing fertile eggs, and such a repast is necessary before every egg-laying session. Indeed feeding appears to stimulate it, even following an extended fast.

Those fleas which hatch from cocoons in quarters abandoned by their tenant must find food to survive. Again, when a mammal dies in the open and the body cools, the fleas must leave and are faced with an identical problem. Normally fleas do not stray far from the host or its abode but even there they have a similar but much lesser task—that of finding the host.

Fleas are not capable of homing in on a host from a distance greater than a few cm and will wander about aimlessly with a potential one much less than a m away. However, they are sensitive to vibrations and to air currents, the latter, as already mentioned, being detected by the sensilium. The insects react to draughts by moving towards them and anyone who has uncorked a bottle containing fleas for the first time cannot fail to have been unnerved by their sudden, vigorous exertions, apparently to move towards its mouth. This is an excellent instance of their ability to sense minor movements in the air. Blowing on fleas makes them very frisky. Quite often they react by leaping, and sudden vibrations produce a similar result. While this exercise is random, it seems an efficacious way of finding a host eventually. It is equally advantageous in escaping an enemy, for such stimuli may bode either well or ill for the flea. The speculative jump is by far the most opportune reaction.

A flea responds to light by moving away from it, which presumably facilitates concealment and keeps the insect well down in the fur of its prey. However, the ubiquitous bird flea, *Ceratophyllus gallinae,* reacts by jumping when there is a sudden fall in light intensity,[117] such as might be produced by the shadow of a passing host. It is possible that some mammal fleas may do the same.

At close range warmth, smell and even carbon dioxide are used to find a 'home', carbon dioxide in the case of the cat flea at least. Generally there is a tendency to travel towards warmth and to seek a temperature around that of the host's body. One siphonapterist collected bird fleas by dragging a hot-water bottle covered with a bird's skin through undergrowth. It is quite possible that mammal fleas which spend the greater part of their time in the nest lose their attraction to heat after a good meal and retire to the surrounding dunnage.

Smell is of great importance in the location of a proper host and the odour of the wrong one may even have a repellent action. Horses are never troubled by fleas, stables are free of them and so, it is said, are the grooms, presumably due to their attendant horsey bouquet. In some cases fleas will starve rather than attempt to suck blood from an accidental host. Some individuals of a particular kind of mammal appear to produce an aroma peculiarly attractive to their usual oppressors or maybe an especially strong scent. This phenomenon is well known among men and women. Older literature on human fleas repeatedly affirms that they find women more attractive than men, suggesting this to be due to the more delicate skin of the fair sex. Such siphonapteran sexual discrimination occurs among other fleas too. The Latin word *pulex* (a flea) is believed by some authorities to be derived from the word *puella,* meaning a girl. In ancient illustrations it is always a woman who is pictured wearing a flea trap.

The siphonapteran sensory equipment and habits in the end achieve a high rate of success, best illustrated by some experiments on rabbit fleas in Britain. About 300 marked specimens were liberated over a securely fenced meadow of about 2,400 sq m (2,000 sq yd) containing three rabbits.[149] Within a few days nearly half of the insects were recovered on the rabbits. Considering the limited opportunities for boarding a rabbit, necessitating the fleas being constantly on the *qui vive,* and the hinderances such as surface tension forces on damp herbage, this is a prodigious achievement.

The chief enemy of a flea is nearly always its host. A great part of the grooming activities of mammals is directed towards the control of external parasites and the nimble fleas must skip lightly to save themselves from falling to the teeth of their unwilling benefactor. They therefore often tend to settle in areas that are least accessible, such as between the shoulder blades and behind the ears. But even in the nest they fall prey to a variety of mites which will attack larvae, cocoons and adults alike. The mite *Euryparasitus emarginatus,* a mere 1.6mm in length (Fig. 47), can deal with a struggling *Hystrichopsylla* which at 5 to 6mm would seem unlikely prey. Fleas are also troubled by certain minute round-worms and by bacteria, but their internal parasites in general are but imperfectly known.

Collecting mammal fleas is not as hazardous as it might at first seem. A mammal which has been dead for any length of time is of little use, as the fleas will have departed. In cold weather, however, they tend to remain much longer than in warm, and a search is often worth-while. Freshly-killed mammals should be placed in a polythene bag, tin or other container which can be tightly sealed. One should not place more than one animal in a container, and two different species should never be put in the same bag, or it will be later impossible to tell from which the fleas came. When it is convenient, a few drops of chloroform are added which swiftly kills the fleas. Where it is intended to dispatch living mice or

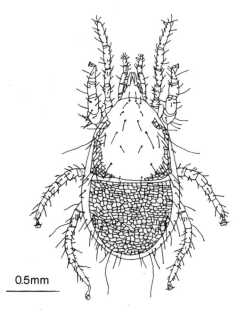

0.5mm

Fig. 47   Flea-killing mite (Euryparasitus emarginatus).

voles this is done at the same time, as the chloroform is fatal to them. The bodies can then be brushed for the insects, and this is best done on a well-illuminated white background, so that the specimens may be easily seen. An old tooth-brush is recommended for brushing. With large mammals an alternative is to hang the body over a bath of water containing a few drops of detergent. The fleas drop into this as they leave their refuges.

There is nothing to be gained by needless killing, and it is quite possible to collect fleas from small mammals and release them unharmed. Blowing against the fur of a small rodent securely held by the scruff of the neck often causes the fleas to show themselves. This is not as perilous a procedure as it might appear, for such forms rarely bite man. Alternatively the host can be rendered unconscious with ether fumes, which knock out the fleas as well, in which case both the fur and the bottom of the container should be examined. Careful etherization practically guarantees the recovery of the animal. I have never had a casualty. Chloroform is often toxic and is not advised for temporary narcotization.

Nests are the most fruitful source for the flea collector. When obtained in the field they should be sealed in polythene bags and looked at later indoors. Nests should never be fumigated because the fleas are then difficult to spot among the debris. They should be searched in small portions in a steep-sided white bowl or, for the more adventurous, a deep-walled tray. As the material is broken up and massaged, the fleas spring out and those in cocoons are stimulated to action. The insects are easily seen as they gambol among the nest fragments, and can be picked up with a wetted needle or forceps. Alternatively a suction device can be employed. It is unwise to deal with much of the nest at one time. The operation is then likely to go appallingly out of control, with far too many of the wily insects skipping about. Strong illumination is a great help in the process and it discourages the fleas from trying to move upwards.

The specimens should be killed and preserved in 70% alcohol. The Royal Entomological Society of London has published an excellent key for their identification (1957) *Handbooks for the Identification of British Insects* (Vol. 1 Part 16. *Siphonaptera*) by Mr. F.G.A.M. Smit.

The study of Irish mammal fleas has been largely limited to collecting and identifying them, but this gives a valuable insight on their choices of host and geographical distribution. Both are of great interest and, as will be shown, the distribution of some fleas falls far short of the range of the host. The reasons are not clear, but local climates and soils may affect the conditions in nests, and we already know that these must be very precise for the immature stages of some species.

The first information on the Hibernian Siphonaptera came in a brief note to the *Irish Naturalist* from Charles Rothschild in 1899, in which he mentioned obtaining examples of the house mouse flea (*Leptopsylla segnis*) and a bat flea, *Ischnopsyllus octactenus*. He also appealed for material. Little further was published until Eugene O'Mahony, as recounted in Chapter 3, began his researches, which form the foundation of our knowledge of the subject today.[185] It comes as a shock to realise that the human flea was not pronounced in a scientific journal as officially occurring in Ireland until 1939. While other naturalists have taken an interest in Irish Siphonaptera since O'Mahony, the bulk of our knowledge comes from his studies, from those of Dr A.J.M. Claassens,[26] while he worked in Cork, and from my own modest efforts.[74,84,86]

There are twenty-two species of mammal fleas documented as occurring in Ireland. Most of the remainder of this chapter will be devoted to their individual idiosyncrasies, distribution and appearance. The distribution maps have been prepared from the available literature and a few additional records of my own. In most cases the lack of records for particular areas represents a lack of collecting rather than an established shortage of fleas.

Pulex irritans, the so-called human flea, is a successful insect. Strictly speaking it is an associate of mammals which have their *pied a terre* in large burrows, into which category the human domicile loosely falls. Man's remote forebears and his nearest animal relatives, being all homeless, cannot therefore have suffered, to any great extent, from *Pulex*. Once man began to occupy a more or less permanent abode the flea began its profitable partnership and has since been transported by human agency over most of the world. It is only lacking in areas where the climate is entirely unsuitable. Curiously enough it is comparatively rare in the tropics. It is likely that pigs were the original hosts. Pigsties sometimes teem with fleas, and fields fertilized with pig-manure may become heavily infested. As already described, the requirements of the larvae are not nearly as narrowly delimited as those of most other fleas, and there have been occasions when adults have swarmed on beaches, the immature insects having grown up in dried seaweed in spots where people had undressed for bathing. O'Mahony discovered them on the 'backstrand' of the North Bull Island, where thousands of Dubliners used to congregate to take the waters, but fortunately not in any numbers. Dogs and cats commonly pick them up. A student once brought me twenty-four from a dog's bed, assuring me that there were many more where they came from. In Ireland *P. irritans* has also been found, presumably having wandered, on a fox, a hedgehog and a rat, and is known from other hosts in Britain. Its tastes are indisputably catholic.

Due to improvements in hygiene and especially the advent of the vacuum cleaner, fleas are now less common in human habitations than before, but are not as scarce as polite society assumes them to be. Human fleas are still around over most of the country and, after talking about them on *Radio Telefís Eireann,* I was sent several letters from housewives on their unwanted lodgers, containing agonised entreaties for an infallible method of ejecting them. Allowing for an understandable reticence among some members of the public to admit to entertaining such unwelcome guests, such infestations are probably not rare. There is no social kudos to be gained by admitting to having sustained flea bites. It seems that central heating may have been an advantageous factor in a minor come-back for the domestic flea.

It should be made clear, if it is not already obvious, that personal cleanliness has very little to do with a flea problem. Free access of transporters such as cats and dogs, the proximity of infected premises and, notably, failure to keep the house clean are the points to watch. One correspondent reported the arrival of hordes of them in her home, in second-hand furniture which suddenly seemed to come to life. Presumably the stuffing contained cocoons, which received the necessary shake-up to hatch.

Pulex is perhaps the easiest of all Irish fleas to recognize, for it has no combs at all. The only other Irish species lacking them is an associate of sea birds which nest in burrows, the Manx shearwater *(Puffinus puffinus)* and the puffin *(Fratercula arctica),* and the sole Irish records are from the Great Skellig Rock, Co. Kerry, and Ireland's Eye, Co. Dublin. Presumably the combless state is correlated with the host's hide, for neither man nor pig have a dense pelage. *Pulex* is one of the largest Irish fleas, females reaching 3.5mm in length.

The flea *Archaeopsylla erinacei,* which comes as large as *Pulex,* normally associates itself exclusively with the hedgehog. One might imagine that they could best disport themselves among the spines, safe from retribution, but in fact they spend their time on the hairy underside. Presumably it is more humid and less draughty there. Hedgehogs are reported as frequently accommodating a hundred fleas, and nearly a thousand were removed from one British individual. Strangely enough, relatively small numbers, fourteen or less, have so far been recovered from the few Irish urchins examined to date. Conceivably this state of affairs may have been purely fortuitous. *Archaeopsylla* has also been taken on foxes from time to time, and may possibly have been picked up on the odd occasions that foxes eat hedgehogs (see Chapter 8). On the other hand a transfer might take place when a fox scrutinises a ball of prickles at close quarters. For all their specificity, hedgehog fleas will attack man savagely when hungry. Despite its undoubted attractiveness, the prudent will therefore hesitate before bringing a hedgehog indoors.

Cat fleas *(Ctenopcephalides felis)* and dog fleas *(Ctenopcephalides canis)* are closely related. Both have a thoracic comb and a horizontal one on the head. The latter is easy to remember and looks particularly fearsome. For all this there are several distinct differences between the species. For example, the dog flea's head is more rounded, and the first spine on the pugnacious-looking comb is much shorter than the second, whereas on the cat flea they are both about the same length. The principal host of *Ctenocephalides canis* is as one would expect, although other members of the dog family are parasitized elsewhere in the world. The fox is said to be so afflicted, but there was only one *Ctenocephalides* in a total of 161 fleas I obtained from 453 foxes.[1/3] Dog fleas on foxes are, in my view, stragglers, and one can easily think of opportunities for the transfer occurring, for instance when terriers are working earths. Dog fleas sometimes teem in houses and will bite man readily enough. I was told of one such massive population at Adare in Co. Limerick and identified several examples from the infested room, *after* they had been massacred with insecticide.

Very little is known of the distribution of *C. canis* in Ireland, but it is probably widespread. Since coming to live in Galway I have discovered that, unlike the dogs in my district of Belfast, many Galwegian canines suffer from them. A former colleague once presented me with 138 and a good deal of loose hair combed from his own animal, a disagreeable beast who deserved every one.

In the tropics cat fleas occur on several mammals, but there is only one true host in these islands, though dogs, naturally enough, are sometimes troubled with them, and they will bite man eagerly. Whereas cat fleas are a common harassment to cats in many parts of England and often form infestations in houses, they appear to be quite scarce in the Emerald Isle. I have been sent fleas from seven cats, all from different localities. Only one was bothered by *Ctenocephalides felis,* the others harboured *Pulex irritans* or rabbit fleas, the latter doubtless acquired while hunting. If cats were regularly troubled with their own fleas, I should certainly have received more of them. Claassens examined seven Cork felines and found nothing, but four out of the twelve dogs he looked at were flea-ridden.

Besides the usual nuisance and embarrassment, there is a more sinister aspect to cat and dog fleas, for they are the species most frequently implicated in the transmission of the dog tapeworm (*Dipylidium caninum*) to children. The eggs of the latter pass out with the dog's droppings, fragments of which are devoured by the flea larva, in which the eggs hatch. The embryos bore into the body of the larval flea and, when the insect becomes adult, the young worms form cysts about themselves. The dog, in its efforts to dislodge its close acquaintances, may nip an infected one and swallow a cyst along with the other matter squeezed from the insect. The cyst develops in the dog's intestine into a mature tapeworm. Children probably pick up tapeworms by having their faces licked by a dog which has just squashed a flea. Such intimacy between dogs and children is therefore to be discouraged.

The rabbit flea (*Spilopsyllus cuniculi*) is responsible for the spread of myxomatosis in Europe and has thus attracted much research. Over a large part of its life it is sedentary, passing its time with its well-serrated stylets sunk in a rabbit's skin. They are normally found in clusters on the inside of the host's ears, a site which the rabbit is clearly unable to reach with its teeth. When a *Spilopsyllus* first finds itself on a rabbit, it moves against the lie of the fur and thus eventually ends up on the head: fixing itself to an ear is then only a minor problem.

This flea enjoys a remarkably close relationship with its provider, and its procreation is under the direct control of the reproductive hormones in the rabbit's blood, a quite astonishing response evolved by the parasite the better to pursue its nefarious profession.[175] Experiments in Great Britain have shown that during the last ten days of pregnancy the concentrations of certain hormones in the doe rabbit's bloodstream rise steeply, triggering off the maturation of the eggs in the female flea. Just before the litter of rabbits is born, the flea's rate of feeding increases markedly, and consequently the number of defaecated pellets of dried blood, which will be essential later for the growth of the larvae. A few hours after birth the fleas leave the doe and feed voraciously on the young. Here, after the prolonged period of celibacy on the adult, they copulate. It is believed that this is stimulated by the high concentrations of growth hormones in the nestlings. The eggs are laid, and after two or three weeks the fleas return to the doe. In this way the larvae hatch in ideal surroundings.

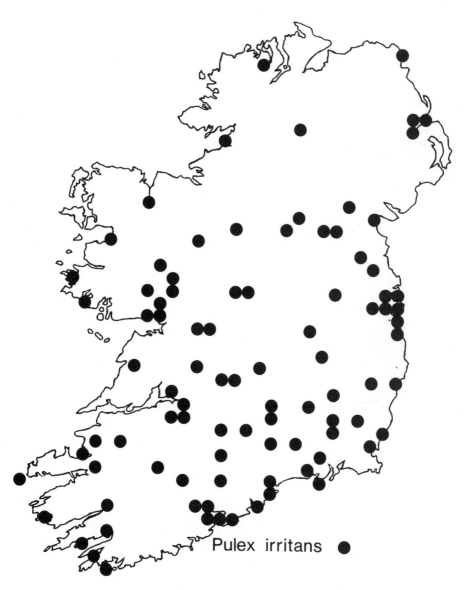

Pulex irritans ●

Fig. 48   The recorded distribution of the human flea (Pulex irritans) in Ireland (based on the Ordnance Survey by permission of the Government of the Republic of Ireland: permit No. 2291).

151

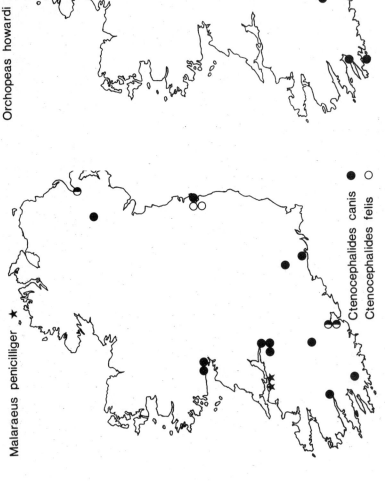

Orchopeas howardi ■

Leptopsylla segnis ■
Rhadinopsylla pentacantha □

Fig. 50 *The recorded distribution in Ireland of the grey squirrel flea (Orchopeas howardi), the house flea (Leptopsylla segnis) and the rare field mouse flea 'Rhadinopsylla pentacantha' (based on the Ordnance Survey by permission of the Government of the Republic of Ireland: permit No. 2291).*

Malaraeus penicilliger ★

Ctenocephalides canis ●
Ctenocephalides felis ○

Fig. 49 *The recorded distribution in Ireland of the bank vole flea (Malaraeus penicilliger), the dog flea (Ctenocephalides canis) and the cat flea (Ctenocephalides felis) (based on the Ordnance Survey by permission of the Government of the Republic of Ireland: permit No. 2291).*

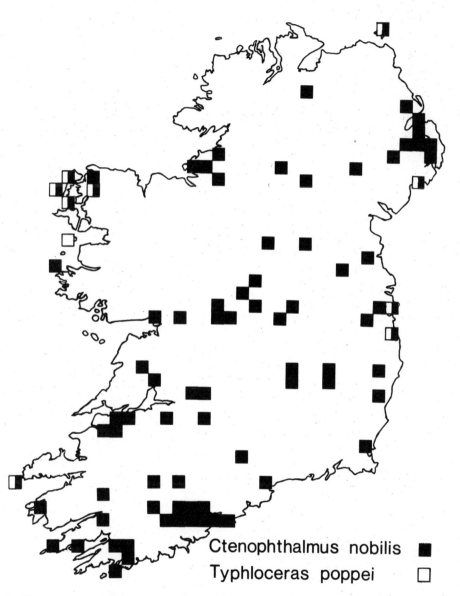

Fig. 51 *The recorded distribution in Ireland of the field mouse fleas 'Ctenophthalmus nobilis' and 'Typhloceras poppei' (based on the Ordnance Survey by permission of the Government of the Republic of Ireland: permit No. 2291).*

Spilopsyllus sometimes finds its way on to hares and, as already remarked, cats while out rabbiting. A correspondent from Tynagh, Co. Galway, presented me with thirty-three from her cat. On both these accidental hosts the fleas still tend to congregate about the ears. Puffins and shearwaters, nesting in burrows as they do, are known to contract *Spilopsyllus.* Their own flea (*Ornithopsylla laetitiae*) is, not surprisingly, a close relative.

Rabbit fleas are by far the most common on foxes, there being ample opportunities for them to get aboard. Contracting rabbit fleas must be a constant hazard for a fox while it is excavating a breeding stop. The collection of Siphonaptera from foxes mentioned earlier comprised no fewer than 116 rabbit fleas,[173] thirty-nine badger fleas (*Paraceras melis*), one dog flea, two hedgehog fleas, two bird fleas and a rat flea. Considering Reynard's bill of fare, there are no surprises here and, of course, foxes frequently occupy badger setts. Foxes, as already pointed out, spend much more time above ground than is generally supposed and, in my opinion, they probably have no true flea of their own.

There is a story, frequently told in the British Isles, of how the fox rids itself of fleas. A forestry worker once told me he had seen the phenomenon himself; but I am still sceptical. The fox seizes a lump of wool, moss or hay in its mouth, and then proceeds to back slowly into a river. The fleas, which have no liking for baths, struggle upwards through its hair, the fox continuing to reverse, and immerse, by degrees. Finally they reach its head and, when this too is submerged, they progress on to the wool, which is then released by the fox, at first to float and eventually to take its tormentors to a watery grave.

The field mouse is parasitized by no fewer than four different fleas, *Ctenophthalmus nobilis, Hystrichopsylla talpae, Rhadinopsylla pentacantha,* and *Typhloceras poppei.* The first three are also parasites of bank voles. In fact in Britain, where there is a variety of small rodents, *Ctenophthalmus* is to be found on most of them and does not seem to be particularly discerning; field mice, brown rats, voles, moles and shrews all suffer from it, and *Hystrichopsylla* seems to have somewhat similar tastes, though it eschews rats. *Ctenopthalmus nobilis* is by far the most common of the four. It is ubiquitous in Ireland and a spot-check of the fleas on any field mouse or bank vole will, in most cases, show that they belong to this species. The three backwardly directed spines in the comb on each side of the head are quite characteristic.

The giant *Hystrichopsylla* is the only Irish flea one can recognise without the use of a microscope—on its size alone. It is a handsome animal. The usual combs are well developed and there are a series down the back as well. The females, along with those of *Typhloceras,* are the only ones in Ireland to have two spermathecae. These siphonapteran behemoths are only occasionally met with. However, I once found seven on a single mouse, which is approximately paralleled, from the point of view of size, by a man harbouring seven young rats in his clothing.

Rhadinopsylla is a nest flea, and not commonly found on rodents when they are abroad. Even so, it is surprising that only one has ever been found in Ireland, significantly from the *nest* of a field mouse dug out by O'Mahony at Clontarf, in the Dublin suburbs. Perhaps around 500 field mice have been examined for fleas in Ireland without producing a second.

Typloceras poppei only parasitizes field mice. Where it occurs it is common, though its numbers fall short of those of *Ctenophthalmus,* but it is restricted to quite small areas. In Ireland all of these are near or on the coast. On Irish islands where any quantity of field mouse fleas have been collected, *Typhloceras* has been found. There is no ready explanation of this, but the survival of the larvae may be dictated by precise conditions in the nest which are more often fulfilled near the sea.

Only one specific vole-flea has been found in Ireland, though there are seven in Britain. This is *Malaraeus penicilliger*, which has only been taken at Tarbert, Co. Kerry, and near Glin in Co. Limerick, this despite a good deal of collecting in Cos. Cork and south Kerry, and, more recently, at Adare in Co. Limerick. Curiously enough, though it apparently occurs throughout the range of the bank vole in Great Britain, it is localized on parts of the continent. This may be yet another example of flea's precise requirements, but there is no real explanation to date. It is interesting that the district where *Malaraeus* is found corresponds with the mooted point of introduction of the bank vole (Chapter 2). This tends to confirm the district suggested. The fleas must have arrived with the vole, so, if they are found in only one locality, then it is likely that that is where they arrived. The alternative—that they colonized new territory and died out at the original point of introduction—is improbable.

The house mouse carries *Leptopsylla segnis*, which has been found on no other Irish mammal. As with several other species, it is probably widespread in Ireland. The limited collecting accounts for the sparseness of the records.

The brown rat must be regarded as the chief host of *Nosopsyllus fasciatus*, which at times ends up on other rodents, especially the field mouse. These two mammals often live in close proximity in the field and so interchange of fleas might be expected. Interestingly enough, Claassens found that all the rats he examined had more field mouse fleas (*Ctenophthalmus*) than rat fleas (*Nosopsyllus*). *Ctenophthalmus* is also found on stoats, for reasons which will by now be obvious.

The pigmy shrew has two fleas, *Palaeopsylla soricis* and *Doratopsylla dasycnema*, to itself in Ireland. Both of these appear to be equally common. Occasionally they straggle on to a rodent and, as there has been very little systematic scrutiny of shrews for fleas, most of the Irish records have come as rarities on field mice.

The badger flea (*Paraceras melis*) has been discussed earlier with reference to foxes. *Paraceras* is an odd species with exceptionally large antennae and excessively long labial palps, extending well beyond the first joint of the forelegs. It will be remembered that these palps are used to protect and guide the stylets on to the skin. Their inordinate length seems to suggest that this may be a tricky job on badgers, which have a thick pile of densely-packed hair.

The red squirrel suffers from *Monopsyllus sciurorum*, which is a near relative to many bird fleas. To fleas, at any rate, bird and squirrel nests are similar and it is possible that the ancestors of some bird-fleas lived on arboreal rodents and that the switch was made over several generations. Where the grey squirrel has replaced the red in Britain, these fleas have made the necessary adjustment to the new provider, and the have also been taken on the latter in Ireland. The pine marten too contracts them, presumably when out after squirrels. I have also obtained a *Monopsyllus* from a field mouse. It has in addition been taken as a straggler on various mammals in England and, as one might anticipate, birds. Its anatomy is, not surprisingly, very similar to that of several bird fleas. In the same way, bird fleas sometimes stray on to squirrels. *Monopsyllus* bites man with vigour. The most unpleasant and inflamed flea-punctures I have sustained personally were suspected to be of the *Monopsyllus* brand.

The grey squirrel flea *Orchopeas howardi* arrived in Ireland with its introduced host. It has, however, only been taken on one squirrel, simply because few people have bothered to look for it. In Britain it wanders on to red squirrels occasionally.

With the constant stress which has been laid on the importance of nests to the Siphonaptera, it may seem odd that bats have fleas. However as these mammals habitually use certain roosting places, the accumulations of their droppings on the floor beneath provide an excellent nursery for the larvae. Just as bats are quite different from other mammals, their fleas are quite distinct. They have long slender legs which enable them to crawl up vertical surfaces to reach their hosts. The head comb is instantly recognizable: two stout blunt spines well ahead of the mouthparts. Some also have an attractive translucent band along the front of the head. Characteristically there are additional combs along the back. Though some bat fleas find their way on to bats which are not their true hosts, they are practically never found on other animals. The only instance I can trace is of one on a short-eared owl at Ballymoney, Co. Antrim.[26] It seems logical to suspect that the bird had made a meal of the insect's former sustainer.

It is probable that the types of summer and winter quarters inhabited by bats will, to some extent, influence their fleas. There indeed seems to be some connection between the type of roost and the species of fleas present, but much has still to be learned.

The pipistrelle, which sleeps in buildings, often in confined spaces, and in cracks in rocks, provides for the abundant *Ischnopsyllus octactenus* and the much rarer *Nycteridopsylla longiceps,* which appears to be highly localized. The long-eared bat harbours *Ischnopsyllus hexactenus* and roosts openly under roofs, or sometimes in roomy holes in rocks or trees. *Ischnopsyllus intermedus* is found only on Leisler's bat in Ireland, which hides in hollow trees, though occasionally in roofs. *Ischnopsyllus simplex* is a flea found on bats which roost in buildings but hibernate in caves. In Ireland it has been obtained twice on Natterer's bat, but it may well be found on the whiskered bat in future as this is a preferred host in Britain.

Considering the lack of interest in siphonapterology, a surprising amount has been done in amassing data on Irish fleas, but there is a great deal still to do. It is obvious that precise host preferences are not always clear. The distributions of some fleas are also odd, incompletely known, and do not lend themselves easily to explanation. But there has been a great increase in interest in fleas in the British Isles in the past twelve years, though a relative one, of course! The outlook in this field of scientific endeavour is bright. By the end of the century we may not only have precise distributions, but a fair knowledge of the underlying, determinant factors.

10 The Otter

There is no doubt but this beast is of the kind of beavers, saving in their tail, for the tail of a beaver is fish, but the tail of an Otter is flesh. It hath very sharp teeth, and is a very biting beast. So great is the sagacity and sense of smelling in this beast, that he can directly wind the fishes in the water a mile or two off. . . . The skin doth not lose its beauty by age, and no rain can hurt it.

Historie of Foure-footed Beastes   Rev. Edward Topsell

The most elusive of all Ireland's mammals is the otter. It is rarely seen, even by country people. This may seem strange as, next to the badger and deer, it is the biggest Irish beast, but it is also aquatic, nocturnal and exceedingly wary of man. Besides, in comparison with badgers and foxes, otters are thinly spread. This is not intended to imply any current diminution in their numbers. It is simply that, adapted as they are to water and deriving their sustenance from it, they are bound to be less numerous than, say, foxes, which are at home anywhere in the countryside and even in city suburbs. A glance at a large-scale map of Ireland will illustrate the point. Otters, though they may wander far from fresh waters and the coast, are ultimately tied to them, and such areas *in toto* comprise only a small fraction of the whole of the island. It is essential to bear this in mind and to remember the unobtrusive nature of the animal before passing judgement as to whether or not otters are scarce in a district.

Fig. 52   Otter.

157

The otter has an elongate, powerfully-built body which is, nevertheless, extraordinarily supple. The tail is long and tapered, pointed at the tip and thick at the base. Indeed it is impossible to say where the tail stops and the hind-quarters begin. There is no very obvious neck and the head, disproportionately small and very much flattened, also merges imperceptibly with the rest of the body. The overall effect is one of superb streamlining. The eyes, which face forward, are situated rather on top of the head, not unusual in aquatic animals if one thinks for a moment of a frog or a hippo, and command a good view in front and above, if not below. The nostrils too are on top of the head and allow the otter to breathe whilst almost totally submerged. The small ear flaps surround apertures which, along with the nostrils, can be closed when the animal dives, but the eyes remain open. The senses of sight, hearing and smell are all acute, though the latter is not as miraculous as the Rev. Topsell considered it. The handsome, bristly whiskers sprout from two prominent pads on either side of the snout but there are others, elsewhere on the face and on the chin. Whiskers are especially important to otters, particularly in turbid waters where vision may be severely limited. They are used in detecting currents and thus allow their owner to sense, for example, turbulence due to rocks in a river bed or, indeed, water movements caused by fleeing fish. The legs are relatively stumpy, the front pair rather shorter than the hind. The feet all bear five toes furnished with claws and are webbed.

The otter's crowning glory is its hair, which is dark brown on the back and a grey below which extends on to the cheeks. At the throat the colour may be almost white, though I have not noticed this on any of the few Irish skins I have examined. The guard hairs are long and stiff and, when dry, have an almost metallic lustre. On the back they are greyish at the base and brown at the tips. The fawn underfur is extremely dense and matted, so thick in fact that the skin is never wetted. The underfur traps a layer of air, which is retained while the otter is submerged and acts as an insulation against loss of heat. The bubbles which mark the animal's progress beneath the water are not only released from the nostrils. Some escape from the underfur as well. When the otter steps on to dry land the guard hairs adhere together in clusters, giving the coat a spiky appearance, but they dry quickly after a shake. No doubt the oil in the fur causes most of the water to run off on emergence from the water. Otters groom themselves assiduously and presumable this is not unconnected with a diet of fish which is inevitably a messy one.

The skull (Fig. 53) is long, low and very flattened. The canine teeth are well developed, sharp and well to the front: ideally positioned for gripping slippery prey. The cheek teeth, though bearing many cusps, are broad, partially flattened and adapted to crushing, which is essential in dealing with the bones of fish or in crunching crayfish (*Astacus fluviatilis*). As in the fox and stoat, the skull bears ridges for attachment of the powerful masticatory muscles. In addition the lower jaw is locked to it. This is obvious in a cleaned skull and indeed it takes force to separate the jaws. Their resultant action is therefore an extremely powerful one, operating entirely in the vertical plane.

Irish otters are, quite possibly, darker in colour than those in Britain. At a meeting of the Zoological Society of London in 1834,[161] Mr William Ogilby produced a stuffed Irish otter on behalf of a Miss Moody of the Roe Mills near Limavady, Co. 'Derry. On account of the intensity of its colouring, which was reputedly almost black, and on various other characters, he considered the Irish otter a distinct species. This was quite an assumption on a single beast!

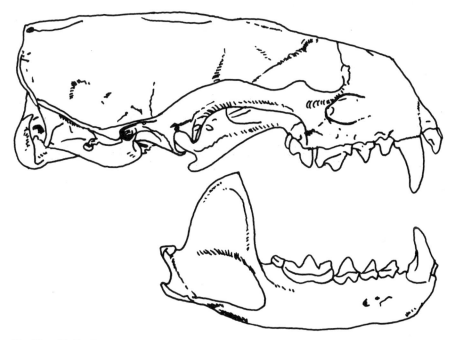

Fig. 53   Skull of otter.

Thompson records that he subsequently changed his mind. In 1897 the London Zoo purchased two otters from Co. Down[19] and it was remarked that they, too, were generally darker in colour than was thought normal. However, no one thought the matter worthy of further investigation until 1920, when M.A.C. Hinton, curator of mammals at the British Museum,[115] received three further specimens from Co. Galway. These were, again, almost black and Hinton formed the opinion that the Irish otter should be considered discrete, but as a subspecies and not as a species. Finally Mr Michael Dadd, an English zoologist,[32] attacked the question systematically in 1970 by measuring the degree of colouration of the English and Irish skins in the British Museum collections with a reflectance spectrophotometer, an electronic instrument for measuring colour intensity. Although this may seem an over-elaborate method, as the differences are evident to the eye, it does reduce the problem to figures. On the limited number of specimens available, Dadd found that there was complete separation between the two forms. The Irish skins were much darker and the paler colour beneath the throat was much smaller in area, practically absent altogether (as suggested by Ogilby), while it was prominent in English otters. I have only been able to examine a few dead Irish otters with their skins still on and have never seen an English one, so I cannot pass a personal opinion. Scharff, who was able to look at six Irish skins, commented that none was darker than chestnut brown,[179] but cautiously withheld any further comment as there was no English material for comparison. I have myself tried in vain to obtain the use of a reflectance spectro-photometer to investigate the skins in the Irish museums. Perhaps airing the puzzle may encourage someone else who can lay his hands on one to do it. There is certainly some evidence that the Irish otter is a distinct subspecies. However, assertions as to minor differences in size and proportions between the two forms, made on various occasions, have no solid basis in fact.

White or partially white otters have been reported in Ireland occasionally. Completely white ones were seen by S.J. Hurley of Killaloe, Co. Clare. One of these he mentioned in the *Fishery Gazette* of 1893, where he also recalled seeing one with a white circle round it neck some years before. In the *Field* of 1898[120] he was 'happy to mention the appearance of two other specimens'. Hurley was an otter enthusiast, keeping them as pets and watching them in the wild, or hunting them. He even referred to them as 'dear creatures'. Unfortunately the sum total of his publications was a few short chatty notes in the *Field* and similar periodicals. In one of these he talked of having published 'a history of my tame otters and cormorants', but I have been unable to trace this.

Scharff, in 1909,[179] wrote that on some skins small, widely-spaced tufts of the underfur are white. One of the Williams brothers, taxidermists in Dublin, informed him that perhaps about 1% or so of skins were marked in this way. In that year the Dublin Natural History Museum acquired a specimen from Lough Sheelin, lying between Cos. Cavan and Westmeath, which had small white spots all over, the whiteness extending on to the guard hairs. Seven years later Scharff was to see another similarly speckled otter,[181] from Kilcolgan in Co. Galway. Roderic O'Flaherty's fearsome white-faced otter (Chapter 3) might have been yet another instance of whitening.

The fur of the otter is highly prized and combines all the best qualities, for it is thick, handsome, waterproof and exceedingly hard wearing. Consequently the animal has been hunted and trapped in Ireland for a very long time. In a pipe roll of Henry IV[102] we read that in 1408 John, son of Dermod, was charged with two otter skins for his rent on Radon (Rathdown, Dublin) for the year, five skins for the previous two-and-a-half years and 162 for arrears of rent for many years past. The *Libel of English Policie*,[14] written about 1430, in a passage on trade of Chester deals with the products of Ireland and runs

I caste* to speke of Irelonde but a lytelle.	[venture]
Commoditees yit I woll entitelle,	
Hydes, and fish, samon, hake, herynge,	
Irish wollen, lynyn cloth, faldynge*,	[coarse woollen cloth]
And marternus* gode, bene here* marchandyse,	[martens] [are there]
Hertyns* hydes, and other of venerye,	[fawns]
Skynnes of otere, squerel, and Irysh hare,	
Of shepe, lambe, and fox, is here chaffre*,	[their business]

Of[14] a similar date is a mention of Nicholas Arthur of Limerick trading in horses, falcons, skins of otters, martens, squirrels and other soft-furred animals, his first trading voyage having been in 1438. In the eighteenth century things had not changed and Rutty informs us that the otter

> . . . is frequent here, and chiefly valued for its Skin, which is sometimes exported, and the Furr dressed with the Skin, is used for Muffs, Waistcoats, &c.

William Maxwell in his *Wild Sports of the West* (1832) recounts his adventures in Connaught and refers fairly often to a local character who made his living by trapping and shooting otters or by hunting them down with dogs. The latter is a fierce business and the quarry can give a terrible account of itself in its native element. The following is a somewhat coloured narrative by the hunter himself of a fight between his dogs, Badger and Venom, and a bitch otter.

Badger, who had been working in the weeds, put out the largest bitch I ever saw; I fired at her, but she was too far from me, and away she went across the Lough, and Badger and Venom after her. She rose at last; Badger gripped her, and down went dog and otter. They remained so long under water that I was greatly afraid the dog was drowned; but, after a while, up came Badger. Though I was right glad to see my dog, I did not like to lose the beast; and I knew, from the way that Badger's jaws were torn, that there had been a wicked struggle at the bottom. Well, I encouraged the dog, and when he had got his breath again, he dived down, nothing daunted, for he was the best *tarrier* ever poor man was master of. Long as he had been before at the bottom, he was twice longer now. The surface bubbled, the mud rose, and the water became black as ink: 'Ogh! murder,' says I, 'Badger, have I lost ye?' and I set-to clapping my hands for trouble and Venom set up the howl as if her heart was broke. When, blessed be the Maker of all! up comes Badger with the otter gripped by the neck. The bitch swam over to help him, and I waded to the middle, and speared and landed the beast. Well, then I examined her, she had her mouth full of *ould* roots and moss, for she had fastened on a stump at the bottom, and the poor dog was sorely put-to to make her break her hold. I mind it well: I sold the skin in Galway, and got a gold guinea for it.

The usual bloody welcome afforded a family of otters is well described in the rambling *Sportsman in Ireland* (by 'Cosmopolite', 1840), everything possible being done to kill the maximum number. Later in the century, Thompson remarked that accounts of the destruction of otters in various parts of Ireland occurred frequently in newspapers. Sir Ralph Payne-Gallwey, in his classic monograph on wildfowling *The Fowler in Ireland* (1882), wrote of knowing men who spent their lives trapping the animals for their skins, who spoke of a very large variety known as the 'King of Otters' or 'Master Otter'.

The slaughter continues today and I know for certain that gin traps are still used to take them in Co. Galway. It is quite probable that the same is true of other counties. Advertisements for pelts occur frequently in the local press and at the time of writing (1975) up to £6 is offered for a good skin. A substantial number, too, perish in fish traps, and others die in eel nets and lobster pots. The uncircumspect animals break in after fish, crabs or lobsters, stick fast, cannot extricate themselves in time, and drown.

Besides the value placed on their skins, otters have long been considered a danger to fishery interests. Although it is doubtful whether they are ever so numerous as to have any serious economic effect, except perhaps in hatcheries, it is understandable that their hunting should annoy some fishermen. Local bounty schemes have been operated on various occasions, but it is difficult to collect information on them, especially details of the numbers of rewards paid. The Foyle Fisheries Commission funded such a programme for several years and published, in its report, the annual kill from 1958 to 1968, when the practice was discontinued. At the latter end an allowance of £2 was made for each animal. The data are as follows:

Year ending	'58	'59	'60	'61	'62	'63	'64	'65	'66	'67	'68
Otters	14	35	28	38	32	19	34	25	26	24	20

The last figure (20) represents nine months only.

In 1938 Moffat[157] remarked that Fishery Conservators on the Liffey, Slaney, Barrow and other rivers were paying rewards of between 10s and 18s (50p and 90p) but the otter had a price on its head much earlier than this. Irish statutes in Queen Anne's (11th) and George II's (17th) reigns offered bounties for killing otters, martens, 'weasels' and various predatory birds. In the time of George III an ordinance on game enacted, *inter alia*

That from and after 1st day of July, 1787, any persons who shall take, kill or destroy otters, martins, weazels, rats, cormorants, kites, scal-crows or magpies, shall receive for every otter or martin 5s [25p] ; for every weasel, 1s; for every cormorant of kite, 6d. [2½p] and for every scal-crow or magpie, 3d; and for every rat, 1d.

The latter act was repealed under William IV.

In 1834 Ogilby[161]mentioned a premium for the destruction of otters in Co. Antrim and that many people made a profession of hunting them, living on the reward and the proceeds from selling skins. Thompson also alluded briefly to such rewards.

Of some interest are the peculiar wooden objects,[6,23] believed to be otter traps, unearthed from bogs in Ulster in the last century: one from Aghadowey, Co. 'Derry, another from Clonetrace, Co. Antrim, and a further nine from Castlecauldwell in Co. Fermanagh. The latter were taken to be coffins of some forgotten race of dwarfs by the men who found them. Turf-digging on that part of the bog was afterwards suspended for it acquired a reputation for the super-natural. The general structure of all of these artefacts is illustrated in Fig. 54. They took the form of a flattened spindle, around 1m in length, with a rectangular hole in the centre, which was about a third of the total length of the object and bevelled on one side. A broad groove, with overhanging edges, extended almost the full length of the opposite side. In this groove, and only slightly shorter than it, lay a rod or valve which was retained in position by a pin at each extremity, running across and above it. Two small bows of springy wood, like miniature versions of those used in archery but without the string, were inserted, one at each end, between the valve and one side of the groove, thus retaining the valve firmly against the opposite side. The bows were, of course, prevented from coming out by the overhanging edges. To set the trap, the valve was forced against the bows with a lever and secured in the 'open' position with pegs. Opinion is divided as to the method of operation after this. In all probability the trap was fixed on the surface of the water, with the bevelled side down. Bait of some kind was then placed on the top. The otter, pushing its head from below through the hole to reach the bait, moved the valve slightly and so allowed the pegs to fall out. The bows were thus released and forced the valve against the unfortunate otter's neck, holding it fast, if not choking it. The reasons for believing that these engines were designed to take otters are fairly plain. The traps would have taken much more work to make than any simple fish-trap we know and, as only one fish could have been taken at a time, they seem unlikely to have been constructed for that purpose. Besides, the design seems unsuited for fish and the trap too large for birds. In any event, if set on the surface of a lake or river to take water-fowl, the bevelled edges would have no function, for a bird would most likely insert its head from the top, where a sharp or smooth rim would be of no consequence. The smoothing off of the lower edge, on the other hand, would materially assist the progress of an animal entering from beneath. It is inconceivable that the mechanism should be set other than on the water's surface. No large and presumably intelligent animal would force its head through the slot when it could bypass it with ease.

Compared to the toll exacted by pelt hunters, the effects of the three packs of otter-hounds in Ireland at present can be considered negligible, especially as the organizers are bound to discourage trappers and shooters in their areas.

With man's hand turned against it for centuries, the otter has managed to survive and there is no reason to suppose that it will go under in Ireland now. The public are more aware of their wildlife and, possibly, the killing of otters is

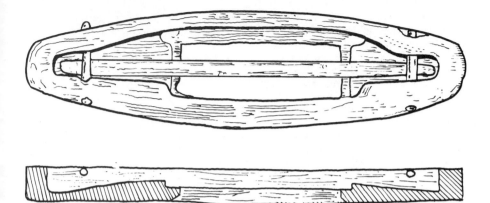

Fig. 54   Ancient otter trap—one of several unearthed in Ulster during the nineteenth century.

subject to less indifference than formerly. Ireland also has far to go before it is anything like as heavily populated or developed as Britain, and so indirect competition with the otter by man is small. While two entirely unsubstantiated suggestions of a drastically depleted Irish otter population have been made in Britain in the past twenty years,[97,193] there is no evidence of this at all. It is significant that no Irish naturalist of any standing has suggested a reduction in numbers. Moffat,[157] in 1938, regarded it as a common species whose numbers seemed to be constant. R.L. Praeger, in the *Natural History of Ireland* (1950), considered that it was holding its own and, twenty years later, Professor Fergus O'Rourke in *The Fauna of Ireland,* had exactly the same impression. Mr C. Moriarty, a naturalist who is also a member of the Fisheries Division of the Civil Service in the Republic, regards the otter as 'still a reasonably common animal' in his *Natural History of Ireland* (1972). The bounty figures from the Foyle Fisheries Commission indicate no down-turn in the population, and I am quite convinced that otters are common in Lough Corrib, Co. Galway. Finally, the recently published *Provisional Distribution Maps of Amphibians, Reptiles and Mammals in Ireland* (1975), which includes a map of Ireland showing 10km grid squares where the organizers have obtained records of otters from 1950 to 1973, suggests that they are widespread. The 200 odd records could not have been accumulated if they were scarce. For comparison there are around 350 for the hedgehog, surely one of the easiest Irish mammals to see, even if only as a squashed remains on the roadside.

   Otters are to be found near practically any kind of unpolluted waters in Ireland: lakes, rivers, streams and even on the wetter bogs. Fast-flowing streams provide rather fewer opportunities for catching fish since, as will be seen later, the slower moving species, typical of still waters, are taken more often. Otters may be present in the remotest areas and one was hooked on a fishing line in 1875 on the lonely lakes at the head of Black Valley in Co. Kerry.[184] Cover and unfrequented resting places are an asset. Stringer says of their habitat

. . . the places he most frequents are, rivers, loughs, and overflowed fenny bogs; his places of repose or rest are commonly in the rocks of the sea, hollow banks of rivers in obscure and unfrequented islands that happen to be in either river or lough, or in any wet bogs that are grown over with rank wood or great roots, or great tussocks growing in such places . . .

Otters are also to be found around the coast and have been spotted on several offshore islands. Both Ogilby and Thompson referred to their abiding in sea-caves and holes among the rocks of the north Antrim coast. A specimen was found drowned in a lobster-pot in Cork Harbour in 1873[105] and Mr Frank Clark, formerly Senior Technician in the Zoology Department, University College, Galway, came across a similar accident off Inishmore in the Aran Islands,[80] Co. Galway, in 1970. In the last century otters were reported as frequenting the coasts of Inishboffin and Inishark[22] in the same county. They have also been recorded on Rathlin Island, Co. Antrim, and I heard the islanders talk about them more than once while I stayed there. On Cape Clear Island, Co. Cork, the ornithologists manning the bird observatory[183] have seen them six times and sometimes heard their whistling; on two occasions this went on intermittently for more than a week. Otters are also known on Belmullet, Co. Mayo, which is practically an island.

Like other members of the weasel family, otters bound rather than run and though swift and sinuous in their turns and dashes on land, their top speed is not great, probably because of the disparity in length between the fore and hind limbs. Sometimes they will sit up on their hind legs supported by the tail and look about them, which gives them a singularly sagacious appearance. Although solitary animals over much of the year, both young and old are very playful. While they may chase each other both in and out of the water, they also play on their own with pebbles or twigs or nearly anything small and moveable. Otter species in general show a remarkable dexterity of the fore paws. Sliding, either in mud or snow, is greatly enjoyed.

When swimming, the tail, body and all four legs are used for propulsion and steerage, the action being both lithe and powerful. Very often the only parts visible above the surface are the head and tail. Moffat, who recommended otter-watching at full moon, thus thought it quite possible at first to mistake one swimming for two water birds, one following in the other's wake. Considerable co-ordination and precise, rapid manoeuvre are obviously necessary in catching fish seeking to avoid capture in their element, and pursuit may last some minutes.

Evidence of otters is not so difficult to see and the tracks or 'seal' are obvious in mud. The five toes are usually plain and the webbing is diagnostic. Sometimes marks made by the rudder are seen with the seal. Another indication of otter activity is the remains of a meal, and they often have regular dining places. Quite frequently fish are abandoned on land after only a few bites and otters may fish for sport, or are wantonly murderous, depending on how one happens to look at it. The droppings or 'spraints' are also a clue to be on the look-out for. Spraints have a strange musty odour which is impossible to describe but, once smelt, is never forgotten. They are often deposited at definite stations: rocks, mounds or fallen tree trunks by the water, but I, and others before me, have seen places where mud and wisps of grass have been scraped together and a dropping left on top. Fresh spraints are slimy, black or blackish but fade as they become older. Sprainting places seem to be visited by more than one otter and no doubt serve in some form of communication. The otter has a pair of scent glands by the anus, the secretions of which are likely communicated to the droppings, presumably accounting, to some extent, for their characteristic smell.

During the day otters lie up in 'holts', as their burrows are called, drains or hollow trees. They have also been known to climb trees. The holt frequently has an entrance below the level of the water, where the animal may issue forth unnoticed. As regards drains, there is a bizarre account in the *Field* of 1874 of an otter using one which ran from a cottage on the River Lagan. Tracks had been seen around the end of the drain next the river and, out of curiosity, a terrier was sent up it. A tremendous noise ensued from beneath the cottage. The floorboards were taken up and, beside the hearth, was revealed an otter at bay. The drain was apparently used regularly and the animal may have found a snug berth under the warm hearth-stone. Sometimes an otter will build a 'couch' for itself, a sort of open nest, usually of reeds, in some secluded retreat. As with much of the natural history of the beast, Stringer was familiar with its habits of repose.

... if warm weather, he will lie on a root or tussock, or will sometimes lie on the bank of a river in some bush, where he can slip down into the water upon the least annoyance; if in very cold or wet weather, or very hard frost, he will not lie so open, but gathereth old grass or reeds, or old hay hanging on the bushes or banks of rivers by a flood, and will make a bed very warm like a goose nest in some hollow bank of a river, or in some tree root growing on the river's side, or in the hollow or inside of some great tree root that happens to be in any overflowed bog, and lies above water; for he commonly when going into his byle or lodging creeps up into it through the water, and hath his bed above the surface of the water, and so there is no way to suspect, nor reason to believe him there, unless that hounds wind him through the earth, and if so, when he finds men begin to dig or make any disturbance, he will slip down the same way he came up, and go perhaps fifty or sixty yards under water before he vents.

Although knowledge of the distances moved by otters is somewhat sketchy, it is generally believed that they can be considerable, largely for two reasons. First, individuals often loiter in one locality for a short time and then move off again, which smacks of vagrancy. Secondly, otters are sometimes encountered at great distances from the nearest water.

There are a few chance observations on the otter's food in Ireland which I will attempt to summarise. I have eschewed mere opinions or assertions, of which there are many, and confined the list to definite observations. While this may result in the loss of some data, it is the only way of maintaining an objective viewpoint.

Thompson mentioned the stomach contents of only one specimen: several three-spined sticklebacks (*Gasterosteus aculeatus*). In the *Field* of 1881[50] there is an account of an otter catching a trout while being hunted. There is a hearsay record of a bream (*Abramis brama*) being taken in the same periodical six years later.[118] The otter trapped in the lobster pot off Inishmore had fish in its stomach too:[80] a sea scorpion (*Cottus* sp.) and parts of an edible crab (*Cancer pagurus*). In the *Field* of 1862 is a description of an otter engaging two salmon simultaneously near Foxford in Co. Mayo.[114]

The first he seized hold of, but after a severe struggle, lasting several minutes, it got away; he went in pursuit of the fish again, and met a second salmon, which after some hard work in a rapid stream he succeeded in mastering, and carried to the weirs, where he left it on a wall. He then immediately returned to the spot where he had lost the first . . . and as it was not able this time to make any fight owing to its previous injuries, the otter carried him off to where he had the other . . .

Moor hens (*Gallinula chloropus*), commonly called 'water hens' in Ireland, are killed by otters from time to time. There are two references to this in the *Field*. In 1874 remains of a meal of moor hens were found at 'an island'.[135] In 1885 a fisherman near Monaghan saw two of the birds rise from a river and fly inland.[207] An otter appeared suddenly, bounded after them, caught the hindmost in an instant, and was back in the water almost immediately afterwards. From the same journal of 1881 comes a description of a cormorant (*Phalacrocorax carbo*),[204] coming up from a dive, being seized by the leg by an otter, which towed it to the shore and devoured its head. Moffat[155] recalled seeing the remains of a full-grown heron (*Ardea cinerea*) at an otter's feeding place in his native Wexford. Hurley caught an otter in the act of dining off a goose,[110] though he did not record the species. Barrett-Hamilton had evidence of some kind of their feeding on ducks. Though he never published it, the fact is implicit in a letter to him from A.G. More on March 12th 1889 (in More's *Life and Letters*).

Few mammals seem to be eaten and so the story of the pursuit of a hare is

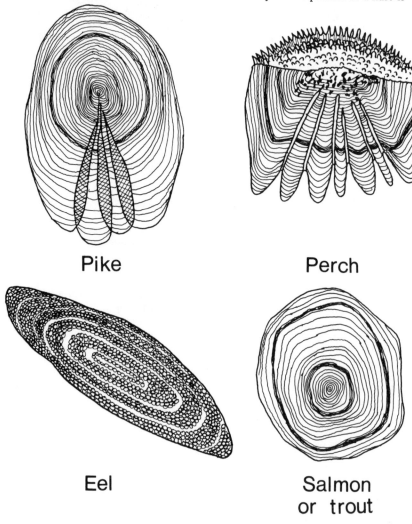

Pike

Perch

Eel

Salmon
or trout

Fig. 55   The scales of some Irish freshwater fish (not drawn to scale).

166

rendered all the more curious.[127] In the *Field* of 1901, a correspondent wrote of how he chanced to see an otter bounding along the shore at Ross Point in Lough Melvin, Co. Leitrim. It turned inland up a ditch covered with scrub out of which a hare then appeared, ran along the shore and stopped. The otter came into view again, continuing on the hare's trail but, presumably noticing the boat, took to the water.

I have carried out two small systematic investigations of the Irish otter's food. One was on the material in the guts of thirty-four otters obtained in Co. Galway[80] from 1969 to 1971. All but one were from Lough Corrib or the River Corrib. The second investigation was on eighty spraints collected on the Agivey River, Co. 'Derry,[94] and one of its tributaries, the Moyaghill river, from October to December 1970.

Some of the Galway otters were deliberately killed, but a large proportion had drowned themselves in fish-traps of one kind or another. As the fishermen sold the pelts, all but one of the carcasses they gave me were already skinned. This was inevitable. The expense in buying them would have been too great and I would not have been happy if I had felt that I was encouraging the destruction of the animals.

The contents of both stomachs and intestines were examined. The latter were included so as to extract the maximum amount of information from the small sample of animals available, the contents of the stomachs being dealt with in the same way as those of foxes. Each intestine was cut open along its length and scraped into saline, in other words a solution of common salt. The resultant unattractive mixture was shaken in a tall glass cylinder and then allowed to settle. Hard parts fell to the bottom and the softer ones floated. The liquid and washings were decanted and the process repeated. When the sediment, mainly composed of bones, scales and teeth, was clean enough, it was removed for scrutiny.

Any bird material was treated in the same way as that from foxes' stomachs. The fish were identified against a prepared series of teeth, vertebrae (back bones) and scales. No drawings of the vertebrae have been included here, for they are complex structures and the differences difficult to describe briefly. Nevertheless, differentiation between the major groupings of fishes is not particularly arduous if one assembles a representative collection of bones from the species of fish inhabiting the lake or river from which one has obtained the otters. The task is facilitated by there being relatively few species of Irish freshwater fish. The scales are usually easy to tell apart, and, if present, simplify the work enormously. A representative selection is illustrated in Fig. 55. Fragments of frog bones present no problems if a prepared skeleton of a frog or even a drawing of it is available for reference purposes.

Only twenty-nine of the guts contained food, and the results from them are summarised in Table VIII. The cyprinid fish in the Corrib system are gudgeon (*Gobio gobio*), bream, minnow (*Phoxinus phoxinus*) and rudd (*Scardinus erythrophthalmus*) so the identification of the cyprinids was, in fact, none too precise. This was simply because there were no scales or other diagnostic hard parts present which would have allowed a more accurate classification. The scales of pike and of the salmonids—salmon, trout or possibly even char (*Salvelinus colii*)—were all less than 3mm in diameter, suggesting small fish. None of the chunks of eel (*Anguilla anguilla*) in the stomachs was greater than 35mm in diameter. The feathers were all grey-black in colour and came from birds belonging to the Order Ralliformes—the rails. As moor hens and coots (*Fulica atra*) were the only common rails in the district, they were the most likely victims.

Table VIII.

Percentages of the stomachs and intestines of some Co. Galway otters in which various items of food were detected.

	Stomachs (21)	Intestines (28)
Eels	71	46
Perch	10	32
Pike	5	18
Cyprinid fish	10	7
Trout or salmon		14
Sticklebacks		4
Frogs	14	29
Birds	5	4
Crayfish	5	7
Diving beetles		14
Earthworms		14

Crayfish were reduced to numerous small pieces of shell which were easily discerned. The diving beetles (*Dytiscus* sp.) were identified from their legs and their large, partly-damaged wing cases, the earthworms from partially digested portions in every instance.

There are some marked differences in the frequencies with which the various foods occurred in the stomachs and in the intestines. As some otters might have eaten part of the catch in the fish-traps before drowning, this could have weighted the results from the stomachs in favour of the coarse fish captured in the traps. By far the most common coarse fish captured were pike, and, to a lesser extent, perch (*Perca fluviatilis*), both of which were more frequently detected in the intestines. Only two otters were drowned in eel nets. The discrepancies between the contents of stomachs and intestines are much more likely to be due to three other reasons.
(1)   Eels have an extremely high content of fat or oil, but the digestive substances secreted in the mammalian stomach are soluble only in water. Thus the digestion of a meal of eels in the stomach may be comparatively slow, and it may stay there longer than would one of other fish.
(2)   With the large amount of soft material in the stomach, relative to the cleaned hard parts from the intestine, a few scales or even bone fragments of the fish less commonly taken might have been overlooked.
(3)   Identification was often from a small number of scales or vertebrae in the intestine. It is quite probable that these could have adhered to the sides of the intestine long after the bulk of indigestible matter from a meal had passed

through. Thus some species of fish could have been overestimated in the intestine.

Clearly the otters in the Corrib were feeding mainly on eels, perch, frogs and smaller quantities of other fish, together with beetles, earthworms and the odd moor hen or coot. Perch, eels and pike are all abundant, but pike probably swim too fast for otters to catch them with any regularity. Salmonids were found in only 14% of intestines (never in stomachs) which probably overestimates their importance as discussed in (3) above.

The analyses on the Agivey and Moyaghill rivers present a complete contrast. Seventy-four spraints contained recognizable material and the results are displayed in Table IX. The feathers were, once more, all grey-black and from rails. This time it was possible to identify four of the five cases of cyprinid fish as being of rudd.

It is obvious that the chief food in this instance was, judging by the size of the vertebrae, young trout. Mr Kenneth Vickers, of the Northern Ireland Ministry of Agriculture, informed me that he would expect small salmonids to be very common in the lesser streams flowing into the Agivey river. This, taken in combination with the fact that the collection of spraints was made during the trout breeding season, goes far to explain the results, which are a somewhat specialised case and not a justification for a general pogrom on otters by fishermen. The findings in Galway are much more likely to be generally representative. The otter's predilection for eels is also well documented in Britain. It is, in this context, noteworthy that eels devour the eggs of both trout and salmon.

Stringer's opinion on the otter's diet was that it consisted entirely of fish, frogs and worms, and that eels formed the bulk of its food. However he saw salmon, trout, eels, pike and bream all left lying, only partially eaten. He was most emphatic in his assertions that fish which the otter found dead were never touched. He also claimed that: 'no man living can affirm a wild otter to have eaten flesh,' but was too cautious to venture to an absolute statement. He was content to say that if there were otters that killed ducks, then it was not every otter. He cited as evidence an instance of an otter swimming past a flock of ducks, leaving them unmolested.

Very little is known of reproduction in Irish otters, and it is only since the

Table IX.

Percentages of seventy-four spraints from Co. 'Derry containing various items of food.

Eels	9
Perch	15
Pike	1
Cyprinid fish	7
Trout or Salmon	81
Frogs	9
Birds	7

last war that it has been agreed in Britain that they may breed at any time of the year.[193] I examined the Galway specimens' reproductive tracts while dissecting them and discovered nothing incompatible with this. The males were certainly fecund in all seasons. Stringer was quite explicit on this point: 'The otter breedeth at any time of the year,' and his may well be the first authoritative statement of the facts. The Victorians and Edwardians believed that spring was the whelping season, and Hurley made an intriguing and ambiguous comment on the matter in the *Irish Sportsman* of 1892.[119]

As a rule they pair in the week before Christmas, and bring forth their young about February 24th to 28th. I mean adult otters of course. I have in my time procured baby otters all the year round—well, in every month of the twelve, but these were the young of female otters that had bred as they arrived at maturity.

Hurley was more taken up with fancy theories than the obvious conclusions which might be drawn from the evidence of his own eyes—that otters breed throughout the year—full stop. On the same page as his comment is a letter from 'Crubeen', that he had seen young ones killed by 'Mr Yates's otter hounds' at various times during the twelve seasons (*sic*).

It is well known that males may fight fiercely over a bitch otter in heat and it appears that these attacks are concentrated on the genital region. In corroboration, the penis bones of two of the Galway otters I dissected had been fractured and had fused again. (Perhaps I should digress to explain that a penis bone is quite a common accoutrement in mammals. Domestic dogs and cats have them. So do many of the wild mammals of Ireland.) Stringer watched at least one of these battles.

... if in a river or lough where otters are plenty, there will be sometimes two or three brace of dogs of male-otters following her, yea, and they will fight and tear each other, till they leave blood on the river banks. Their noise, when they fight so, is very loud and shrill, not much unlike the noise of cats when fighting, but you may hear the otters much further ...

Mating is described in most books as taking place in the water. There are no records of this for Ireland, but the fisherman who supplied me with most of the bodies in Galway assured me that he had witnessed such an event in the water and that it is prolonged, which squares with descriptions elsewhere. The precise gestation period has yet to be established with certainty. Hurley suggested sixty-three days[119] and there is some measure of agreement on this. The litter size is usually stated to be two or three,[189] with up to five in exceptional cases.[193] Of the four bitches I dissected with placental scars (the significance of which will be recalled from Chapter 7), one had one, another had two and the remaining two had three each, which indicates litters of from one to three. Stringer gave two to five.

The form which the breeding holt takes varies but, when near water, there is an entrance below the surface. Parental care is prolonged and cubs stay with the bitch for a considerable time, though the exact period is not known. The young are surprisingly reluctant to enter the water, and must be encouraged or inveigled into it by their mother. According to Dr. Ernest Neal,[158] who is best known for his work on badgers, the underfur is not dense enough to be waterproof until the cubs are three months old, which is when they first learn to swim. Hurley[119] was of the opinion that weaning commenced at seven weeks. Stringer was well aware of the relatively helpless condition of the young and thought that many of them drowned in floods. Portmore, where he lived, lies

170

between Lough Neagh and Portmore Lough, and may well have been subjected to frequent flooding.

. . . it is a great chance that any of their young come to perfection, that is, to live to be three or four months old, so as they can prey for themselves, unless such as are bred in April, May, or June, for thòse bred then are two or three months old before they are caught with a flood, which kills more otters than all the huntsmen in Europe; for the otter kindleth her young most commonly in such close hollow banks of rivers as aforesaid, and no way into the place but by coming up under water, and perhaps not two foot [c. 60cm] above the surface of the water when at the lowest, and to be sure, if a flood be before the young be two or three months old, farewell young otters, for I can affirm, young otters are above three months old, and indifferent large, before they ever prey for themselves, or leave the byle or nest where they are bred. When a flood catcheth the young, I do not believe, that one in ten doth get out of the nest undrowned . . .

However Stringer also considered the bitch otter a poor mother, which runs quite contrary to the views of most otter enthusiasts. In support of this, he cites two examples which, on their own, are inconclusive, and he probable formed an opinion on insufficient data.

There is more than one instance of an otter being kept as a pet in Ireland, though I am not prepared to vouch that the claims by their masters as to their versatility were, in all cases, unembellished. Thompson mentioned one belonging to Lord Belmore, of Florencecourt, Co. Fermanagh, which had been trained to catch fish, and Richardson (Chapter 4) noted that the Duke of Leinster's game-keeper owned one similarly accomplished; he also wrote at length on an otter he had kept himself. Hurley had several at various times and insisted that he had used one successfully as a retriever while wildfowling. Another of his pets, which eventually succumbed to distemper, used to go off fishing at night, returning to scratch on the door for admittance in the morning.[110] He also mentioned foster-ing a pair of young otters successfully on a cat,[110] which happened to have a litter of kittens at the time.

Besides the alleged detrimental effects of otters to fishery interests, there have been a few reports of more direct confrontations with man. Moffat mentioned rare attacks by otters on humans, but all of them were hearsay.[155] One was in Mayo in early 1927. Another, in Co. Cavan some fifteen years pre-viously, involved an animal, which had been shot and wounded, calling three others to its assistance. The final instance was recounted to Moffat by a man of advanced age in Co. Wexford, who claimed to have been attacked, many years before, while working in a turnip field. A further hearsay account appeared under a *nom de plume* in the *Field* of 1888[45] in which an otter attacked a farm labourer's dog. The labourer then fired and wounded the otter, which screamed and whistled, whereupon two other otters appeared; but all three were success-fully driven off. It is unfortunate that none of these episodes was described first-hand, and so all of them must be treated with a measure of reserve.

11

Wolves

The lean and hungry wolf,
With his fangs so sharp and white,
His starvling body pinched,
By the frost of a northern night,
And his pitiless eyes that scare the dark
With their green and threatening light.

Book of Highland Minstrelsy   Eliza Harris

As the wolf has been extinct in these islands for nearly two centuries, any attempt to document its history in Ireland must result in an essay essentially more literary than scientific. The vast majority of those who wrote about the animal from first-hand knowledge were concerned with it as a threat to life and livelihood. Few of them had any pretensions to be naturalists and, if they had, would hardly have chosen wolves as the most suitable species for study. The present chronicle is therefore, for the most part, a fragmentary and eclectic assemblage of contemporary correspondence, ancient statutes, tradition and second-hand reminiscence. Nevertheless, I flatter myself that it is not wholly lacking in interest.

Informed modern views on the wolf—that it is, in normal health, harmless to humans—are in sharp contrast to the long standing one: that it preys upon man whenever it has the opportunity and is, indeed, the very embodiment of evil. Fairy-tales, folklore and current metaphor have all served to reinforce the latter belief. Nevertheless by human standards the personal life of the wolf is most unimpeachable. It is monogamous, both sexes make conscientious parents, and contention within the pack is limited by a series of conventional vocal and visual communications. Furthermore, there is no reliable information to support the idea that wolves, in normal health, are a danger to man himself. If wolves preyed on men, even occasionally, then there are sufficient numbers of both to produce at least a single reliable, recent account of this happening. But such an account does not exist. Whenever it has been possible to investigate fully reports of people being killed by them, they have invariably proved to be spurious. A wolf infected with rabies is quite a different proposition and will undoubtedly attempt to bite, given the chance. But so will other mammals in a similar condition.

In North America there is only one report of a wolf attack on man in a scientific journal, in Canada in 1942, and the details suggest that the animal was rabid. On the other hand there have been numerous encounters between wildlife research workers and wolves and in these the latter always retreated; in some cases parents were involved and cubs were being taken from a den. Perhaps the most convincing testimony is that in an area with one of the highest densities of wolves in the world, the wilderness section of Algonquin Park, thousands of children camp every year unmolested.[150]

In Europe and Asia reports of the wolf's hostility to man are more common. But here too there is little in the way of solid fact to back them up. Neither the Russians not the Scandinavians have been able to raise a single well-authenticated instance of a non-rabid wolf attacking a man.

If wolves go for man at all, it must be extremely rarely. This is not a case of scientists dismissing what we all know perfectly well to be true. People are

172

Fig. 56   Wolf.

173

manifestly capable of believing and disseminating the most arrant nonsense, and are particularly credulous in regard to the ways of animals. The wolf ravening for human flesh is a myth. Most stories about it probably have their basis in assaults by wolves with rabies, which must indeed be terrifying. Exaggeration does the rest. In any event, as we shall shortly see, our ancestors had good cause of a different kind to detest and fear the wolf.

Detailed data on the food of wolves come mainly from North America.[52] Although the menu varies locally, in winter it consists mainly of the larger grazing mammals, such as caribou (*Rangifer tarandus*), elk (*Alces alces*) and deer, according to availability. In summer, lesser prey can form up to half of the diet, and this ranges from an assortment of rodents down to birds, reptiles, fish, crabs, insects, worms and berries. But the prey is predominantly the bigger herbivores, and it is this, more than anything else, that has brought wolves into conflict with man, for, naturally, they will also kill sheep and cattle. It is in the main due to their depredations in this direction that wolves have earned such enmity.

Anyone who has seen the slaughter wrought by stray dogs among sheep can begin to appreciate the havoc a pack of wolves could perpetrate, and the speed and pertinacity of a wolf is greater than that of most dogs. Men have hated the wolf because it could destroy their stock: because it could deprive them of their living overnight. The ramifications of the destruction of the last of the English wolves, which was complete in the reign of Henry VII, can be seen in the effects on the wool trade. As long as there were wolves, sheep had to be protected at night, and this usually meant housing them in some way. Driving them in involved labour, as also did nightly feeding and watering and the growing and gathering of fodder. When the wolf was no more the sheep-house became an anachronism, overheads plunged and the production of wool became even more remunerative. The subsequent turning back by landlords of arable land to pasture for sheep, probable a direct result of disappearance of the wolf, and resultant loss of employment, was one of the main grievances in the social upheaval of the sixteenth century.

Once the wolf roamed over the whole of the northern hemisphere in all terrain saving tropical forest and arid desert. Today its range has been greatly curtailed as a direct result of human persecution. In western Europe it is found in the Balkans, where its range is continuous with that in Russia, but elsewhere on the continent it has been reduced to relict populations: in the Iberian Peninsula, Italy, Scandinavia and a small part of France. But even in these districts its hold is a precarious one.

Those who pass over the countryside of Ireland today can have little conception of its wildness five hundred years ago. Formerly a great part of the British Isles was clothed with thick forest which for centuries formed an impenetrable haven for wolves, and attempts to annihilate them were entirely prevented. It was only when this forest was substantially cleared that the wolf in Britain and Ireland became an endangered species. But although it became extinct in England in the late fourteen-hundreds, the last killed in Scotland was no earlier than 1743 (according to popular chronology) and it was apparently over thirty years later that it was effectually extirpated in Ireland. As we shall see, once forest-clearances commenced in earnest there, the days of the wolf were numbered.

No relics whatsoever of Irish wolves slain in historic times have come down to us. Those there are have been dug from the floors of caves, which often formed the homes of the larger carnivores in prehistoric times, and into which they dragged the animals on which they preyed. The bones of both hunters and hunted were sometimes preserved in the silt in the caverns, deposits of sand and clay excavated from the soluble rocks by the action of water. The remains of wolves have been discovered in the caves of Shandon, Kilgreany and Ballinamintra in Co. Waterford, in those of Kesh, Co. Sligo, and at Castlepook and Carrigtwohill in Co. Cork. At the same sites have been found the bones of reindeer, mammoth and the giant Irish deer. Perhaps the wolves, but just as likely other predators, had killed them for food. Remains of the giant deer have, in fact, been found mainly in the white marl or black silt that frequently lies beneath peat bogs, often in large numbers; these areas were formerly swamps or shallow lakes. Such occurrences have never been satisfactorily explained, but it has been surmised *inter alia* that the deer may have perished in the waters in their efforts to escape from wolf packs which were pursuing them.

A reminder of the wolf at the dawn of Irish history are the ring forts, of which an estimated 40,000 are scattered over the face of Ireland. Each is composed of one or more banks or ditches within which there were originally dwellings. Examples date between 1000 B.C. and 1000 A.D. The fort was simply to protect the denizens of the district and their animals from attack by human foe, and to guard their flocks from the nocturnal depredations of the omnipresent wolf. Driving cattle and sheep into shelter at night is a persistent theme running throughout the history of the wolf in Ireland.

Though legend has it that Conall Cairnech, a contemporary of Cuchullain, was hunted by 'three red wolves of the Martini', the earliest reference to wolves in Ireland is, naturally, by Augustin in 655. According to R.L. Praeger in his *Natural History of Ireland* (1950), the Ancient Laws of Ireland (Brehon Law Tracts) inform us that the early Irish kept wolves, among other animals, as pets and that Nennius, writing in the eight century, describing the 'Wonders of Eri here according to the Book of Glen-da-loch,' lists the only noxious animals in the land as the mouse, the wolf and the fox. Giraldus Cambrensis remarked that

In Ireland, the wolves often have whelps in the month of December, either in consequence of the great mildness of the climate, or, rather, in token of the evils of treason and rapine, which are rife here before their proper season.

This is a perfect example of his moralising. A more fabulous tale concerns two wolves which conversed with a priest, who was luckily able to return them to their human form by the appropriate rites. There is likewise a curious reference to a wolf speaking with a human voice in the (unpublished) annals of Clonmacnoise (A.D. 688).[160]

The Monastery of St Saviour at Glendalough, believed to be of the twelfth century, has the capitals of the chancel arch adorned with grotesque carvings of both men and animals. In O'Donovan's voluminous *Ordnance Survey Letters,* those for Wicklow in 1838 mention that the carvings are considered by some authorities to represent wolves, which no doubt were abundant in the wild country of this district at the time.

Ranulphus Higden, the monk of Chester, remarks in passing on the presence of wolves in Ireland in his *Polychronicon* of the fourteenth century.

The wolves of Ireland were, quite likely, noticed more often in England as the sixteenth century advanced. This was partly because a generation of Englishmen had been born who knew not wolves in their own land, and who were, perhaps, mildly interested in their presence across the channel. Stories must also have been brought back by soldiers returning from punitive expeditions. Even

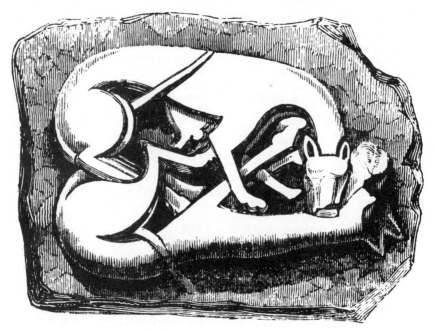

Fig. 57   Ancient carved stone from Ardnaglass Castle, Co. Sligo, supposed to depict a dog killing a wolf.

Shakespeare alludes to the wolf in Ireland in *As You Like It,* when Rosalind likens lovers' plaints to 'the howling of Irish wolves against the moon'. A few historians speak of wolves as having become more plentiful at the beginning of the seventeenth century. This may well have its basis simply in a build up in the writings about them, rather than in a genuine increase.

An intriguing incident occurred after the English authorities converted an abbey church at 'Derry into a fort and magazine around 1567, which gave great offence to the local people. Fittingly a 'large and hairy wolf' subsequently caused an explosion in it.[7]

In 1570 the Jesuit Edmund Campion refers in his *History of Ireland* to wolf-hunting, observing that, 'The Irish are not without wolves, or greyhounds to hunt them; bigger of bone and limme than a colt.' Whether the description pertains to the dogs or their quarry, or both, is not altogether clear.

A contemporary of Campion, George Turberville, a gentleman of Dorset, was the author of a *Book of Hunting* (1575) which says of wolves

The Wolf is a beast sufficiently known in France and other countires where he is bred; but here in England they be not found in any place. In Ireland, as I have heard, there are great store of them; and because many noblemen and gentlemen have a desire to bring that countrie to be inhabited and civilly governed (and would God there were more of the same mind) therefore I have thought good to set down the nature and manner of hunting the Wolf according to mine author.

The method used was as follows. An open spot was chosen in the woods some distance from where the wolves were known to be lying up. A horse was then killed and its fore-quarters trailed around the paths and clearings in the vicinity,

176

and then both parts of the carcass returned to the chosen site of operations. One or two pairs of wolf-hounds were concealed in the undergrowth. At nightfall the wolves emerged, struck the scent and followed it to the dead horse, on which they proceeded to feed. Just before dawn the hunters placed the dogs so as to prevent the quarry returning to cover. The wolf was allowed to pass the first dog, or brace of dogs, before all of them were slipped, so that he was ambushed and, with four dogs, set upon from all sides. The whole business seems unlikely, for it would depend for its success on keeping the dogs quiet and remaining down-wind of the wolf.

In 1584 Robert Legge compiled a *Book of Information,* by order of Sir John Perrot, Lord Deputy of Ireland at the time, which recommends that to encourage

... destruction of ravening and devouring Wolves, some order might be had, as when any lease is granted, to put in some clause that the tenant endeavours himself to spoil and kill Wolves with traps, snares, or such devices as he may devise.

The scheme was, in point of fact, not put into effect until many years later.

About this period it is said that wolves were committing great ravages amongst the flocks in Munster, and after the destruction of Kilmallock by James Fitzmaurice in 1591, it was stated to have been the haunt of wolves. Later, Fynes Moryson, secretary to Lord Deputy Mountjoy from 1599 to 1603, in his *Description of Ireland,* recorded how the cattle had to be driven in at night

... for fear of thieves (the Irish using almost no other kind of theft), or else for fear of Wolves, the destruction whereof being neglected by the inhabitants, oppressed with greater mischiefs, they are so much grown in numbers as sometimes on winter nights they will come and prey in villages and the suburbs of cities.

Barrett-Hamilton also credits Fynes Moryson with a cynical Latin verse which, translated, reads

For four vile beasts Ireland hath no fence:
Their bodies lice, their houses rats possess;
Most wicked priests govern their conscience.
And ravening wolves do waste their fields no less.

Yet another Lord Deputy, Lord William Russel, who held the office from 1594 to 1597, makes it plain in his journal that both he and Lady Russel were fond of hunting. Under 26th May 1596, it is written that they hunted wolves. As the vice-regal court was then at Kilmainham, it would appear that wolves were to be found not far from the city of Dublin. As will be seen, this was reportedly still true more than sixty years later.

O'Donovan, in a foot-note to his translation of the *Annals of the Four Masters* (1851), quotes O'Sullivan in his *History of Irish Catholics* as saying that after the battle of Kinsale, in 1601, the hungry wolves sallied forth to attack men weak with hunger.

In 1609 a letter from Sir Arthur Chichester to Sir John Davys included the following passage in reference to the plantation of Ulster.[108]

If the Irish do not possess and inhabit a great part of the lands in some of those escheated countries, none but Wolves and wild beasts would possess them for many years to come; for where civil men may have lands for reasonable rents in so many thousand places in that province, and in this whole kingdom, they will not plant themselves in mountains, rocks and desert places, though they might have the land for nothing.

The colonization of Ireland alluded to in the last quotation led inexorably to the extinction of the wolf, both directly through a more or less sustained campaign against it in the sixteen-hundreds, and indirectly by the massive destruction of woodland organised by the colonists.

According to Dr. McCracken in her *Irish Woods since Tudor Times* (1971), an eighth of Ireland was still forested in 1600, and it must be borne in mind that even this figure is somewhat misleading, for there were sizeable areas of the country where trees would not grow: the mountains, bogs and the karst country of the mid-west. Two hundred years later the area under timber had been reduced to a fiftieth, the bulk of the clearance having taken place by 1700. Thus there were many instances of leases stipulating that tenants should clear so many trees annually in the early part of the seventeenth century. Conversely, towards its close, restriction on cutting wood was the rule, and a series of acts sought to prevent deforestation and to promote planting. Early in the new century too Ireland changed from being a net timber-exporting nation to a net importer.

There were several causes for the decimation of the woodlands, but they are all traceable to the settlement from the end of Elizabeth's reign which resulted in a kind of industrial revolution in Ireland.

The woods had, of course, been gradually reduced for the use of men in earlier times, but in the sixteen-hundreds they were exploited to the full in industry, such as house-building, ship-building, glass-making and, above all, for charcoal to smelt iron. Timber was also shipped out in great quantities. The clearing of trees was necessary too for the expansion of agriculture, and was done as part of a deliberate policy of eliminating the fastnesses of wolves, of both the two-legged and four-legged varieties. As regards the former, it is easy to appreciate how the vagabond population may have been supplemented by the socially unsettling conditions of the time. Outlaws had, nevertheless, been plentiful for hundreds of years prior to this age. These rebels, usually known as 'wood-kernes' or, later, 'tories', were hunted down with much the same measure of mercy afforded the wolf which went on all fours.

The constant threat of the wolf and tory and the trouble that had to be taken to avoid their depredations are illustrated by a quotation from Blennerhassett's *Directions for the Plantation of Ulster* (1610).

Sir Toby Caulfield's people (county of Armagh) are driven every night to lay up all his cattle, as it were inward, and do he and his what they can, the wolfe and wood-kerne, within culiver shot of his fort, have oftentimes a share.

According to Thomas Gainsford's *Glory of England* (1618), in Ulster the wolves obliged the populace to '. . . house their cattle in the bawnes of their castles, where all the winter nights they stood up to their bellies in dirt'. These statements readily explain contemporary determination to be rid of woods, wood-kernes and wolves.

The improvement brought by deforestation, in one direction at any rate, may be gauged from a comment by the Earl of Cork who, in 1632,[144] wrote

The place where Bandon Bridge is situated is upon a great district of this country and was within the last twenty-four years a mere waste bog and wood serving as a retreat and harbour to woodkernes, rebels, thieves and wolves and yet now (God be praised) as civil a plantation as most in England.

That more forceful measures for the eradication of the wolf were contemplated early in the reign of James I is clear from the *Heads of a Bill in the Irish Parliament, 1611*, which sketched out

An Act for killing Wolves and other vermin, touching the days of hunting, the people that are to attend, who to be their director, an inhibition not to use any arms. The Lord Deputy or Principal Governor to prohibit such hunting if he suspects that such assemblies by colour of hunting may prove inconvenient.

The authorities were plainly most anxious that such hunting parties should not become a cloak for insurrection, and the proposed act, probably because of this, was permanently shelved. However, James was prepared to give English free enterprise his blessing in the form of one Henric Tuttesham, as can be seen from the *Patent Rolls James I.*

The King being given to understand the great loss and hindrance which arose in Ireland by the multitude of wolves in all parts of kingdom did by letters from Newmarket 26th November 1614 direct a grant to be made by patent to Henric Tuttesham, who by petition had made offer to repair to Ireland, and there use his best skill and endeavour to destroy the said wolves, providing at his own charge, men, dogs, traps and engines and requires no other allowance save four nobles sterling [about £3], for the head of every wolf, young or old and of every County, and to be authorized to keep four men and twelve couple of hounds in every County for seven years.

Light relief is provided by a letter to Sir James Crofts in 1624,[108] which contains an amusing anecdote.

A pleasant tale I heard Sir Thomas Fairfax relate of a souldier in Ireland, who having got his passport to go for England, as he past through a wood with his knapsack upon his back, being weary, he sate down under a tree wher he open'd his knapsack and fell to some victuals he had; but upon a sudden he was surpriz'd with two or three *Woolfs*, who, coming towards him, he threw them scraps of bread and cheese till all was done; then the *Wolfs* making a nearer approach unto him, he knew not what shift to make, but by taking a pair of bagpipes which he had, and as soon as he began to play upon them, the *Woolfs* ran all away as if they had been scar'd out of their wits. Whereupon the souldier said, 'A pox take you all, if I had known you had lov'd musick so well, you should have had it before dinner'.

In contrast a grim but equally apocryphal incident was recounted in 1642 in a tract entitled *Ireland's Tragical Tyrranie.* This concerned a family of fourteen persons named Adams who, during the rebellion of the previous year, were compelled to seek shelter in the woods and were all devoured by wolves. A sceptic might feel forced to enquire who it was, then, that survived to tell the tale.

Hardiman, who edited O'Flaherty's *H'Iar Connaught* referred to in Chapter 3, mentioned therein that after the war of 1641 wolf hunters were appointed in various districts including Connaught, but he does not reveal the source of his information.

The panic caused in Britain by the rebellion just alluded to triggered off the Civil War, for the King and Commons disagreed violently as to who was to lead the army to quell it. The insurrection dragged on until the war ended in England and King Charles lost his head. Cromwell was then able to put down the rebellion in a swift and barbarous fashion. The further draconic measures he envisaged for the subjugation of the country need not concern us here except insofar as they were directed at wolves. Effective steps were taken in this direction.

On 27th April 1652 an order was made to prevent the export of wolf-dogs from Ireland. What these dogs looked like and whether their appearance changed much over the ages with selective breeding is a matter of debate. Whether they resembled the modern Irish wolf-hound or grey-hound, or neither, is not altogether clear. However, they were definitely much in demand over a long period of history. Symnachus recorded that as early as the fourth century a number of dogs of great size were sent from Ireland to Rome in iron cages. Other reputed devotees of the breed included Cardinal Richelieu, the Shah of Persia and the Great Mogul. In Cromwell's time the order was designed to stop those leaving Ireland from taking their noble pets with them and thus hindering the annihilation of the wolf.[160]

Declaration against transporting of Wolfe Dogges.

Forasmuch as we are credibly informed, that Wolves doe much increase and destroy many cattle in several partes of this Dominion, and that some of the enemie's party, who have laid down armes, and have liberty to go beyond sea, and others, do attempt to carry away several such great dogges as are commonly called wolfe dogges, whereby the breed of them, which are useful for destroying of wolves, would (if not prevented) speedily decay. These are, therefore, to prohibit all persons whatsoever from exporting any of the said Dogges out of this Dominion; and searchers and other officers of the customs, in the several partes and creekes of this Dominion, are hereby strictly required to seize and make stopp of all such dogges, and deliver them either to the common huntsman, appointed for the precincts where they are seized upon, or to the governor of the said precinct.

Wolf hunts were also organized as appears from a document of 20th December in the same year (1652): 'Ordered that measures be taken for the destruction of wolves in the Barony of Castleknock, Co. Dublin'.[49] At least two wolf-hunters were officially licensed,[144] Richard Toole on 1st December 1652 and, on 11th March in the year following, Captain Edward Piers. Toole, and Maurice McWilliam, his servant, were allowed to move up and down the country with two fowling pieces to destroy wolves. The instructions to Piers were more elaborate. He was leased all the forfeited lands in the Barony of Dunboyne, Co. Meath, for five years from May 1653 for £543 on condition of maintaining a hunting establishment for killing both foxes and wolves. He was to keep a pack of dogs, consisting of three wolf dogs, two English mastiffs and thirty-two hounds, and employ a huntsman, two men and a boy, an orderly hunt to take place thrice a month. The team was to be split between Dunboyne and Dublin. To make sure that he fulfilled his side of the contract, he had to pay an additional £100 rent per annum, to be defalked in wolf and fox heads—six and twenty-four of each respectively in the first year down to one and five in the last two years.

In the same year (1653), the authorities also concerned themselves with the relief of the poverty stricken and in a *Declaration touchinge the Poore*[160] (12th May) there is a grisly reference to children being 'fed upon by ravening wolves'. A further step was taken on 29th June by the introduction of a system of bounties to encourage wolf-hunting in the following[160]

Declaration touching Wolves.

For the better destroying of wolves, which of late years have much increased in most parts of this nation, It is ordered that the commanders in chiefe and commisioners of the Revenue in the several precincts, doe consider of, use and execute all good wayes and meanes, how the wolves, in the counties and places within the respective precincts, may be taken and destroyed; and to employ such person or persons, and to appoint such daies and tymes for hunting the wolfe, as they shall adjudge necessary. And it is further ordered, that all such person or persons as shall take, kill, or destroy any wolfes, and shall bring forth the head of the woulfe before the said commanders of the revenue, shall receive the sums following, viz., for every Bitch wolfe, six pounds; for every Dogg wolfe, five pounds; for every cubb which prayeth for himself, forty shillings [£2] ; for every suckling cubb, ten shillings [50p] ; And no woolfe after the last of September until the 10th of January be accounted a young woolfe, and the Commissioners of the Revenue shall cause the same to be equallie assessed within their precincts.

This seems to suggest that wolf cubs were first available in early January, which would rather tie in with the reference by Giraldus Cambrensis to wolves whelping in December. This is, nevertheless, the veriest conjecture. All the present information points to litters in spring. The amounts paid represent, for those days, almost incredibly high sums, and presumably the lure of such rewards was necessary because the taking of a wolf presented a difficult, not to say hazardous task. It was also quite probably expensive, if Edward Piers' establishment is anything to go by.

A document of 1665 reads[49]

Lord Deputy and Council of the Commissioners of Asscessments for the County of Galway Call their attention to the fact that the sum of £243. 5. 4½d was due to the Treasury from the counties of Galway, Mayo, Sligo and part of Leitrim formerly within the precinct of Galway, advanced for wolves destroyed there in the pursuance of the late Commissioners of the Commonwealth for the destroying of wolves etc.

The exact date is not given but in December of that year the inhabitants of Mayo petitioned the Council that the Commissioners of asscessment might be at liberty to compound for wolf heads, which was ordered accordingly.[160] The levy for these enormous bounties obviously fell heavily on some districts.

In a statement of the receipts of expenditure on expenses for the taking of wolves from July 1649 to November 1656, a staggering total of £3,847. 5s was accounted for.[49] Caution must be exercised in attempting to calculate the numbers killed from this figure, for the odd 5s, and the anomalous 5s. 4½d in the amount mentioned earlier, implies incidental expenditure of some kind. It is plain from an order of 1659, copied from the Commonwealth Records, that 'toyles', snares or nets for catching the animals, were provided from public money.[10]

Whereas some money hath been issued on accompt to Coll. Daniell Abbot and others for providing of Toyles for taking of Wolves, which have been bought over for public use, and understanding that part therof is at present at Greenhill near Kilcullen Co. Kildare, Ordered that Captn. Tomlins, Comptroller of ye Trayne do forthwith take care that ye sd Toyles and other materials thereto belonging bee brought from Greenhill or any other place, and layd in the publique stores, and there kept untill further directions shall be given concerning ye same.

In the *Calendar of State Papers, Ireland,* two letters from Sir George Rawdon to Viscount Conway document, in passing, a campaign in south Antrim against the wolf. The 'Collen' referred to is today known as Collin Mountain, and Tunny Park is the district lying along the edge of Lough Neagh between Glenavy and Portmore.

Moyra, 11th July, 1657.
... sent ... on Monday to find the first passage to Chester; also the dogs which it is a pity to send out of the country, especially one of them. They have been about 'The Collen' and above Mr. Doynes this six weeks, and had some courses at wolves which exceedingly infest this country.

Lisburn, 7th October, 1665.
... The wolf haunts that park (Tunny) of late and hath killed 3 or 4 of a few muttons, ... so I have put Totnall upon setting traps and watching with guns and Simon the keeper who is an excellent shot but I perceive no great woodman, yet I hope will do well being careful and not given to drink ...

181

P.S.:- The keepers and all our gun men are watching the wolves that haunt the Tunny Park almost every night.

Arthur Stringer, Lord Conway's huntsman, did not mention wolves at all in his book of 1714. Presumably they had disappeared from the area by that date.

Similar losses were being felt in Co. Down,[31] as revealed in a letter from Christopher Croaffts to Sir John Perceval in 1663. 'We are much troubled with wolves, for we lost at Wailshistowne [Walshestown?], three sheep; another night at Ballyadam, four sheep.'

In *The Chronicles of a Puritan Family in Ireland* (1923), the author, the Rev. G.N. Nuttall-Smith, affirmed that wolves were still hunted in the neighbourhood of Dublin about 1660, which does not seem unlikely.

After the Restoration wolves were still thought sufficiently common in Ireland for Sir John Ponsonby to report in 1662 from the *Committee of Grievances*, as recorded in the *Journal of the House of Commons*, that a bill should be brought in 'to encourage the killing of Wolves and foxes in Ireland'. Life as a bounty-hunter too must have seemed remunerative enough to prove attractive, as appears from a petition of 1663 to the Duke of Ormond, then Lord Lieutenant of Ireland.[172] In this a certain William Collowe indulged in some particularly obsequious verbal grovelling to obtain permission to hunt wolves in a way 'more than ordinary, and never knowne in this Kingdome'. He also wanted everyone else restrained from stealing this supposedly original method, the nature of which we can only guess at. An endorsement shows that Ormonde approved the presentation of the document, but we are not told of the eventual outcome.

In the *Travels of the Grand Duke Cosmo III in England* (1669) the author speaks of wolves as common in Ireland and mentions that mastiffs were in great demand for hunting them.

As late as 1673 wolves were still sufficiently plentiful to be regarded as common in Co. Cork, if a letter from Lord Broghill,[21] then residing at Charleville, to the Earl of Dorset is to be believed. The former even possessed a tame one. That they were still being killed in the county is also testified to by an item in the Council book of the Corporation of Youghal.[24]

22 Ap. 1676. Item. That 3 li. 15s. 4d. charged on the Town and Liberties of Youghal, by order of the late Justices of Assize, 29 July, 1675, towards the taking of wolves and foxes, be paid by the Mayor out of the Town revenue.

John Dunton wrote a number of letters on his travels through Ireland which are now with the Rawlinson Manuscripts in the Bodleian Library at Oxford. The precise date of the extract below I have not traced, but it was in the latter half of the seventeenth century and gives an insight into the social inconveniences caused by the wolf, and that, as usual, the cattle had to be driven in at night. The passage refers to a night spent somewhere in Connaught.[147]

I had just compos'd my selfe to sleep when I was strangely surprized to heare the cows and sheep all comeing into my bed chamber. I enquired the meaneing and was told it was to preserve them from the wolfe which everie night was rambling about for prey. I found the beasts lay down soone after they had enter'd and soe my fears of being trodden upon by them were over, and truly if the nastiness of their excrements did not cause an aversion hereto, the sweetness of theire breath which I never was sensible of before, and the pleasing noyse they made in ruminating or chawing the cudd, would lull a body to sleep as soon as the noys of a murmuring brook and the fragrancy of a bed of roses.

182

This sort of arrangement may have laid the basis for the offensive, proverbial Irish 'pig in the kitchen'.

It is interesting that, as late as the reign of William and Mary, Ireland was sometimes known by the nickname 'Wolf-land'.[108]

The first indication of a decline in the numbers of the wolf comes from the William Molyneux papers, collected for Moses Pitt's ill-starred atlas. Teague O'Roddy prepared the notes for Co. Leitrim in 1683 and he stated that

The wolves, which were very numerous, are now very scarce, owing to the Justices at Quarter Sessions having leavied twopence a hearth in every Barony, out of which they grant a reward for each wolf killed.

It is quite likely that, if this was true, they were also thin on the ground over a large part of the country. A wolf pack may have a range between 315 and 1,250 sq km (150 to 473 sq miles)[52] and as conditions for wolves worsened in Ireland, they may have been forced to move greater distances in search of prey and in returning to suitably safe cover to lie up in. Besides, a night's visit to a district by a single marauder would have been enough to convince many that wolves were anything but scarce. When the literature describes them as locally reduced in numbers, this may well have applied over a much greater area. It must be emphasized too that, unlike several commentators, O'Roddy was a man on the spot.

From 1683 onwards the paucity of wolves is mentioned more and more frequently. However for around twenty years there were also assertions to the contrary, in some regions at least. Dr. McCracken, in her aforementioned book on the Irish woods, mentions leases in the area west of Lough Neagh binding tenants to kill a certain number of wolves during their tenancy. These documents she believed to date from the early eighteenth century. In an account of the British Isles published at Nuremberg in 1690 (cited in Lord Macauley's *History of England*), the wilds of Co. Kerry are referred to as a haunt of wolves, and Lawrence Eachard in his *Description of Ireland* (1691) lamented that the country was 'much troubled with wolves'. J. Howel,[8] alderman of Cork City, in a letter dated 1698, wrote of having both wolves and foxes in the district. In the country around Schull and Berehaven, also in Co. Cork, Bishop Downes[147] in his visitation notes for 1699 speaks of the area as still harbouring wolves. Finally their abundance is mentioned by Guy Miege in *The Present State of Great Britain and Ireland,* which was first printed in 1707, and he notes that the Irish prayed for the wolves lest they should be devoured by them. Hardiman (in *H-Iar Connaught*) erroneously gives the date as 1738, which is that of the eighth edition, but himself admits that an abundance of the animals at so late a date was unlikely. Apart from a poem of 1719, *McDermot, or the Irish Fortune Hunter*, in which wolf-killing is represented as a popular sport in Munster[108] (where the crest of the O'Quins is a wolf's head, erased, argent), there is no sign that the beasts were anything but scarce after 1707. Taken along with O'Roddy's remarks, it appears that they were brought under control at the close of the seventeenth century.

At this point a brief digression is necessary to include a superstition regarding wolves which is evident in a letter from Lady Wentworth to her son Lord Strafford in 1713. She says[5]

I have made your daughter a present of a wolf's tooth. I sent to Ireland for it and set it hear in gold. They are very lucky things.

The possession of a wolf's tooth was supposed to an infallible way of retaining one's own.

The wolf reportedly persisted in Ireland until near the end of the eighteenth century. It has been possible to compile a kind of catalogue of 'last Irish wolves': for many districts came to regard their own final representative of the species as the last in the country as a whole. It is quite easy to see how the exaggeration crept in on recounting events which must have cast a strong spell on the imagination. It will become obvious that the dates given for these events are sometimes confused. Opinion also differs in some counties as to where the final individual was hunted down, though in others there is a degree of accord. Apparently in most cases the details were not committed to paper for a long time and, as one would expect, there is much hearsay. Clearly detective work is a couple of hundred years too late, and I make no apology for the anomalous and undigested information presented here.

In 1841 a Mr Charles Webber[203] presented the Royal Irish Academy with a stone on which was carved in rude bas-relief what was believed to represent a dog killing a wolf. A reproduction of it appears in Fig. 57. It was supposed to commemorate the destruction of the last wolf, and came from Ardnaglass Castle in Co. Sligo. There was a legend that the chieftains of Leitrim hunted the animal through various districts and killed it in a small wood. The area is still marked Carrownamadhoo on maps: 'dog's quarter'. But the stone clearly dates from very much earlier than the seventeenth century and the story has an ancient ring about it. It does, however, illustrate how yarns of this nature may become established as serious accounts of the demise of the last Irish wolf.

The 'last wolf' of second greatest antiquity was one in Co. Antrim, near Belfast. The earliest record I can trace is by a Belfast schoolmaster, J. Compton, who brought out a small volume in 1823 under the title *A Compendious System of Chronology*. Against the year 1692 there appears the following item. 'The last wolf seen in Ireland is killed with Irish wolf-dogs on the hill of Aughnabrack, near Belfast, by Clotworthy Upton, of Castle-Upton, Templepatrick'. I have been told that it was speared, or so the story goes. *Breach* is, as we shall see, Irish for a wolf, and Aughnabrack means 'the hill of the wolf'. The hill is commonly known to Belfast-men as Wolf Hill. A killing at Nappan, near Glenarm, is the only other one of its kind for Antrim. *Belfast and its Environs* (1842) gives the year as 1712, and William Thompson listed Glenarm as one of the three places in Ireland commemorated with this singular honour. Nappan Mountain would have proved a fitting background for this historic drama. Even today it is one of the wildest and least frequented places in the country.

Waringstown in Co. Down is commonly given as one of the sites where the wolf became extinct, but there are conflicting views on the nature and time of the happening. E.D. Atkinson in *A History of Donaghcloney* (1898) asserted that it took place in 1699, beside an old mill in the centre of the village. O'Donovan described a day excursion to Waringstown in 1834 in his *Ordnance Survey Letters,* where he consulted 'the Rev. Mr Waring, Lord of the Soil' on local history. This must have been the Very Rev. Holt Waring, Dean of Dromore, who succeeded to the property in 1793 on the death of his uncle. Seemingly O'Donovan has all his data from this source, and gives the year of the wolf's demise as 1700. The Dean also had a conversation on the subject with Sir Emerson Tennant about 1834 or 1835, the gist of which is reproduced in J.E. Harting's *British Animals Extinct within Historic Time* (1880), a work which has been assiduously consulted in the preparation of this chapter. Thus Waring recalled, as a boy, repeatedly hearing how a foal belonging to his uncle was killed by a wolf in a stable at Waringstown. But the occasion must have been several years after 1700 at least, for his uncle was born in 1699.

Hardiman traced the dispatch of the remaining wolf in Co. Galway to 1700, in the mountains of Joyce's Country.[160]

O'Donovan (1838) also seems to have suggested that the final wolf in Co. Wicklow was slain at Glendalough in 1710. This is in approximate agreement with the comments in Charles McKenzie's *The Natural History of all the most Remarkable Quadrupeds, Birds, Fishes, Reptiles and Insects from Buffon* (1860), where Glendalough is again cited, but the year is 1700.

Smith, in his admirable *Antient and Present State of the County of Kerry* (1756), observed that certain ancient enclosures had been built to secure cattle from wolves, and that the latter were not finally extirpated until about the year 1710, as indicated by presentments for raising money to destroy them in some old grand-jury books. O'Donovan, in the foot-note in the *Four Masters*, remarked that wolves were last seen in Kerry in 1720.

There is a degree of accord on the date for Co. Cork. The last application made for a wolf-bounty was in 1710. The hero is believed to be one Brian Towsend and the animal was almost certainly killed at Kilcrea.[147]

In an article in the short-lived *Irish Penny Journal* (1841), H.D. Richardson claimed acquaintance with an 'old gentleman between eighty and ninety years of age' whose mother remembered wolves being killed in Co. Wexford around 1730 to 1740. This is shaky enough, but Richardson also intimated that 'many persons of weight and veracity' had asserted that a wolf was killed in the Wicklow Mountains as late as 1770. There is, to the sceptical reader, nothing quite so damning to a hearsay as a vague appeal to authority. Naturally it is impossible at the same time to present evidence to refute this assertion. By this point the critical reader should have had his suspicions aroused as to the validity of any 'last wolf'.

Two tales of wolves in Co. Mayo have been recorded.[159] The last in the county was allegedly destroyed in the Parish of Kilgeevar, near Louisburg, in 1745 and a particularly aggressive specimen it was. A man walking from Roonith to Drummin and Aughagower, having traversed the most dangerous part of his journey securely, met an acquaintance at Cregganbaun and, thinking danger past, gave him his dagger, only to be killed by the wolf further on. The second story, from the same district, tells of a man lying on a bed in his bothy and of a wolf coming in to dry itself at the fire, which it all but extinguished by its repeated shaking. Not content with causing inconvenience, it then sprang upon the blanket on the bed, the man having hid himself beneath it to make the best of a bad situation. He was able to throw the blanket over the wolf and, after a struggle, to dispatch it. This yarn reputedly came in other versions, some featuring a wild-cat. References to wild cats in Ireland are either to feral domestic animals or to 'marten cats', pine martens, which are among the most elusive of all the Irish mammals. An attack by a 'wild-cat', therefore, seems improbable, and perhaps gives a measure of the credance that should be placed on such narratives.

Letters in the Lodge Collection in the Armagh Library seem to suggest that wolves had disappeared there at least some years before 1745.

The memory of the last wolf lingers still in parts of Co. 'Derry. Apparently thirty years ago there were particularly strong traditions of the last wolf around Draperstown and Dungiven.[148] In *Hours in Vacation: In Five Parts* (1853) by

Alfred McFarland, the author states that the last wolf in Ulster was killed about ninety years previously, and therefore *circa* 1763, in the woods near Dungiven. There is yet a further pointer to the Dungiven district in a letter from Bishop Alexander of 'Derry, later Primate of all Ireland, to a certain Mr G.I.D. Lees.[136] It runs

The story I heard from Mr Duncan, who had the little hotel at Dungiven, was told to me when I was a very little boy, probably about 1834. Mr Duncan seemed to me the oldest man that ever wore grey hair. I daresay he was over eighty. Supposing that he was, when the wolf was executed on the hill above Pollpiar about my age in 1834, as he said, that would take us to something between 1750 or 1760. Many years ago in an Annual Registar of 1760, I read of the killing of a wolf in Ireland.

'Pollpiar' seems to be due to someone's illegible handwriting, for there is nowhere of that name in the region. An estate, north of the town, bears the name 'Pellipiar'. Quite independently of this, I have a letter from the Right Rev. Wyse Jackson, informing me that Dean Babington of Cork told him, in his boyhood, that Primate Alexander had spoken to him of the last wolf, and that an old man he had met claimed to have seen the body.

A discordant note is struck by the foot note in the *Four Masters*. A tradition is claimed therein that a certain Cormac O'Neil shot the final wolf living in Glenshane, in the Parish of Dungiven; in 1700. Of course this may not have been meant as the last in the district as a whole, but there is at least some room for doubt.

The Ordnance Survey Manuscripts, written around 1830, reveal that there were claims that the last wolf met its fate in south-east 'Derry. The people of Tamlaght O'Crilly Parish declared that Wolf Hill, marked 'the Wolf's Hill' on modern maps, was the ultimate refuge of the beast. Moreover, in the Parish of Ballyscullion a man told an official that his grandfather killed the last wolf in the woods in that district.

No dates are available from Co. Tyrone, but there is a detailed description of the alleged incident.[108] We are informed that wolves were a great trouble in the county and that sizeable rewards were offered to compass their destruction. A professional wolf-hunter named Rory Carragh was offered an additional incentive to kill the last two, which had slaughtered sheep in a sheep-fold enclosed by a high stone-wall. Carragh undertook the task with the aid of a little boy, the only person who would accompany him, and two wolf dogs. He warned the boy to be on the look out and not to fall asleep. Just the same, the lad was about to doze off when the dog with him leapt with a roar and levelled a wolf. The boy bravely drove a spear through the wolf's neck and, at that moment, Carragh appeared with the head of the other. Another version is that the final wolf in Tyrone was killed by a horse in defence of her foal.[10]

Nuttall-Smith, in his aforementioned book, noted that the last wolf in Ireland perished in the Knockmealdown Mountains, between the counties of Tipperary and Waterford, about 1770. A second passage of his work is also of interest.

Captain E.M. Connolly, of Castletown, told my brother not long ago that he came across a letter of about the same date from Lord Clifden, of Gowran, asking his ancestor to send across his hounds from Castletown, near Celbridge, Co. Kildare, to hunt the Wolves in the Slieve Bloom Mountains.

These mountains divide the counties of Laois and Offaly, and one of the highest summits is still known as the Wolftrap.

Two other dates must be included. One is of 1766 for Co. Kildare.[99] The other, 1782, is quoted by A.G. More (in his *Life and Letters* by Moffat).

The very last 'last wolf', a celebrated and sagacious animal, is accounted for by a letter in the *Field* in 1885 from Captain G.A. Graham, often described as the resuscitator of the Irish wolf-hound. In this he wrote that the last wolf was killed by a pack of hounds owned by 'the grandfather of Mr Watson of Ballydarton' (who was also a master of hounds) at Myshall, close to Ballydarton, Co. Carlow, about 1786. Moffat,[157] being made aware of the correspondence many years later, wrote to Mr Watson's daughter. According to her, the wolf was hunted down from Mount Leinster, where it had been killing sheep, and met its end on the bank of a stream.

When all is said and done the saga of the last wolf is a most unreliable and unsatisfactory one. A great deal of contradiction is evident and there is now, superfluous to state, no way of checking the stories. Evidently most of the wolves were gone by the early seventeen-hundreds, but a few held their own in the more remote parts of Ireland for several years, the final records coming, surprisingly, from the south-east of the country. How accurate the later deaths are we shall never know. The vagaries of human nature sometimes manifest themselves in strange ways and, in collating the data for this chapter, I have been obsessed with the notion that some of the writers felt that they acquired a degree of kudos in discussing the subject, and were vying with each other to produce the latest record. No doubt I am naturally of a distrustful nature. One gentleman who cited a date of 1810 in a magazine informed me, when I wrote to him on the matter, that he could not remember where he had read about it. If there was a contest of this kind, the prize must go to the author of an article on 'The British wolf', in the *Spectator* of 1899 which mused

It is just barely possible, indeed, that an isolated specimen or two of the breed may yet exist among the pathless wilds of Connemara, or some equally savage district—a report of the kind was current about two years ago—and may one day astonish us with an authentic discovery.

In this context it is instructive that Hardiman believed the animal extinct before 1738 and, in Harris's *The Whole Works of Sir James Ware concerning Ireland* (1739-64), the editor remarked that there were no wolves in Ireland then.

The subject is one of consuming interest and provides endless scope for speculation and squabble, neither likely to lead to any reliable conclusion.

The memory of the wolf remains in Ireland in place names. There are few enough in English, but several localities have an Irish name incorporating that of the beast. I am not familiar with Irish and what I write is gleaned from others' efforts. There seem to be more than one name for the wolf including *Fael* (or *Faelcu*) which appears in Feltrim (*Faeldruim*) Hill near Swords in Co. Dublin, which is still locally known to have been once the haunt of wolves. The word *Breach* is much more commonly heard, especially in derivatives of *Breach-mhagh* (wolf field), which are the modern names of various townlands such as Breaghva, Breaffy, Breaghy, Breaghwy, Bregho, Breahig to the extreme corruptions Britway and Brackley. Caherbreagh (*Cathairbreach*), east of Tralee, Co. Kerry, is the 'fort of the wolves'. A curious compound *mac-tire,* meaning 'son of the country', is an oblique reference to the once lonely habitation of the wolf. Thus there is Knockaunvicteera (little hill of the wolf) in Co. Clare and Isknamacteera (water of the wolves), a small lake in Co. Kerry.

The chapter would be incomplete without referring to an article entitled 'The Wolf days of Ireland' by Jonathan Grub, which appeared in the *Zoologist* of 1862.[104] This is a collection of apocryphal stories told to the author by his father who, in turn, had them from *his* mother, who was born in 1731. The scene of events was at Ballyroggin, Co. Kildare, and the characters were Grubb's ancestors, the Malones, in whom the local wolf population seemed to take a decided, distressing and disproportionate interest. The first story is about a woodcutter who foolishly omitted to take his dog, a habitual companion, to work with him. On being approached by a wolf he attempted to ward it off with a heavy wooden stake, at the same time calling to the dog, who eventually arrived and saw the intruder off the parish.

The second story is particularly alarming and depicts a wolf carrying off a small child by its clothes. The infant was quite oblivious of his perilous position and thoroughly enjoyed the escapade until he was, by good fortune, eventually rescued by his parents.

The final tale relates how a member of the family, returning from a journey one night on horseback, was chased by wolves. He put spurs to his terrified steed but his pursuers actually made several leaps upon the horse's hind-quarters, inflicting severe wounds with their fangs. Nevertheless, the traveller, almost deranged with fright, managed to reach his door and cried out to his brother, 'Oh! James, James, let me in—my horse is ate with the wolves'.

Botanical Names of Plants Mentioned in the Text

Apple	*Malus sylvestris*
Arbutus	*Arbutus unedo*
Ash	*Fraxinus excelsior*
Barley	*Hordeum* sp.
Bean (Broad)	*Vicia faba*
Beech	*Fagus sylvatica*
Blackberry or Bramble	*Rubus fruticosus* agg.
Bluebell	*Scilla (Endymion) non-scripta*
Bog-cotton	*Eriophorun* sp.
Bracken	*Pteridium aquilinum*
Cherry	*Prunus avium*
Chestnut (sweet)	*Castanea sativa*
Clover	*Trifolium* sp.
Dandelion	*Taraxacum officinale*
Elm	*Ulmus* sp.
Gooseberry	*Ribes uva-crispa*
Hawthorn	*Crataegus monogyna*
Hazel	*Corylus avellana*
Ivy	*Hedera helix*
Marram Grass	*Ammophila arenaria*
Pea (Garden)	*Pisum sativum*
Raspberry (Wild)	*Rubus idaeus*
Rhododendron	*Rhododendron ponticum*
Rose	*Rosa* sp.
Rowan	*Sorbus aucuparia*
Pineapple	*Ananus sativus*
Sea Buckthorn	*Hippophae rhamnoides*
Sitka Spruce	*Picea sitchensis*
Strawberry (Wild)	*Fragaria vesca*
Turnip	*Brassica rapa*
Walnut	*Juglans regia*
Wheat	*Triticum aestivum*

References

The sources below are from books, newspapers and journals, names of the latter having been abbreviated as in the *World List of Scientific Periodicals* (Fourth Edition. 1963-65). Unlisted titles have been abbreviated to conform. Figures given in parenthesis, before and after volume numbers, refer respectively to series and part. The latter are only included wherever parts have been individually paginated. Titles of newspapers are given in full.

1. Adams, L.E. (1905). Remains of the common mole in Ireland. *Ir. Nat.*, **14**: 72.
2. Akande, M. (1972). The food of feral mink (*Mustela vison*) in Scotland. *J. Zool., Lond.*, 167: 475-479.
3. Alcock, N.H. (1899). The natural history of Irish bats. *Ir. Nat.*, 8: 29-36, 53-57, 169-174.
4. Alexander, G. *et al.* (1967). Activities of foxes and crows in a flock of lambing ewes. *Aust. J. exp. Agric. Anim. Husb.*, 7: 329-336.
5. Allen, F.A. (1909). The wolf in Scotland and Ireland. *Trans. Caradoc. Severn Vall. Fld Club*, 5: 68-74.
6. Allingham, H. (1896). Wooden objects found in peat bogs, supposed to have been otter traps. *J. R. Soc. Antiq. Ir.*, (5) 6: 379-382.
7. Anon. (1855). Illustrative notes to Sir Henry Sidney's memoir. *Ulster J. Archeol.*, (1) 3: 43-52.
8. ――― (1855). (Footnote). *Zoologist*, (3) 9: 268.
9. ――― (1974). Ministry orders hunt for hedgehog. *Vet. Rec.*, **95**: 6.
10. Archibald, C. and Bell, J. (1854). Wolves in Ireland. *Ulster J. Archeol.*, (1) 2: 281.
11. Bacot, A.W. (1914). A study of the bionomics of the common rat fleas and other species associated with human habitations, with special reference to the influence of temperature and humidity at various periods of the life-history of the insect. *J. Hyg. Camb.* (Plague Suppl.), 3: 447-654.
12. Barrett-Hamilton, G.E.H. (1898). Notes on the introduction of the brown hare into Ireland. *Ir. Nat.*. 7: 69-76.

13. ––– (1900). On the geographical and individual variation in *Mus sylvaticus* and its allies. *Proc. zool. Soc. Lond.,*(1900): 387-428.
14. ––– and Hinton, M.A.C. (1910-21). *A History of British Mammals.* Gurney and Jackson. London.
15. Barrington, R.M. (1880). On the introduction of the squirrel into Ireland. *Scient. Proc. R. Dubl. Soc.,* (2) **2**: 615-631.
16. ––– (1882). On the breeding habits of the long-tailed field mouse. *Zoologist,* (3) **6**: 121-123.
17. ––– (1900). *The Migration of Birds as observed at Irish Lighthouses and Lightships.* Porter. London.
18. Bennett-Clark, H.C. and Lucey, E.C.A. (1967). The jump of the flea: a study of energetics and a model of the mechanism. *J. exp. Biol.,* **47**: 59-76.
19. Blandford, W.J. (1897). (Untitled report). *Proc. zool. Soc. Lond.,* (1897): 311.
20. Borrer, W. (1877). Occurrence of the weasel in Ireland. *Zoologist,* (3) **1**: 291.
21. Broghill, Lord. [1874]. Two letters from Lord Broghill to the Earl of Dorset. *Hist. Mss Comm. Rep.* (De La Warr Mss), 4: 280.
22. Browne, C.R. (1894). The ethnography of Inishboffin and Inishark, County Galway. *Proc. R. Ir. Acad.,* (3) **3**: 317-370.
23. Buick, G.R. (1892). Notice of an ancient wooden trap, probably used for catching otters. *J. R. Soc. Antiq. Ire.,* (5) **21**: 536-541.
24. Caulfield, R. (1878). *The Council Book of the Corporation of Youghal.* Privately published. Cork.
25. Claasens, A.J.M. and O'Rourke, F.J. (1964). *Leptinus testaceus,* Muller (Col., Silphidae) a possibly parasitic beetle, new to Co. Cork. *Entomologist's Gaz.,* **15**: 49-50.
26. ––––– (1966). The distribution and general ecology of the Irish Siphonaptera. *Proc. R. Ir. Acad.,* **64B**: 413-463.
27. Clowes, E.P. (1933). Stoat feeding young on rock pipits. *Ir. Nat. J.,* **4**: 217-218.
28. Corbet, G.B. (1960). Wood mice at high altitude in Scotland. *Proc. zool. Soc. Lond.,* **133**: 486-487.
29. ––– (1961). Origin of the British insular races of small mammals and of the 'Lusitanian' fauna. *Nature, Lond.,* **191**: 1037-1040.
30. ––– (1966). *The Terrestrial Mammals of Western Europe.* Foulis. London.
31. Croaffts, C. [1909] Two letters from Christopher Croaffts to Sir John Perceval. *Hist. Mss Comm. Rep.* (Egmont Mss), 2: 5.
32. Dadd, M.N. (1970). Overlap of variation in British and European mammal populations. *Symp. zool. Soc. Lond.,* **26**: 117-125.
33. Darling, J.F. (1883). A black and white stoat. *Field,* **61**: 431.
34. Day, M.G. (1966). Identification of the hair and feather remains in the guts and faeces of stoats and weasels. *J. Zool., Lond.,* **148**: 201-217
35. –––(1968). Food habits of British stoats and weasels.*J. Zool., Lond.,* **155**: 485-497.
36. ––– and Linn, I. (1972). Notes on the food of feral mink *Mustela vison* in England and Wales. *J. Zool., Lond.,* **167**: 463-473.
37. Deane, C.D. (1962). Life of the wild. *Belfast Telegraph,* 19th September.
38. ––– (1962). Irish golden eagles and a link with Scotland. *Br. Birds,* **55**: 272-274.
39. ––– (1973). Still no respite for the badger. *News Letter* (Belfast) 4th December.
40. ––– (1974). Mystery of the mice and an island. *News Letter* (Belfast). 24th August.
41. ––– and O'Gorman, F. (1969). The spread of feral mink in Ireland. *Ir. Nat. J.,* **16**: 198-202.
42. De Barry, R.S. (1874). Maternal instincts of a stoat.*Field,* **43**: 545.
43. Dennis, C.M. and Gooding, C.D. (1965). Predators–lamb killers or scavengers? *J. Agric. West. Aust.,* **6**: 249-250
44. Derg. (1887). Stoats and rabbits. *Field,* **69**: 29.
45. ––– (1888). Otters attacking a dog. *Field,* **71**: 192.
46. Dice, L.R. (1947). Effectiveness of selection by owls of deer mice (*Peromyscus maniculatus*) with contrast in colour with their background. *Contrib. Lab. Vert. Biol.,* **34**: 1-20.
47. Douthwaite, R.J. (1966). Cambridge Irish seabird project. *Camb. Exped. J.,* **2**: 32-35.
48. Dover, W.K. (1877). Absence of the weasel from Ireland. *Zoologist,* (3) **1**: 440.
49. Dunlop, R. (1913). *Ireland under the Commonwealth.* University Press. Manchester.
50. Dunscombe, R. (1881). Otter seizing prey while hunted. *Field,* **58**: 153..
51. Ewer, R.F. (1968). *Ethnology of Mammals.* Plenum Press. New York.
52. ––– (1973). *The Carnivores.* Cornell University Press. New York.
53. Fairley, J.S. (1964). A collection of fieldmice from Rathlin Island, Northern Ireland. *Ann. Mag. nat. Hist.,* (13) **7**: 27-31.

54. — — — (1965). The food of the fox *Vulpes vulpes* (L.) in Co. Down. *Ir. Nat. J.*, **15**: 2-5.
55. — — — (1965). Fieldmice at high altitude in Co. Kerry, Ireland. *Proc. zool. Soc. Lond.*, **145**: 144-145.
56. — — — (1966) An indication of the food of the short-eared owl in Ireland. *Br. Birds*, **59**: 307-308.
57. — — — (1966) Analyses of Barn owl pellets from an Irish roost. *Br. Birds*, **59**: 338-340.
58. — — — (1966). An indication of the food of the fox in Northern Ireland after myxomatosis. *Ir. Nat. J.*, **15**: 149-151.
59. — — — (1967). Food of long-eared owls in north-east Ireland. *Br. Birds*, **60**: 130-135.
60. — — — (1967). An indication of the food of the badger in north-east Ireland. *Ir. Nat. J.*, **15**: 267-269.
61. — — — (1967). Notes on the food of the fieldmouse in Irish woodland. *Ir. Nat. J.*, **15**: 300-302.
62. — — — (1967). The fieldmouse *Apodemus sylvaticus* (L.) in the Burren *Ir. Nat. J.*, **15**: 330-331.
63. — — — (1967). Wood mice in grassland at Dundrum, Co. Down, Northern Ireland. *J. Zool., Lond.*, **153**: 553-555
64. — — — (1967). A woodland population of *Apodemus sylvaticus* (L.) at Seaforde, Co Down. *Proc. R. Ir. Acad.*, **65B**: 407-424.
65. — — — (1969). Destruction of foxes in Northern Ireland. *Ir. Nat. J.*, **16**: 187-189.
66. — — — (1969). Some field observations on the fox in Northern Ireland. *Ir. Nat. J.*, **16**: 189-192.
67. — — — (1969). A critical examination of the Northern Ireland fox bounty figures. *Ir. Nat. J.*, **16**: 213-215.
68. — — — (1969). The fox as a pest of agriculture. *Ir. Nat. J.*, **16**: 216-219.
69. — — — (1969). Tagging studies of the red fox (*Vulpes vulpes* L.) in north-east Ireland. *J. Zool., Lond.*, **159**: 527-532.
70. — — — (1969). Survival of the fox (*Vulpes vulpes*) cubs in Northern Ireland. *J. Zool., Lond.*, **159**: 532-534.
71. — — — (1970). Form of the fieldmouse *Apodemus sylvaticus* (L.) in Ireland. *Ir. Nat. J.*, **16**: 381.
72. — — — (1970). Foetal number and resorption in wood mice from Ireland. *J. Zool., Lond.*, **161**: 276-277.
73. — — — (1970). The food, reproduction, form, growth and development of the fox *Vulpes vulpes* (L.) in north-east Ireland. *Proc. R. Ir. Acad.*, **69B**: 103-137.
74. — — — (1971). More records of fleas from Irish mammals (second series). *Entomologist's Gaz.*, **22**: 259-263.
75. — — — (1971). A critical reappraisal of the status in Ireland of the eastern house mouse *Mus musculus orientalis* Cretzmar. *Ir. Nat. J.*, **17**: 2-5.
76. — — — (1971). New data on the Irish stoat. *Ir. Nat. J.*, **17**: 49-57.
77. — — — (1971). The present distribution of the bank vole *Clethrionomys glareolus* Schreber in Ireland. *Proc. R. Ir. Acad.*, **71B**: 183-189.
78. — — — (1971). A collection of Irish bank vole skulls. *Scient. Proc. R. Dubl. Soc.*, **4A**: 37-44.
79. — — — (1972). The fieldmouse in Ireland. *Ir. Nat. J.*, **17**: 152-159.
80. — — — (1972). Food of otters from Co. Galway, Ireland, and notes on other aspects of their biology. *J. Zool., Lond.*, **166**: 469-474.
81. — — — (1973). Kestrel pellets from a winter roost. *Ir. Nat. J.*, **17**: 407-409.
82. — — — (1974). Notes on the winter breeding of hares in the west of Ireland. *Ir. Nat. J.*, **18**: 17-19.
83. — — — and Clark, F.L. (1971). Barn owl pellets from Co. Galway. *Br. Birds*, **64**: 35.
84. — — — — — (1972). Further records of fleas from Irish birds and mammals. *Entomologists's Gaz.*, **23**: 66-68.
85. — — — — — (1972). Food of barn owls *Tyto alba* (Scopoli) over one year at a roost in Co. Galway. *Ir. Nat. J.*, **17**: 219-222.
86. — — — — — (1973). Further records of fleas from Irish birds and mammals (second series). *Entomologist's Gaz.*, **24**: 347-348.
87. — — — and Comerton, M.E. (1972). An early-breeding population of fieldmice *Apodemus sylvaticus* (L.) in Limekiln Wood, Athenry, Co. Galway. *Proc. R. Ir. Acad.*, **72B**: 149-163.
88. — — — and Deane, C.D. (1967). Analysis of barn owl pellets from Co. Fermanagh. *Br. Birds* **60**: 370.
89. — — — and Foster, R. (1974). Barn owls feeding on bank voles. *Ir. Nat. J.*, **18**: 55.

191

90.   ––– and McLean, A. (1965). Notes on the summer food of the kestrel in Northern
        Ireland. *Br. Birds*, **58**: 145-148.
91.   ––– and O'Gorman, F. (1971). Barn owl *Tyto alba* (Scopoli) pellets from Co. Wicklow.
        Ir. Nat. J., **17**: 62.
92.   –––––– (1974). Food of pine martens in the Burren. *Ir. Nat. J.*, **18**: 125.
93.   ––– and West, B. (1975). Fieldmice from Inishkea South, Co. Mayo. *Ir. Nat. J.*, **18**:
        196-197.
94.   ––– and Wilson, S.C. (1972). Autumn food of otters on the Agivey River, Co.
        Londonderry, Northern Ireland. *J. Zool., Lond.*, **166**: 468-469.
95.   Fenner, F. and Chapple, P.F. (1965). Evolutionary changes in myxoma virus in Britain.
        J. Hyg., Camb., **63**: 175-185.
96.   ––– and Ratcliffe, F.N. (1965). *Myxomatosis.* University Press. Cambridge.
97.   Fitter, R.S.R. (1964). Irish otters and deer in danger. *Wld Wildl. News*, **22**: 5.
98.   Flemyng, W.W. (1913). A gamekeeper's list of undesirables. *Ir. Nat.*, **12**: 162-163.
99.   Forrest, H.E. (1927). Prehistoric mammals of Ireland: IV. *Ir. Nat. J.*, **1**: 234-236.
100.   Foster, N.H. (1917). The Mourne Mountains. *Proc. Belf. Nat. Fld Club.*, (2) **7**: 294-296.
101.   Garvey, T. (1935). The musk rat in Saorstat Eireann. *J. Dep. Agr. Repub. Ire.*, **33**:
        189-195.
102.   Gilbert, J.T. (1859). *History of Dublin.* McGlashen and Gill. Dublin.
103.   Glue, D. (1970). Avian predator analysis and the mammalogist. *Mammal Rev.*, **1**: 53-62.
104.   Grub, J. (1862). The wolf-days of Ireland. *Zoologist*, (1) **20**: 7996-7997.
105.   Hackett, W.A. (1973). Otter in a lobster pot. *Field*, **42**: 138.
106.   Harrington, R. (1973). Hybridisation among deer and its implications for conservation.
        Ir. For., **30**: 64-78.
107.   ––– (1974). The hybridisation of red deer and sika deer in Northern Ireland. *Ir. For.*,
        31: 168.
108.   Harting, J.E. (1880). *British Animals Extinct within Historic Time.* Trubner. London.
109.   ––– (1891). The fox. *Zoologist*, (3) **15**: 321-334.
110.   ––– (1894). The otter. *Zoologist*, (3) **18**: 1-10, 41-47, 379-385.
111.   ––– (1894). The weasel. *Zoologist*, (3) **18**: 417-423, 445-454.
112.   ––– (1912). *The Rabbit.* Longmans, Green. London.
113.   Hawkins, A.E. and Jewell, P. (1962). Food consumption and energy requirements of
        captive British shrews and the mole. *Proc. zool. Soc. Lond.*, **138**: 137-155.
114.   Hearns, P. (1862). An otter-fight with two salmon. *Field*, **20**: 459.
115.   Hinton, M.A.C. (1920). The Irish otter, *Ann. Mag. nat. Hist.*, (9) **5**: 464.
116.   Hopkins, G.H.E. and Rothschild, M. (1953-). *An illustrated Catalogue of the Rothschild
        Collection of Fleas (Siphonaptera) in the British Museum (Natural History),
        London.* British Museum. London.
117.   Humphries, D.A. (1968). The host-finding behaviour of the hen flea *Ceratophyllus
        gallinae* (Schrank) (Siphonaptera). *Parasitology*, **58**: 403-414.
118.   Hurley, S.J. (1887). Otters in the Shannon. *Field*, **69**: 54, 110.
119.   ––– (1892). The otter. *Ir. Sportsman*, **23**: 380.
120.   ––– (1898). White otters. *Field*, **91**: 142.
121.   Hurrell, H.G. (1968). *Wildlife: Tame but Free.* David and Charles. Newton Abbot.
122.   Irwin, R.B. (1896). Weasel in a woodpigeon's nest. *Field*, **88**: 221.
123.   Jameson, H.L. (1897). The bats of Ireland. *Ir. Nat.*, **6**: 34-43.
124.   ––– (1898). On a probable case of protective colouration in the house mouse (*Mus
        musculus* Linn.). *J. Linn. Soc.*, **26**: 456-473.
125.   Jensen, B. (1973). Movements of the red fox (*Vulpes vulpes* (L.)) in Denmark investi-
        gated by marking and recovery. *Danish Rev. Game Biol.*, **8** (3).
126.   Jenyns, L.J. (1841). Notes on the smaller British Mammalia, including the description of
        a new species of *Arvicola* found in Scotland. *Ann. Mag. nat. Hist.*, (1) **7**: 261-267.
127.   J.R.T.M. (1901). Hare chased by otter. *Field*, **97**: 442.
128.   Kennedy, P.G. *et al.* (1954). *Birds of Ireland.* Oliver and Boyd. Edinburgh.
129.   Ker, E. (1874). Irish hare turning white in winter–badger and otters in Ireland. *Field*,
        44: 81.
130.   Kinahan, G.H. (1892). White and piebald stoats. *Zoologist*, (3) **16**: 265.
131.   Kinahan, J.R. (1859, 1860). Mammalogica Himernica: Part 1–Sub-Class, Lissencephala;
        Order Cheiroptera, Insectivoridae;–or, a general review of the history and
        distribution of bats in Ireland; with remarks on Mr Foot's discovery in Clare of
        the lesser horse-shoe bat, a species hitherto unrecorded in Ireland. *Proc. Dubl.
        nat. Hist. Soc.*, (1860) **2**: 154-170. Also in *Nat. Hist. Rev.*, (Proceedings of the
        Societies section) (1859) **6**: 381-397.

132. Kolb, H.H. and Hewson, R. (1974). The body size of the red fox (*Vulpes vulpes*) in Scotland. *J. Zool., Lond.*, **173**: 253-255.
133. Lance, A.N. (1973). Numbers of woodmice (*Apodemus sylvaticus*) on improved and unproved blanket bog. *J.Zool., Lond.*, **171**: 471-473.
134. Langfield, R.W. (1901). Stoat swallowed by a pike. *Field*, **98**: 312.
135. L.D. (1874). Early broods of wild ducks and otters *Field*, **43**: 445.
136. Lees, G.I.D. (1894). The last wolf killed in Ireland. *Land War.*, **58**: 611.
137. Lever, R.J.A.W. (1959). The diet of the fox since myxomatosis. *J. Anim. Ecol.*, **28**: 359-375.
138. Lloyd, H.G. (1968). The control of foxes. *Ann. appl. Biol.*, **61**: 334-345.
139. Lockie, J.D. (1959). Estimation of the food of foxes. *J. Wildl. Mgmt*, **23**: 358-360.
140. ––– (1961). The food of the pine marten *Martes martes* in west Rosshire, Scotland. *Proc. zool. Soc. Lond.*, **136**: 187-195.
141. ––– (1966). Territory in small carnivores. *Symp. zool. Soc. Lond.*, **18**: 143-165.
142. Longfield, R.E. (1928). A pack of stoats. *Ir. Nat. J.*, **2**: 73.
143. McCaughey, W.J. and Fairley, J.S. (1969). Serological reactions to *Brucella* and *Leptospira* in foxes. *Vet. Rec.*, **84**: 542.
144. McCracken, E. (1971). *The Irish Woods since Tudor Times*. David and Charles. Newton Abbot.
145. McFarlane, D. (1964). The effects of predators on perinatal lamb losses in the Monaro, Oberon and Canberra districts. *Wool Technol. Sheep Breed.*, **11**: 11-13.
146. McIntyre, D. (1950). Habits of the otter. *Field*. **196**: 549.
147. McLysaght, E. (1950). *Irish Life in the Seventeenth Century*. Irish University Press. Cork.
148. McMillan, N.F. (1945). The wolf in Ireland. *Ir. Nat. J.*, **8**: 261.
149. Mead-Briggs, A.R. (1963). Observations on the rabbit flea–the vector of myxomatosis. *Ann. appl. Biol.*, **51**: 338-342.
150. Mech, L.D. (1970). *The Wolf*. American Museum of Natural History Press. New York.
151. Millais, J.G. (1897). *British Deer and their Horns*. Sotheran. London.
152. Moffat, C.B. (1890). Habits of the stoat. *Zoologist*, (3) **14**: 380-382.
153. ––– (1905). Duration of flight among bats. *Ir. Nat.*, **14**: 97-108.
154. ––– (1926). The Irish stoat. *Ir. Nat. J.*, **1**: 150-151.
155. ––– (1927). The otter. *Ir. Nat. J.*, **1**: 209-212.
156. ––– (1928). The field mouse. *Ir. Nat. J.*, **2**: 106-109.
157. ––– (1938). The mammals of Ireland. *Proc. R. Ir. Acad.*, **44B**: 61-128.
158. Neal, E. (1962). *Otters*. Sunday Times Publications. London.
159. O'Dowd, J.D. (1940). Stories about wolves. *Bealoideas*, **10**: 287-289.
160. O'Flaherty, R. (1846). *A Chorographical Description of West or H-lar Connaught*. Irish Archaeological Society. Dublin.
161. Ogilby, W. (1834). Notice of a new species of the otter from the north of Ireland. *Proc. zool. Soc. Lond.*, (1834): 110-111.
162. O'Gorman, F. (1965). The mammals of Tory Island, Co. Donegal. *Proc. zool. Soc. Lond.*, **145**: 155-158.
163. O'Mahony, E. (1931). Notes on the mammals of the North Bull, Dublin Bay. *Ir. Nat. J.*, **3**: 199-201.
164. Osterholm, H. (1964). Distance receptors in the feeding behaviour of the fox. *Acta. Zool. Fenn.*, **106**: 3-31.
165. Pack-Beresford, H.D. (1936). Cat kills stoat and stoat kills carrier pigeon. *Ir. Nat. J.*, **6**: 146.
166. Patterson, M.A. and Vessey, S.M. (1973). Tapeworm (*Hymenolepis nana*) infection in male albino house mice: effect of fighting among host. *J. Mammal.*, **54**: 784-786.
167. Patterson, R. (1900). The disappearance of the fox from Co. Antrim. *Ir. Nat.*, **9**: 275-277.
168. Patterson, R.M. (1926). A stoat's mid-day meal. *Ir. Nat. J.*, **1**: 70.
169. Pentland, G.H. (1917). Boldness of a stoat. *Ir. Nat.*, **26**: 20.
170. Portlock, J.E. (1836). On some peculiar habits of the *Otus brachyotus*. *Proc. R. Ir. Acad.*, **1**: 52-53.
171. Praeger, R.L. *et al.* (1902). The exploration of the caves of Kesh, Co. Sligo. *Trans. R. Ir. Acad.*, **32B**: 171-214.
172. Prim, J.G.A. (1867). Petition of William Collowe. *Kilkenny SEast Ire. Archeol. J.*, (2) **6**: 211-212.
173. Ross, J.G. and Fairley, J.S. (1969). Studies of disease in the red fox (*Vulpes vulpes*) in Northern Ireland. *J. Zool., Lond.*, **157**: 375-381.

174. Rothschild, M. (1965). Fleas. *Scient. Am.*, **213** (6): 44-53.
175. ——— and Ford, B. (1966). Reproductive hormones of the host controlling the sexual life of the rabbit flea. *Proc. int. Congr. Ent. (1964),* **12**: 801-802.
176. Rothschild, N.C. (1899). Irish fleas. *Ir. Nat.,* **8**: 266.
177. Savage, R.J.G. (1966). Irish Pleistocene mammals. *Ir. Nat. J.,* **15**: 117-130.
178. Scharff, R.F. (1896). *Canis vulpes melanogaster* Bonap. in Ireland. *Ir. Nat.,* **18**: 141-142.
179. ——— (1909). On the occurrence of a speckled otter in Ireland. *Ir. Nat.,* **18**: 141-142.
180. ——— (1909). Irish stoat with nine young. *Ir. Nat.,* **18**: 160.
181. ——— (1915). The speckled otter. *Ir. Nat.,* **24**: 76.
182. Scott, T.G. and Klimstra, W.P. (1955). Red foxes and a declining prey population. *Sth. Ill. Univ. Monogr.,* **1.**
183. Sharrock, J.T.R. (1973). *The Natural History of Cape Clear Island.* Poyser. Berkhampstead.
184. 'Sixty-one'. (1875). A very bold otter. *Field,* **46**: 477.
185. Smit, F.G.A.M. (1957). The recorded distribution and hosts of the Siphonaptera in Britain. *Entomologist's Gaz.,* **8**: 45-75.
186. ——— (1972). On some adaptive structures in the Siphonaptera. *Folia Parasit.,* **19**: 5-17.
187. South, G.R. (1966). Food of long-eared owls in south Lancashire. *Br. Birds,* **59**: 493-497.
188. Southern, H.N. (1954). Tawny owls and their prey. *Ibis,* **96**: 384-410.
189. ——— (1964). *The Handbook of British Mammals.* Blackwell. Oxford.
190. Standen, R. (1897). Some observations by English naturalists on the fauna of Rathlin Island and Ballycastle district. *Ir. Nat.,* **6**: 173-188.
191. Stebbings, R.E. (1970). A bat new to Britain, *Pipistrellus nathusii,* with notes on its identification and distribution in Europe. *J. Zool., Lond.,* **161**: 282-286.
192. Stelfox, A.W. (1965). Notes on the Irish 'wild cat'. *Ir. Nat. J.,* **15**: 57-60.
193. Stephens, M.N. (1957). *The Otter Report.* U.F.A.W. London.
194. Teacher, D. and Gough, K. (1936). Stoats capturing fish. *Ir. Nat. J.,* **6**: 152.
195. Teagle, W.G. (1967). The fox in the London suburbs. *Lond. Nat.,* **46**: 44-48.
196. Tembrock, G. (1957). Zur ethologie des Rotfiches (*Vulpes vulpes* [L.]) unter besondere Berucksuchtigung der Fortplanzing. *Zool. Gart. Lpzg,* **23**: 289-532.
197. Templeton, R. (1837). Irish vertebrate animal: selected from the papers of the late John Templeton, Esq., Cranmore. *Mag. nat. Hist.,* (2) **1**: 403-413.
198. Thomas, O. and Barrett-Hamilton, G.E.H. (1895). The Irish stoat distinct from the British species. *Zoologist,* (3) **19**: 124-129.
199. Ticehurst, C.B. (1939). On the food and feeding habits of the long-eared owl (*Asio otus otus*). *Ibis,* (1939): 512-520.
200. Ussher, R.G. (1883). Vermin destroyed on an Irish estate. *Zoologist* (3) **7**: 171-172.
201. Walker, J. and Fairley, J.S. (1968). Food of Irish hares in Co. Antrim, Ireland. *J. Mammal.,* **49**: 783-785.
202. Watts, C.H.S. (1968). The regulation of wood mouse (*Apodemus sylvaticus*) numbers in Wytham Woods, Berkshire. *J. Anim. Ecol.,* **38**: 285-304.
203. Webber, C.T. (1841). (Untitled note). *Proc. R. Ir. Acad.,* **2**: 65-66.
204. Weldon, E.F. (1881). Food of the otter. *Field,* **57**: 217.
205. W.H.A. (1894). Stoats climbing trees. *Field,* **83**: 169.
206. Williams, R.P. (1858, 1860). (On a black and white variety of the fieldmouse). *Proc. Dubl. nat. Hist. Soc.,* (1860), **2**: 104. Also in *Nat. Hist. Rev.,* (Proceedings of the Societies section) (1858) **5**: 188.
207. Young, T.A. (1885). Agility of the otter. *Field,* **65**: 21.

INDEX

There is a full list of British mammals on page 2. British species absent from Ireland, and which are not mentioned elsewhere in the text, have been omitted from the index. Latin names of domestic animals have also been excluded. I would recommend readers to look up animals and plants by their common names, unless there is a particular reason for searching under the Latin. Some of the former, cited in the text, could refer to more than one species (e.g. 'mullet', 'sparrow'); in such instances it is impossible to list a Latin equivalent.